Masters of Shape: The Lives and Art of American Women Sculptors

Maria Ausherman

Foreword by Kristen Visbal

Introduction by Carol S. Ward

Photography by Steven Taylor

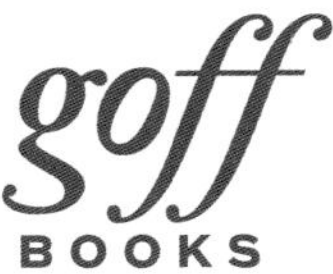

BOOK COVER PHOTO
Memorial to September 11th (Installed 2011) by Meredith Bergmann
Photographer: Steven Taylor

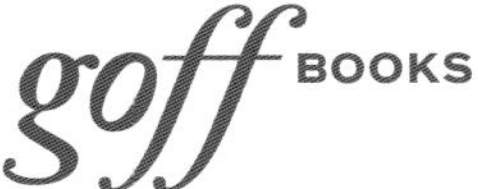

Published by Goff Books, an Imprint of ORO Editions.
Executive publisher: Gordon Goff.

www.goffbooks.com
info@goffbooks.com

Book Design: Anita Stumbo
Goff Books Project Coordinator: Kirby Anderson

10 9 8 7 6 5 4 3 2 1 First Edition

Library of Congress data available upon request. World Rights: available.

ISBN: 978-1-954081-95-6

Color separations and printing: ORO Group Ltd.
Printed in China.

International distribution: www.goffbooks.com/distribution

ORO Editions makes a continuous effort to minimize the overall carbon footprint of its publications. As part of this goal, ORO Editions, in association with Global ReLeaf, arranges to plant trees to replace those used in the manufacturing of the paper produced for its books. Global ReLeaf is an international campaign run by American Forests, one of the world's oldest nonprofit conservation organizations. Global ReLeaf is American Forests' education and action program that helps individuals, organizations, agencies, and corporations improve the local and global environment by planting and caring for trees.

To my mother,
Rieneke Elizabeth VanderGoot Ausherman

And to the memory of my father,
Charles Robert Ausherman

And to the memory of my birth mother,
Maria Isabel Lima Ausherman

"Madam de Stael pronounced
architecture to be frozen music;
so is statuary crystallized spirituality."

—Louisa May Alcott

"Maria Ausherman continues her exploration of women artists in *Masters of Shape,* an inspiring, comprehensive, and beautifully illustrated book chronicling the lives of seventeen pioneering women sculptors. Moving through history, she creates moving portraits of talented artists whose works mirror both their internal worlds and the society surrounding and influencing them. These sculptors dare to speak their truths about inequality and injustice, repression and racism—and do so with bold creativity and immense skill. Savor this book!"

—ANNE LEE, co-author of *Encaustic Art in the 21st Century* (Schiffer Publications, 2015); *Artistry in Fiber: Wall Art; Artistry in Fiber: Sculpture;* and *Artistry in Fiber: Wearable Art* (Schiffer Publications, 2017)

"Embracing the empathy employed by Harriet Hosmer in her sympathetic interpretation of Medusa as a character fated by the actions of others, Maria Ausherman deftly and succinctly opens this study of those who cast, carved, and molded."

—JIM TOTTIS, Vice President of Museum Affairs at Cheekwood Estate in Nashville, Tennessee

"It is so critical that we, as a self-reflective culture, strongly and vigorously pursue hidden histories. In particular, the staggering contribution of female artists has, in the past, been left on the sidelines—but this book goes a long way in pursuing equity in scholarship."

—FRANK VAGNONE, President & CEO of Old Salem Museums and Gardens, and Principal of Twisted Preservation, a consulting firm

"Seeing work from other female sculptors, such as the rawness of Alison Saar's art, has influenced my own art practice and is encouraging the creation of a new series of work. Ausherman's book will inspire other artists, too." —JOYCE MORROW JONES, Mixed media fiber artist and sculptor

"Maria Ausherman repeats her powerful profiling of women who formed our culture and overcame obstacles of gender and race in the last hundred and fifty years: in her first book on photographers and in this beautiful book featuring American women sculptors of the last 150 years. Ausherman corrects the error of art historians in ignoring women artists simply by celebrating them insightfully, and so well."

—PATRICE MAYNARD, Waldorf teacher and publisher

Table of Contents

Acknowledgments

I FIRST BECAME ACQUAINTED with sculptures as a teenager during the 1970s living in North Carolina. During one spring vacation, my family drove from Chapel Hill to camp close to the ocean at Huntington Beach State Park at Murrells Inlet, South Carolina. After getting situated at our site, my parents, two young brothers, sister, and I crossed the street and strolled along what was then only a narrow road to visit Brookgreen Gardens. There, we ambled through a forest path where classically inspired sculptures stood—and still stand—amid garden clearings.

That walk through woods and gardens opened up a new world of art for me. Archer and Anna Hyatt Huntington acquired Oaks Plantation, the former rice plantation where my family and I walked. Within two years, the Huntingtons transformed 9,200 acres of beachfront property, rice fields, undulating river views, marshy tidal swampland vistas, and forest land of sandy pine trees and moss-draped oaks into a botanical garden. Now a national landmark, it is the home for the nation's largest and most comprehensive collection of nineteenth-century and modern American figurative sculpture.

That day at Brookgreen Gardens I learned that sculpture serves many purposes. The best sculptures of people evoke a whole life and are not fixed on a particular moment. Sculptural portraits are formed from many impressions and are designed to be seen from many angles at different times of day in changing light. Monuments are often created to honor real people so that their legacies continue to be remembered. Other monuments honor imaginary figures who spark our imagination, give us pleasure, and remind us of virtues to live by. Sculptures can be places where people congregate and talk about anything in the world. Their purpose is to heal, to inform, and to inspire.

Often, we forget or don't think to give credit to sculptors, but they are the ones who create monuments that have the capacity to elicit a wide range of emotions and thoughts. The sculptors are truly the unsung heroes, even when they are not acknowledged for their artistry, creativity, and courage at a time when it was, like most things, men's work. Not only have women sculptors made an extraordinary amount of good quality sculptures, large and small. Influenced by their circumstances of class, race, gender, and time period, they have brought their own points of view.

Pioneering sculptors have been chosen for this book with the hope they will never be forgotten for leading the way. Present-day sculptors such as Penelope Jencks, Meredith Bergmann, Alison Saar, and Kristen Visbal have been chosen as well for their contributions to their art and for how they are leaving their mark on the political scene and modern design. Together, the artists featured in this introductory book are helping to redefine the medium, question history, and evolve the future of their profession.

Many people deserve credit for their assistance. Foremost is my friend Carol Ward, art historian and director of the Lexington Historical Society, who had faith in this project and wrote the Introduction. Steven Taylor, my husband, who is a wonderful photographer and traveling companion, is responsible for photographing many of the sculptures. Special thanks to the talented sculptor Kristen

Visbal for writing the Foreword. I am especially indebted to editor Lisa Messinger for generously reviewing the manuscript and suggesting corrections and modifications.

Special thanks to all those who helped to find or take photographs and gave permission to reproduce images: Chamisa Redmond, Alexis Valentine, and Kenneth Johnson of the Library of Congress; Andrea Ko and Elena Munoz-Rodriguez of the Newark Museum of Art; Helen Connor of the Davis Museum at Wellesley College; Anke Voss of the Concord Free Library in Concord, Massachusetts; Monica Park of the Brooklyn Museum of Art; Sophie Teer and Rachel Elwes of Ben Elwes Fine Art in London; Diana Edkins and Robert Dunkin of Art Resource; Daniel Trujillo of the Artists Rights Society; Jude Fowler Smith of the Art Gallery of New South Wales in Australia; Allen Phillips and Stacey Stachow of the Wadsworth Atheneum Museum of Art; James Kohler of the Cleveland Museum of Art; Derek Ostergard of the Malvina Hoffman Estate; Steve Comba of the Benton Museum of Art at Pomona College in Claremont, California; Aliya Kalla of L.A. Louver in Venice, California; my nephew Noah Ausherman; and my daughter Chloe Chapman.

Sincere thanks to Gordon Goff, Federica Ewing, and Kirby Anderson of ORO Editions for finding this project worthy of print and appreciating how much the photographs add to the text. I'm also grateful for the graphic design work of Anita Stumbo.

On a more personal note, I am thankful for my family—my mother Rieneke Ausherman, my daughters Chloe and Lydia Chapman, and their families, including granddaughter Emma Jane Decker, my sister Judy Ausherman, my brothers Chuck and Steve Ausherman, and their families, and my husband Steven Taylor—for their love and encouragement.

—Maria Ausherman

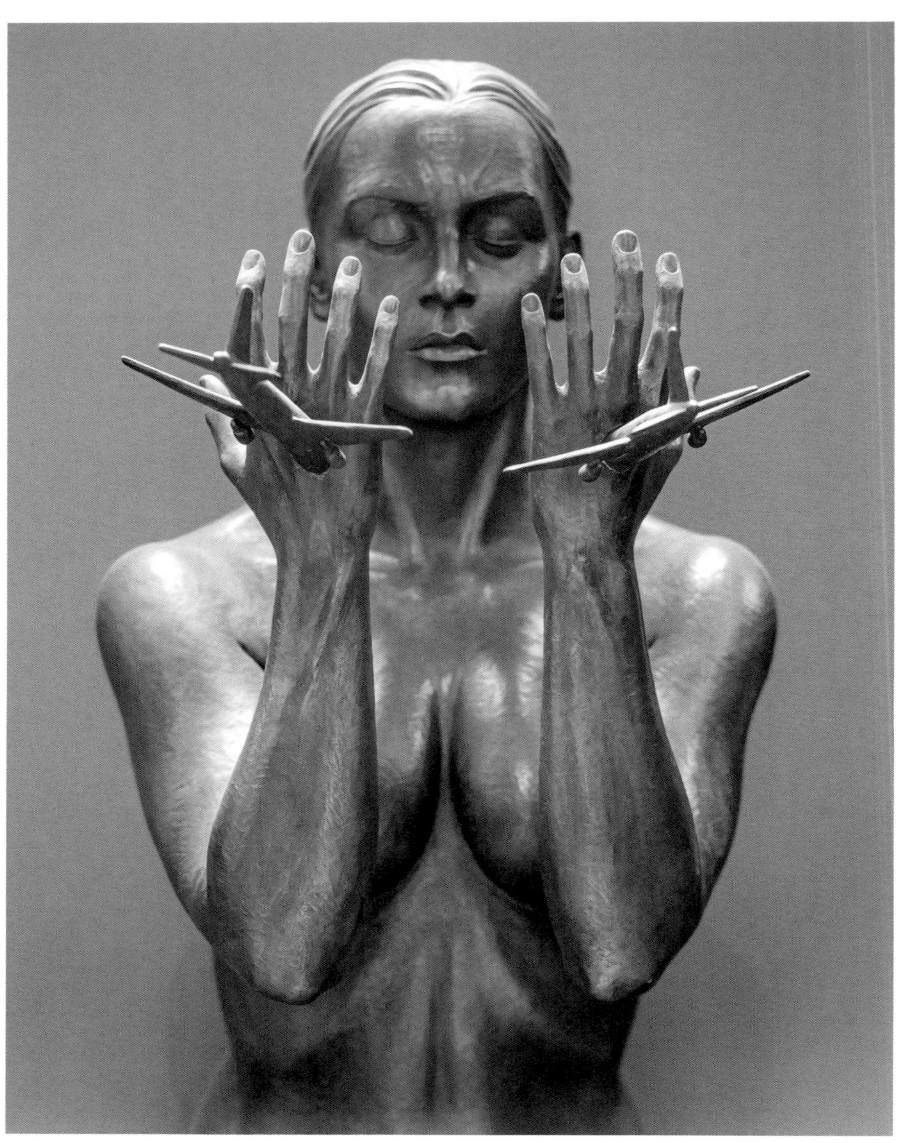

Memorial to September 11th, Installed 2011

Meredith Bergmann's sculpture at the Cathedral of St. John the Divine in New York City is a memorial to the tragedy of September 11th. The symbol of female empowerment and resiliency shows a young woman with her eyes closed in prayer and her palms turned inward to concentrate her inner strength and absorb the attack of two jets that have flown into her hands.

Foreword

THE SINGULAR COLLECTION of women portrayed in *Masters of Shape* exhibits the high tensile strength and malleability of a spider's silken thread. Artists who, through sheer tenacity, originated an artistic bedrock on which we, as sculptors, walk. Bound by a steely gusset, these women leave a formidable imprint on American art history. Nearly every one of them had the fortitude to take a stand for what they believed in, be it abolitionism, women's suffrage, women's rights, the spirit through which race or war is seen, or the promotion of the female form in art and how we perceive it. These strong feminine forms contrast with the eighteenth-century artistic feminine ideal where women appear heavily adorned, slight in stance, and act as ornamentation. Instead, we see the robust, full-hipped *Mother and Child* by Elizabeth Catlett and Alison Saar's *Grow'd* depicting a black woman in strong royal repose. Anna Hyatt Huntington's *Joan of Arc*, the first monument by a woman and New York's first feminist sculpture, thrusts her sword towards the sky, acting as the courageous leader we female sculptors follow.

Art reflects awareness. The physical labor, heavy materials, and endless hours seemed not to deter these female sculptors from their course. They embraced a traditionally masculine profession with aplomb, passion acting as the rudder through which they navigated their lives. Two hundred years later, art created by women commands just 2% of the art market, represents 13% of the art represented in museums, and in 2017, the University of Luxembourg concluded these works auction for a whopping 47.6% less than those artworks created by men. We, as artists, still have a long way to go to overcome this bias, making this book even more poignant for the valiant spirit which characterizes American women sculptors.

I joined these spirited women by advocating for gender equity with *Fearless Girl*, a strong and defiant young girl cast in bronze. The figure originally stared down *Charging Bull*, a sculpture that has become synonymous with the male-dominated Wall Street financial community. *Fearless Girl*, rendered quickly to unveil for International Women's Day 2017, is a harbinger of the role women will play in business tomorrow. The figure propagates education for girls, women in leadership, equal pay, and equal promotion on the job. The form is simple, the message literal. The response is global. *Fearless Girl* sent a message that women intend to stand up for their rights and will not back down. I join Anne Whitney, Harriet Hosmer, Edmonia Lewis, Janet Scudder, Augusta Savage, Elizabeth Catlett, Penelope Jencks, Meredith Bergmann, Alison Saar, and Gertrude Vanderbilt Whitney who felt her work would be taken more seriously if she were a man, in promoting equal rights.

So, what compels a sculptor? I can only speak for myself. I was driven to create and am largely self-taught like Margaret Foley. Sculpture, a hand-eye coordination, is intuitive. It can be perfected through study, technique, and exposure but, it must be there to begin with. Like many of the women sculptors in the book, I came from upper-class means, influenced by an artistic mother who painted and occasionally created sculpture. There was enough leisure afforded by finance to devote to such subjects as the creation of art for the pure beauty of it. What is significant, however, is that both of my parents encouraged me to be whatever I chose, never imposing any restrictions or gender bias. That's the real reason I cannot understand why or how women could be treated differently or paid less for the same job. In the awareness of the discrepancy in rights came purpose in art and the drive to convey which adds depth to the sculptor's work. It seems I share the same conviction regarding equality that these women who came before me and my contemporaries have. We, as artists, are the voice of society. We, as women, send a different message. We translate issues into tangible form. Since the beginning of time, equality has escaped us. Change comes slowly but, through the socially conscious artist, new ideas are conveyed.

Aesthetics ruled my creations until *Fearless Girl* when I found myself surprised at just how effective realism is at conveying a message. The women sculptors presented in this book work in realism; it's the way the realism is used that matters. Gertrude Whitney's compelling *Titanic Memorial*, a towering thirteen-foot granite figure of a partially draped man, casts the men of the Titanic as Christ-like in white stone, a symbolic homage to those who gave up their seats for women and children, never returning from that ship. Anna Hyatt Huntington's *Fighting Stallions* speaks to the raw power of nature. Edmonia Lewis's *Forever Free* bears the stamp of Lewis's abolitionist view, a call for racial equality.

Many of the mid-nineteenth century sculptors depicted here were expatriates who settled in Rome and who seemed to bridge old-world classic European style with American art in the delicate folds of drapery over powerful forms. They bridged the gender gap through excelling at the male profession of sculpture. In fact, women weren't supposed to have a profession. If they made art, it was small and easily rendered in the home. But these ladies were the first, working through realism to establish women in the arts and to portray the feminine subject.

All of us have traveled, studied, or lived in Europe, influencing the style of what we create. Emma Stebbins was the first to receive a public art commission through New York for her *Bethesda Fountain.* Anne Whitney depicted women in non-traditional stances, looking up as in *Lady Godiva* and paving the way for change. Louisa Lander created *Virginia Dare*, a sculpture that introduced nudity and the depiction of woman. The influential Harriet Hosmer was considered the first professional female sculptor. Edmonia Lewis was the first black sculptor of international recognition. Vinnie Ream was the youngest artist and the first woman to win a government commission presenting her *Abraham Lincoln* at twenty-three years old. These American women sculptors documented the ethnic races, immortalized notable members of society, and spoke freely, both literally and figuratively.

Patrons such as Gertrude Vanderbilt Whitney, whose greatest legacy is the Whitney Museum of American Art, embraced modernism and served to establish credibility in America art. Anna Hyatt Huntington, with her husband Archer Milton Huntington, established fourteen museums and Brookgreen Gardens sculpture park in South Carolina, housing the largest collection of American realist works. These women helped to establish our American art tradition and contributed to the landscape of monumental art in America.

Art is at its best when it addresses the issues of its era. The objective gives the work heart and substance. The women chronicled in this book are the women who elevated American art through the mastery of technique and style. New York City plays a central role in their lives, as in mine, as a community for sharing information and a canvas on which to present art. These women transcend gender roles and, through their growing awareness and discontent, initiate feminist art in a response to racial and gender bias. They speak through their art. Their response is natural. How long will it take? How long, really, before true socio-economic equality is achieved between genders? When will racial bias ebb? The style of art women in America create may change, but the message will always reflect our culture.

—Kristen Visbal
Visbal Fine Bronze Sculpture

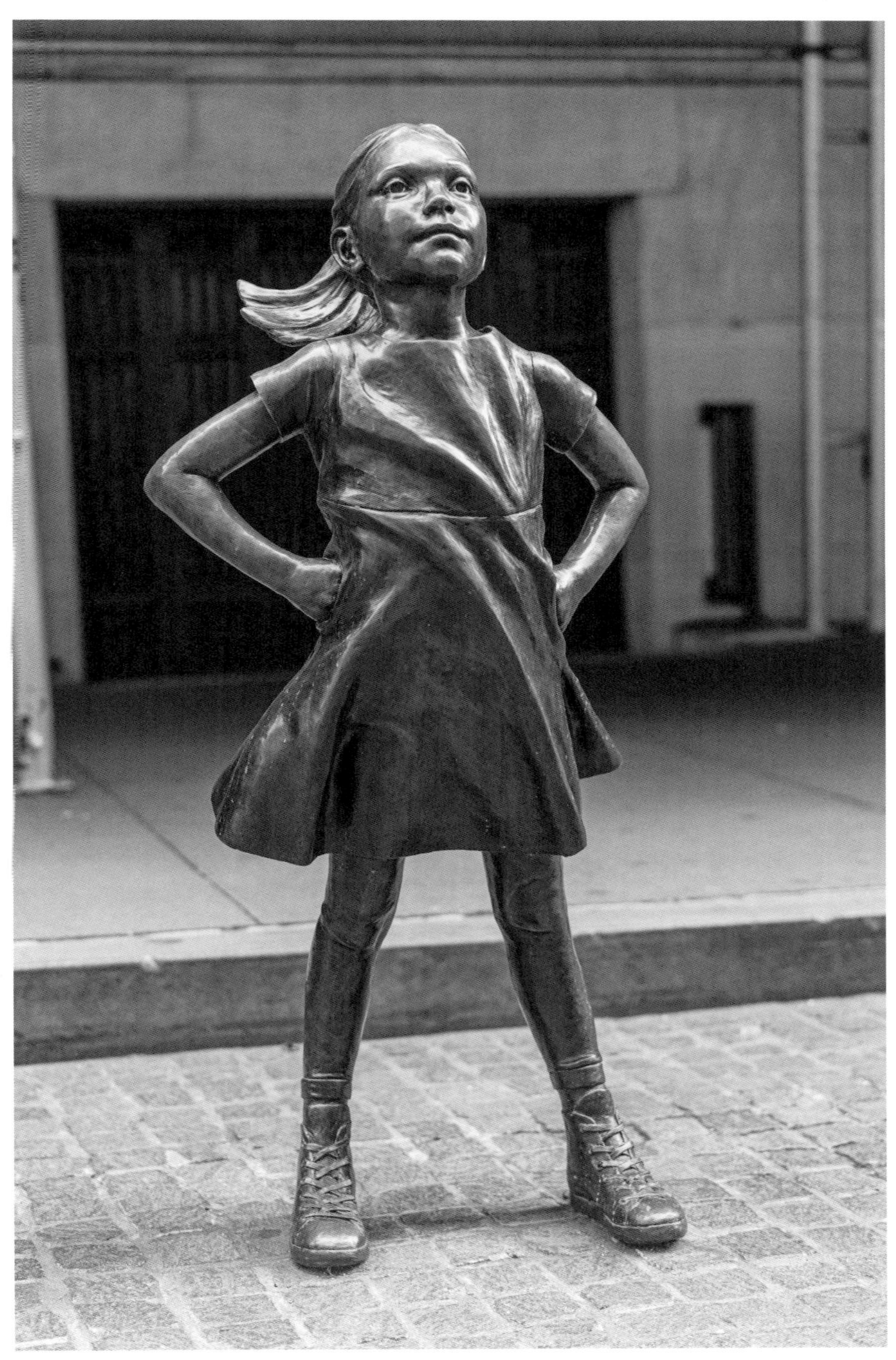

***Fearless Girl*, 2017**

Introduction

"SOMETHING MUST BE DONE!" This famous quote originated at the start of the American Revolution during the Battle of Lexington when Abigail Harrington shouted to her son to go out and defend their town. It was taken up as a suffragette call to arms when Caroline Wellington sewed the words on a banner carried in the 1913 Women's March in Washington, D.C. Now it is the inspiration for Meredith Bergmann, one of the sculptors discussed in this book. Meredith's sculptures in Boston and New York City create a dialogue between the past and the present, with an eye to the future, and she has turned that eye to Lexington to create a new piece entitled *Something Is Being Done*, the first monument in the birthplace of America dedicated to women. It may seem foreign to us that this is only just happening, but it speaks to a longer and more complicated history of women being depicted in sculptures and being sculptors themselves.

There is a long history of women in sculpture. The first sculpture known is the *Venus of Willendorf*, dating from 25,000 years ago, of a naked woman with over-exaggerated breasts and sexual features, long determined to be visual signs of heightened fertility. We can then look throughout the annals of art history to see sculptures of women: Greek and Roman goddesses, slave figures from the Baroque and Rococo eras, mythological figures from the nineteenth century, and through contemporary art movements with pieces by Jeff Koons, Murakami, and Marc Quinn. All women, all nude, or mostly nude, and presented in passive stances presented for the male gaze. Because what do all the creators of these sculptures have in common? They were, or are, all men. While there is no doubt the pieces are beautiful, create moments of feeling, and are integral parts of the art historical canon, they intrinsically speak differently to the viewer due to the creation of the female form by a male and for a traditionally male audience. One is reminded of the story of Pygmalion, an ancient Greek sculptor who fell in love with the female sculpture he created because she was so beautiful and lifelike.

We know, as this book so rightfully showcases, that there were female sculptors working throughout history, but why don't we know more about them? Why are they only recently getting the accolades they deserve and have been denied for so long? Partly, as the Guerrilla Girls asked in 1989, "Do women have to be naked to get into the Met Museum?" This iconic question is followed on their art/advertisement with the explanation that "less than five percent of the artists in the Modern Art Sections are women, but eighty-five percent of the nudes are female." Herein lies the salient problem: What the public tends to learn and know about art is based on what is in museums and galleries, what critics tell us we should like, and what exhibition is the hot thing to go explore. Up until recently, that did not include women artists at the forefront.

The fact that we still feel the need to separate out female sculptors so they can get noticed in and of itself seems antiquated and out of date. This book will introduce the reader to the rich history of seventeen artists, knowing there are so many more out there to explore and research. These women artists are diverse; their subject matter is extremely and intensely personal, and just as with sculptures of women done by men, their works take on a new life and meaning knowing that the sculptor was female. We can delve into the mind of each artist, explore what was going on historically to have her create the piece in the style and manner she did, and discover how she developed the technical skill to create it.

The other vital aspect the book brings to light is the medium of sculpture itself. The relationship between artist, artwork, and viewer is dramatically different when considering a sculpture compared to a drawing or painting. The standard viewing of a traditional two-dimensional work is passive, with a very clear understanding of where a viewer should stand and how they should address the work and explore it visually. For a sculpture, there are so many aspects to consider in this relationship, including medium, placement, scale, and accessibility. A sculpture creates a *conversation* with the viewer and the space it inhabits—a phrase Meredith Bergmann used in a recent meeting I was lucky to join. For me, it is a much more dynamic relationship and perhaps why I tend to be drawn more and more to sculpture in museums and galleries, especially outdoors, because more so than painting, these sculptures invite me to build a different type of relationship with them.

What struck me examining the women represented in this book was that some of our most well-known and beloved sculptures throughout history, especially in the nineteenth and twentieth centuries, were created by women. Historical texts discuss male artists to such an extent that women have largely been left out of the narrative, not based on their not being proficient artists, skilled at their craft, or classically trained just as their male counterparts, but because art historical canon is so driven by the male perspective that unfortunately women are moved to the sidelines—until now.

The early women sculptors outlined in this book typically focused on subjects that were more in the feminine sphere. Janet

Scudder was influenced by Renaissance masters like Donatello to create figures of children and elves for the gardens of her wealthy clients, becoming not only one of the most successful women sculptors of the early twentieth century but also a trendsetter who helped popularize outdoor sculpture. Bessie Potter Vonnah also focused on outdoor sculpture, and one of my favorite pieces in Central Park, in New York City, is her sculpture in honor of Frances Hodgson Burnett, the author of *The Secret Garden*, where the placement of the piece around a lily pond is a prime example of how a sculpture's setting is just as important as the sculpture itself. Similarly, the famous *Angel of the Waters* fountain at the heart of Central Park was created by a female sculptor, Emma Stebbins. This public art commission was the first ever awarded to a woman in New York City. Another trendsetter discussed in this book is Gertrude Vanderbilt Whitney, who although we would classify her sculptures as rather traditional in nature, was the first major proponent for contemporary art (of her time) and founded what we know today as the Whitney Museum.

There is also a group of female sculptors who historically had ties to the Boston area; they all had to deal with blatant sexism and hardships that male sculptors never encountered. Harriet Goodhue Hosmer's sculptures became her children as she remained single throughout her professional career—something women still grapple with today. The best-known woman sculptor of her day, Hosmer helped her fellow female artists as they trained and worked in Italy and back in the United States. This was especially useful for someone like Edmonia Lewis, who feared accusations of someone else doing her work. Unlike her male counterparts who hired Italian workers to assist them, Lewis carved all her own works, sculpting heroines she wished to emulate. Another example of the pervasive sexism of the time concerns Louisa Lander, who was attacked by colleagues for supposedly "being overly familiar with a model." Unlike her male counterparts, this rumor would cause permanent damage to her career, a double standard that still exists today. Vinnie Ream similarly was accused of plagiarism as she worked on Lincoln

Memorial, and luckily found a circle of friends in the American expatriate community of sculptors, including Harriet Hosmer, Edmonia Lewis, Margaret Foley, Anne Whitney, and Emma Stebbins, whose studio was next to Ream's. The community these women created helped them navigate the dangerous waters of a male-dominated art form and the art critics who wanted to bring them down with baseless accusations. Similarly to Ream, there were female sculptors who focused on historical figures and social causes–Anne Whitney with her pieces, such as Africa (concerning the Emancipation Proclamation), a statue of Samuel Adams for the Capitol Building in Washington, D.C. and Charles Sumner in the Boston Public Garden (that stands at Harvard Law School).

A number of female sculptors have used their medium to address social causes. Three of them included in the book focus on African American experiences in America, both historically and today. Augusta Savage created portraits of everyday people, but perhaps her most well-known piece was *The Harp* for the 1939 New York World's Fair, unfortunately, torn down at the end of the fair. Inspired by spirituals and James Weldon Johnson's poem, "Lift Every Voice and Sing," Savage's sixteen-foot sculpture depicted twelve stylized singers as the strings of an enormous harp, all held in a large hand. Elizabeth Catlett moved to Harlem in the 1940s and became part of a group of intellectuals living there. Her pieces speak, in a more abstract way, to what it was like to be black in the middle of the twentieth century, and she uses motifs from African masks and historical sculptures to bring the past and present together.

Two of the three most contemporary of the sculptors discussed in this book, Alison Saar and Meredith Bergmann, look at women's role in both history and contemporary society. They use their artwork to expand the narrative about women's bodies and the marginalization of women and to bring historical women to the forefront. Surrounding Saar's sculpture of *Harriet Tubman*, natural elements represent the woods Tubman and her Underground Railroad passengers traveled to freedom. On her skirt, images relate to the slaves she helped. The base, meanwhile, focuses on her life. Bergmann's work spotlights women throughout history and their role as both women and key players in changing the face of America. Her sculptures portray the women in a hyper-realistic way, with a very emotional touch.

As you read through this catalog of women sculptors, I hope you'll note the quote by Meredith Bergmann that stood out to me. With her pieces, she hopes she is "breaking the bronze ceiling." This book plays a role as well by shedding more light on sculptors throughout history who are immensely talented in their craft and happen to be women as well. I hope that through this scholarship, these artists further gain their rightful place alongside their brother sculptors.

—Carol S. Ward
Executive Director
Lexington Historical Society

1

Emma Stebbins

(1815–1882)

EMMA STEBBINS was born in New York in 1815 to Mary Largin and John Stebbins. One of nine children, Stebbins grew up in a wealthy household with parents who encouraged her artistic abilities. Her father was president of the North River Bank, and her brother, Henry, would become head of the New York Stock Exchange. Talented at an early age, Stebbins studied oil painting at the studio of portrait painter Henry Inman. Before she was thirty years old, she was elected an associate of the National Academy of Design, where she exhibited. Two years later, she showed copies of oil paintings at the Pennsylvania Academy. Until age forty, she worked as an amateur painter and sculptor in her upper-middle-class home in New York City.

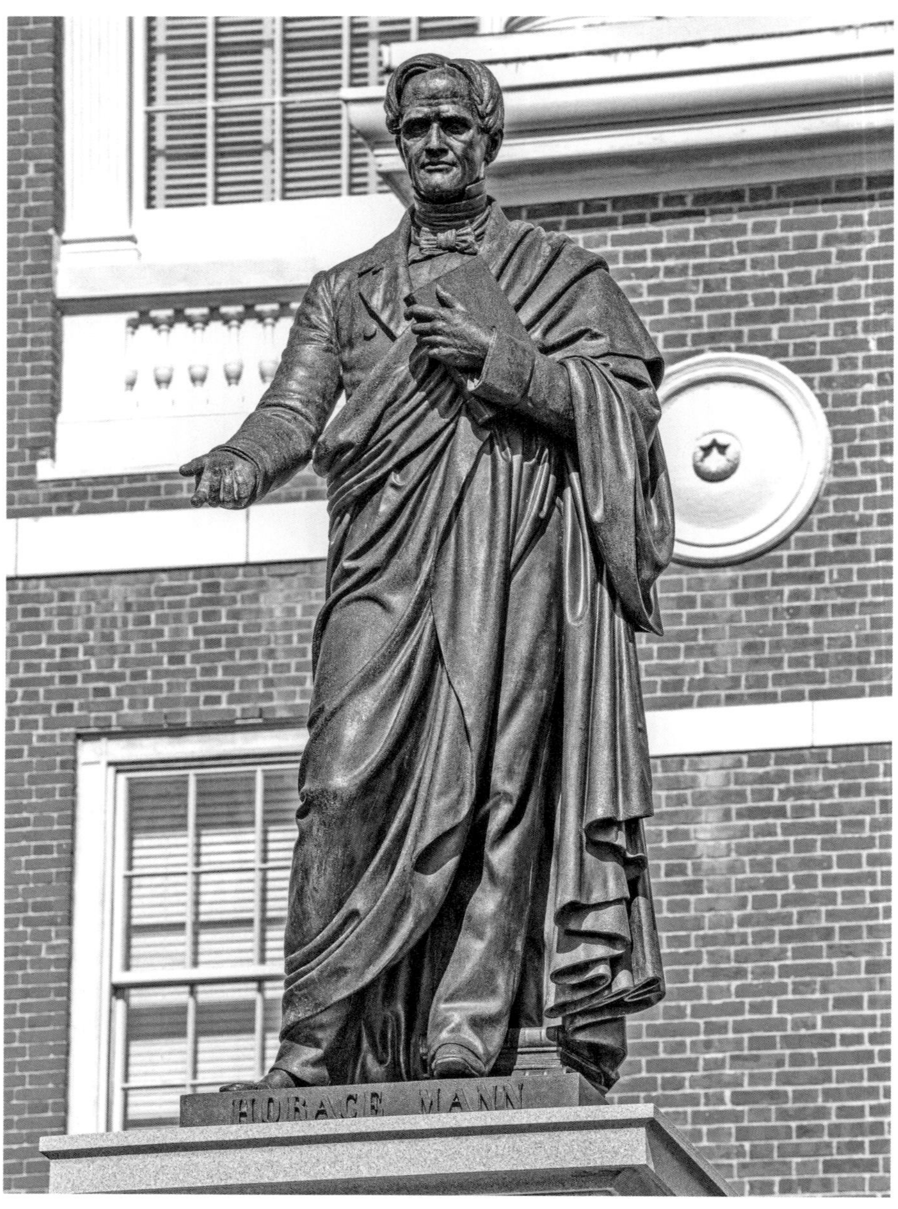

Horace Mann, 1865

Stebbins created the Horace Mann sculpture while living in Rome. Known for his commitment to public education, Horace Mann (1796–1859) was an educational reformer who believed education should be universal and free, and that its aims should be civic virtue and character.

At the age of forty-one, Stebbins left home to train in Rome, where she turned to sculpture. Welcomed into the expatriate community of American artists who lived there, she studied with Paul Akers, an American sculptor from Maine. She soon became friends with sculptor Harriet Hosmer and actress Charlotte Cushman, who was a leader in the expatriate community and a mentor to female artists and writers. Cushman fell in love with Stebbins and stopped supporting Hosmer so she could find projects for Stebbins instead. Stebbins and Cushman would become lifelong companions and frequently entertained at the home they shared. One of Stebbins' first sculptures was a bust of Cushman, praised in *The New York Times* as "the finest achievement in marble yet reached by female genius in Rome."

Stebbins competed with Harriet Hosmer for a commission to create a statue of educator *Horace Mann*, who was known as the "apostle of female education." Stebbins was awarded the commission, and her bronze of Mann stands in front of the State House in Boston, wearing a Roman cloak over modern clothes. He holds a book in his left hand and beckons with his right hand.

Stebbins's best-known commission is her *Angel of the Waters* (1873) for Bethesda Fountain in Central Park. Calvert Vaux, one of the two designers of Central Park, which began construction in 1857, situated the fountain on Bethesda Terrace at the end of the promenade near 72nd Street. The terrace was designed to be the centerpiece of the park, where visitors could come and enjoy the view of the Lake, Central Park's largest man-made body of water. Stebbins's brother, Henry, was a member of the Central Park Board of Commissioners and helped to secure the commission for Emma, and her family helped pay for the casting of it in bronze in Munich.

A central location where people today continue to congregate and relax, the fountain showcases the eight-foot-tall angel, which stands with wings outstretched and one foot on the upper basin. In one hand, she holds a lily, while the other hand is extended in a gesture of benediction. Cherubs around the base represent Health,

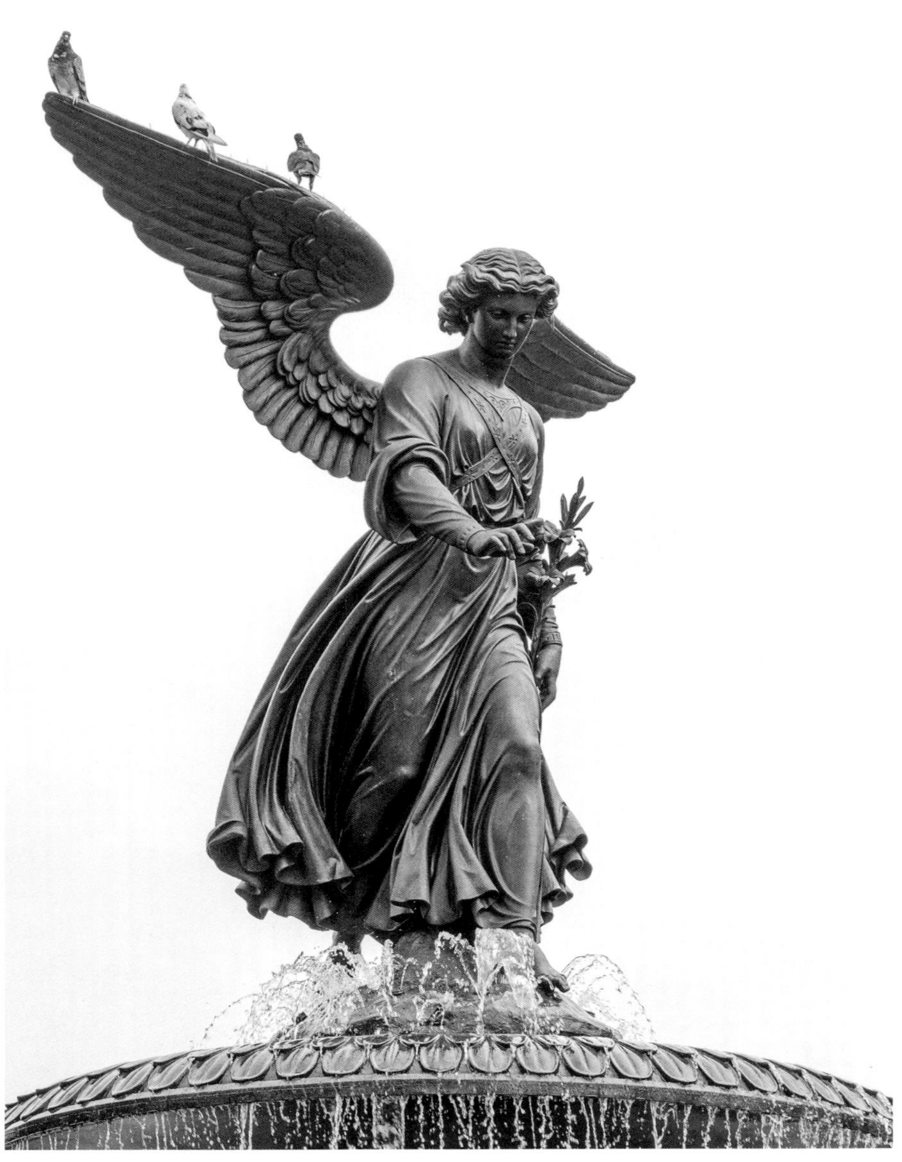

Angel of the Waters, 1873

The *Angel of the Waters* sculpture was the first public art commission ever awarded to a woman in New York City. The Angel stands atop the Bethesda Fountain, which is the focal point of Bethesda Terrace, the centerpiece of Central Park where visitors gather to view the nearby lake.

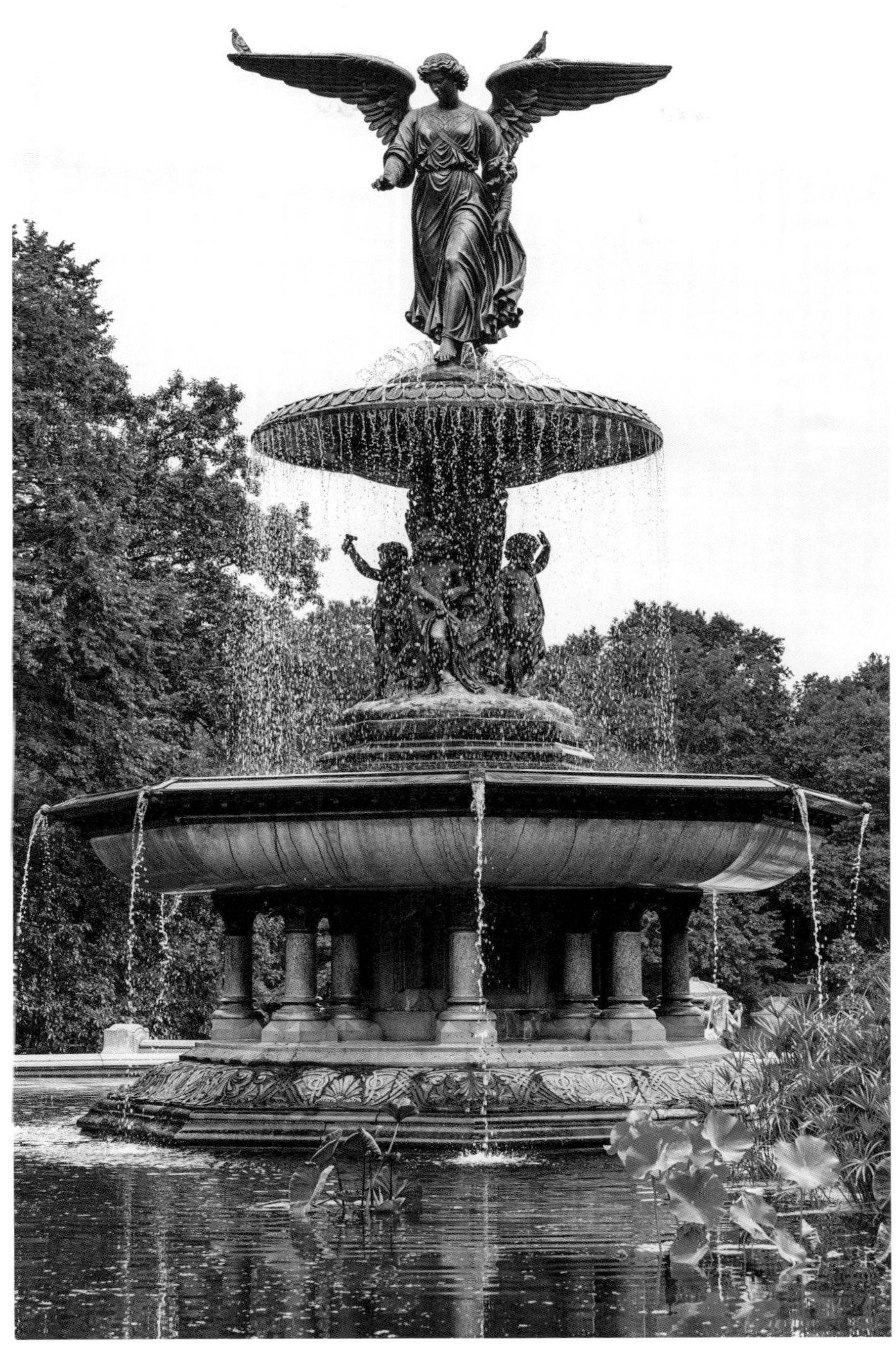

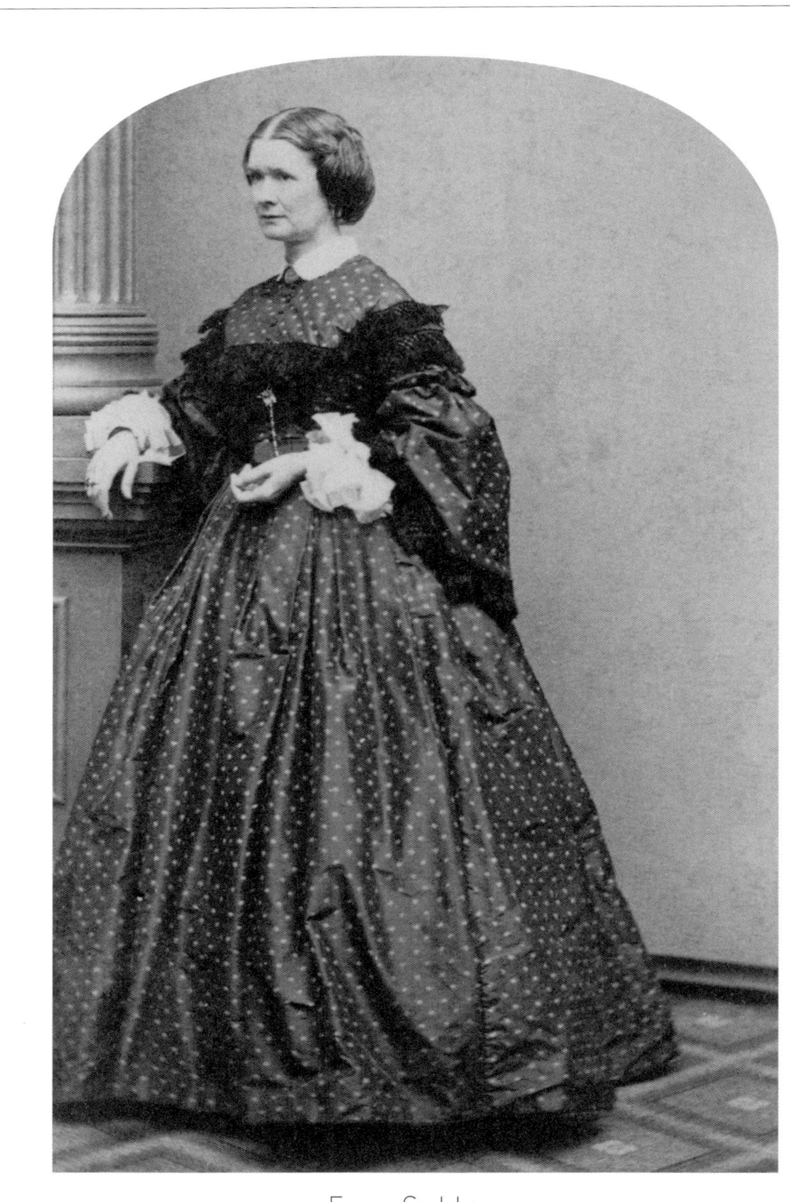

Emma Stebbins

"I did my little part as well as I could and with some of the saving grace of truth and love to sanctify it—whatever its failures," Emma Stebbins wrote of her career to fellow sculptor, Anne Whitney[1] in 1874.

Temperance, Purity, and Peace. Stebbins based the sculpture on the biblical story of the angel who imbues the waters of Bethesda with healing powers. Conceived as a tribute to the Croton Aqueduct, a complex water distribution system built in 1842 that brought badly needed fresh water to the city, the public art commission was the first ever awarded to a woman in New York City.

Cushman and Stebbins lived in Rome together for twelve years. But when Cushman began to battle breast cancer, Stebbins followed her back to Newport, Rhode Island, where they settled in a villa. Despite the pain of her condition, Cushman toured the country to make one more theatrical comeback before her death in 1876. She was well-received by the public. William Cullen Bryant recited an ode in her honor, and an impromptu parade on Fifth Avenue developed after the show. Stebbins wrote Cushman's biography, *Charlotte Cushman: Letters and Memories of Her Life*, published in 1878. In 1882, Emma Stebbins died in New York at age sixty-seven, most likely from lung disease caused by years of inhaling marble dust. She is buried in the Green-Wood Cemetery in Brooklyn.

Anne Whitney

(1821–1915)

BORN IN Watertown, Massachusetts, in 1821, Anne Whitney came from a wealthy, liberal, and supportive family that, like Harriet Hosmer's, traced its roots to the Massachusetts Bay Colony. Since Whitney could not be educated at Yale or Harvard because she was a woman, she was tutored at home and also spent a year at Mrs. Samuel Little's Select School for Young Ladies in Bucksport, Maine. She went on to study in Rome, Munich, and Paris before returning to the United States. In 1846, she opened a small school in Salem, Massachusetts, which operated until 1848, when she left Massachusetts to travel.

Whitney began to write poetry and was published throughout the 1850s in magazines such as *Atlantic Monthly* and *Harper's*. She became part of the New England literary scene, developing friendships with author Ralph Waldo Emerson and Unitarian leader Theodore Parker, among other prominent figures in the community. Whitney was a staunch supporter of social reform movements, such as the abolition of slavery and feminism. She gave poetry readings to raise money for the establishment of a women's hospital, an effort led by Elizabeth Blackwell, one of the nation's first women doctors. Whitney's sonnets attracted the attention of the leading feminists of the day.

Shortly before her two volumes of collected poems were published in 1859, Whitney decided to become a sculptor. Encouraging her to make the career change at the age of thirty-six, her brother built a small studio for her at their house. Throughout the 1860s, she experimented with sculpture and created portrait busts, mainly of relatives.

While Whitney was living in Brooklyn to study anatomy at a local hospital, she met and fell in love with aspiring painter Abby Adeline "Addy" Manning. The women would become lifelong companions.

Eager to learn more about sculpture techniques, Whitney studied privately for two years with Boston sculptor William Rimmer, one of the country's best anatomy instructors. Although women were not permitted access to life drawing classes where they could sketch the male nude form, soon after her studies with Rimmer, Whitney created *The Lotus Eater*, the first male nude made by an American woman. While in Boston, she befriended Harriet Hosmer and Edmonia Lewis, to whom she gave private lessons.

Addressing abolitionist and feminist concerns, Whitney's first life-sized sculpture was of a fully clothed *Lady Godiva* (1862), an eleventh-century Englishwoman who rode nude on horseback to prevent unreasonable taxes from being imposed by her husband on his tenants. Whitney based the strong, resolute figure on Tennyson's poem "Godiva" but depicts Godiva at the moment when she decides to accept humiliation in exchange for social good. The following year, when the Emancipation Proclamation was signed, Whitney created *Africa* (1863), a portrayal of an African woman rising from slavery. The reclining figure shades her eyes from the blinding light of freedom as she awakens from her long slumber.

In 1867, at the age of forty-six, Whitney and her partner, Addy Manning, moved to Rome, where their sculptor friends, Harriet Hosmer and Edmonia Lewis, were living. The couple remained there for four years, establishing contact with other prominent American artists like Emma Stebbins and Vinnie Ream.

Whitney's finest work while in Rome was *Roma* (1869), an allegorical image of the poverty-stricken, decaying city, represented as an old peasant woman. Within the hem of her dress are pictured medallions of famous Italian artworks, including the *Apollo Belvedere*, *Laocoon*, and *Dying Gaul*, all of which are meant to remind us of the city's greatness. Nonetheless, the hunch-backed woman holds pennies in her right hand and in her left, a license to beg. The sculpture was an expression of Whitney's sympathy for the citizens of Rome, who were experiencing political and social instability because of the struggle to unify the secular government and the papacy. Deemed offensive to papal authorities, the sculpture was banned in Rome, so Whitney smuggled it out of the country and displayed it in London, Boston, at the Philadelphia Centennial, and at the 1893 Chicago World's Columbian Exposition. It was later installed at Wellesley College in Massachusetts, to which Whitney and her family had close ties and where she taught for a time.

Whitney returned to America in 1871, and in 1876 created a statue of *Samuel Adams* for the Capitol Building in Washington, D.C. The statue of Adams defiantly standing with arms crossed and a scroll in one hand was so well received in Boston that a bronze version was placed in Adams Square in front of Faneuil Hall.

Following the death of abolitionist *Charles Sumner* in 1874, the Boston Art Committee sought to memorialize him with a statue to be erected in a place of prominence in the Boston Public Garden. They requested submissions from local artists, and Whitney anonymously entered her design. She was awarded the commission, but when the Committee discovered that the artist was a woman, they rescinded the commission, and her statue languished for almost three decades until it was resurrected in 1902. The sculpture now stands outside Harvard Law School.

Although she encountered injustices in her own life, one success led to another as Whitney created sculptures inspired by what she

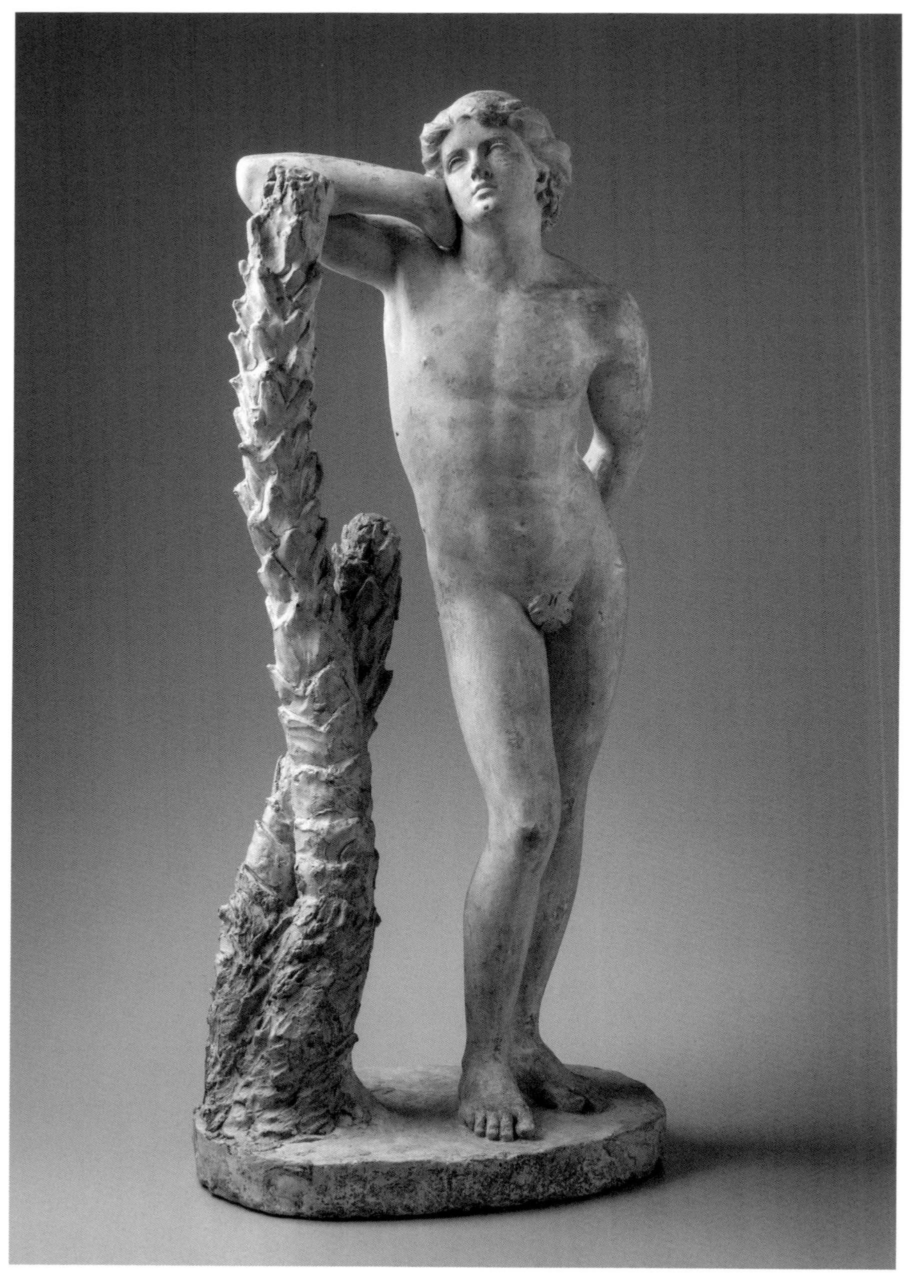

The Lotus Eater, 1868

The original marble nude but for a fig leaf was based on a Tennyson poem, which in turn was based on a passage in Homer's *Odyssey.*

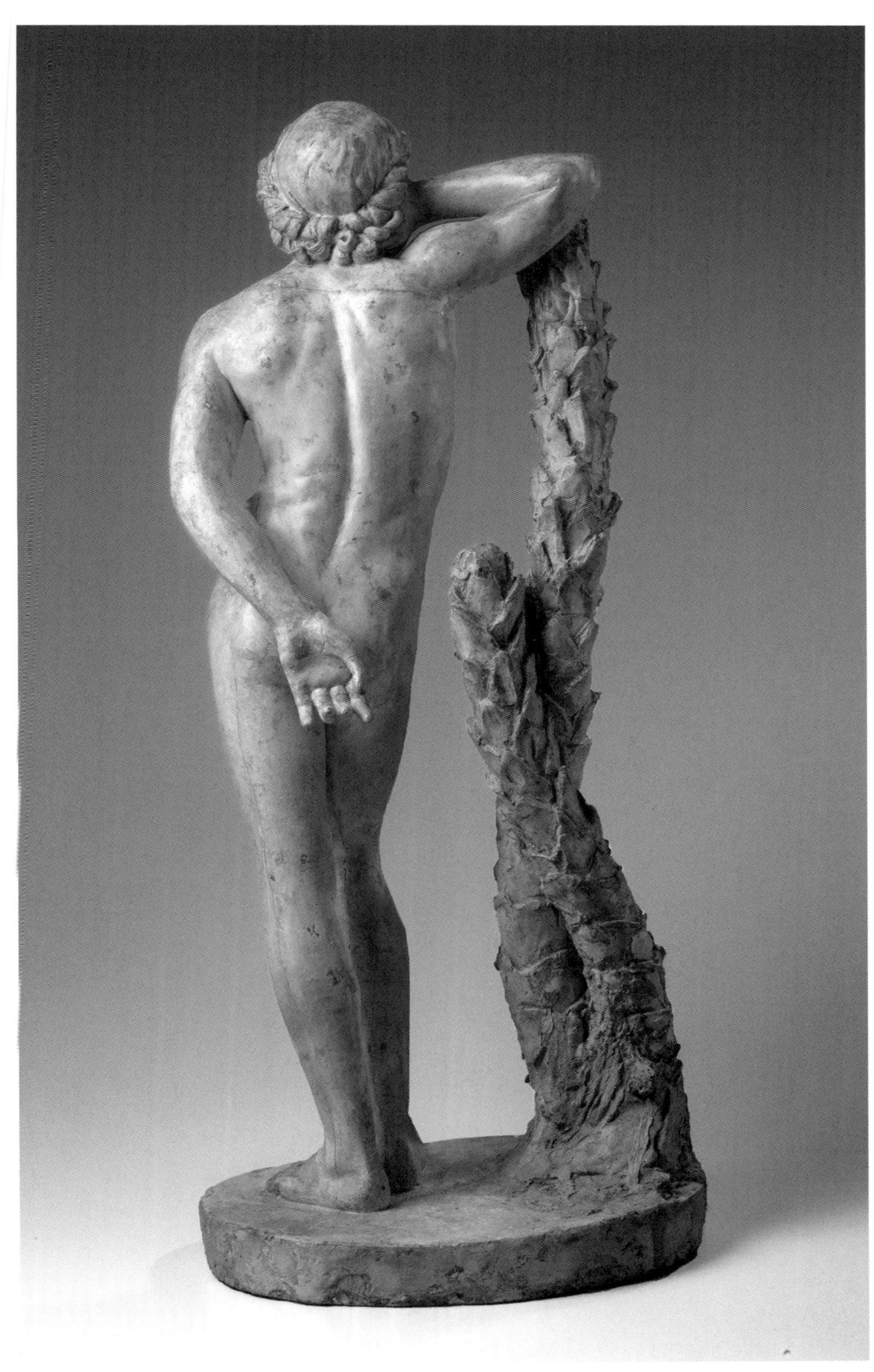

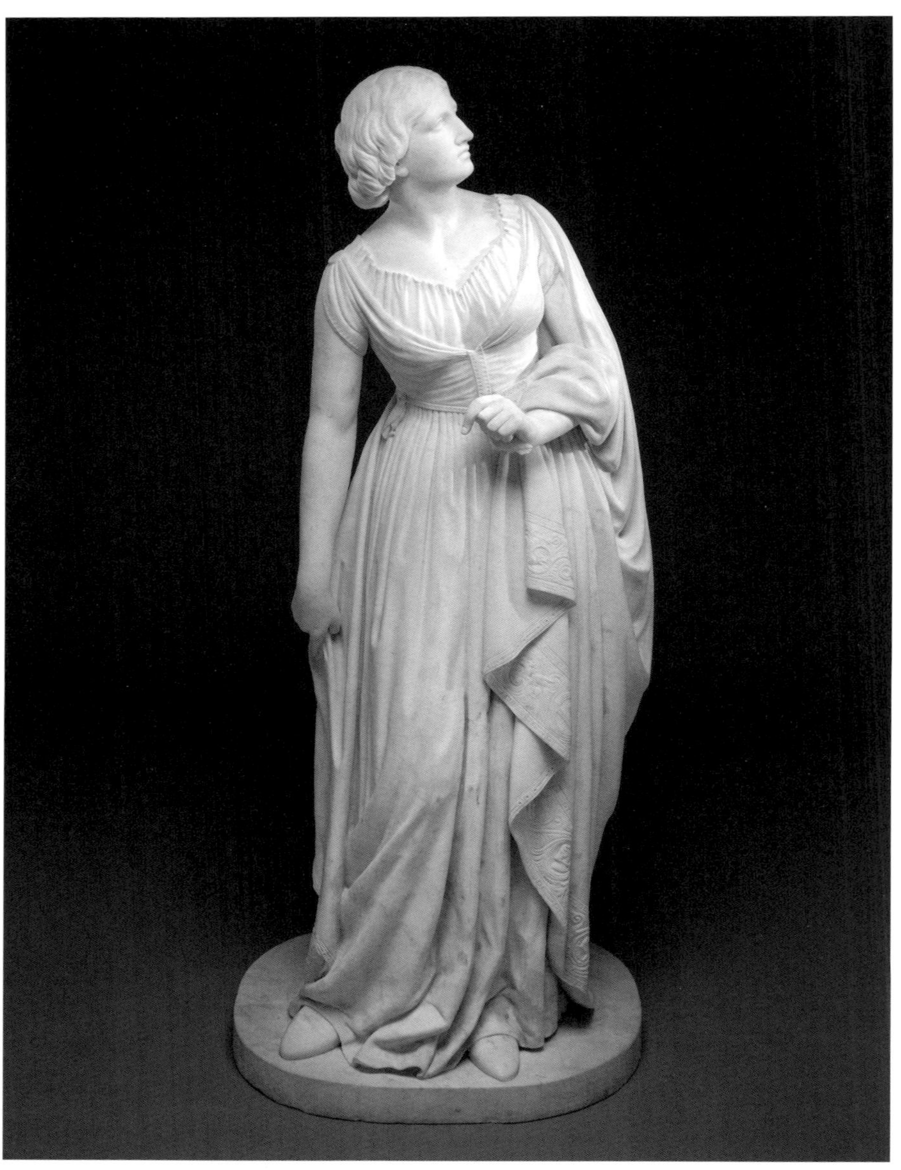

Lady Godiva, 1862

Whereas most visual interpretations depict Godiva's nude ride, Whitney chose to represent the moment when she accepts her husband's challenge. Still fully clothed, she looks upward, recalling the heavenward gaze of saints, thus underscoring the morality of Godiva's decision, because she undertook the ride for the sake of her subjects.

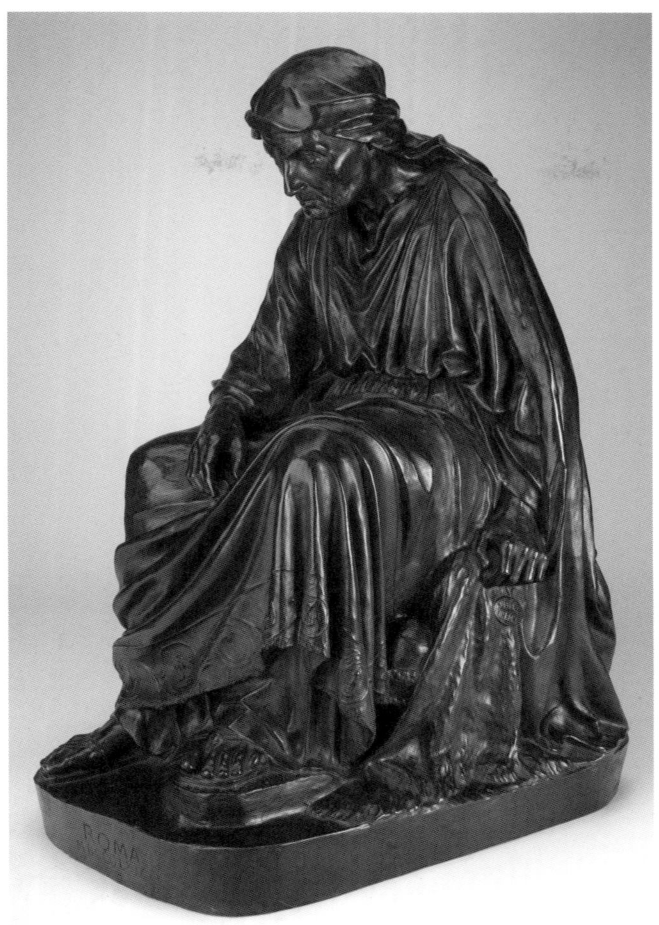

***Roma*, 1869**

Roma represents the plight of Roman citizens under the rule of the papacy.

viewed as social injustices—from the poverty on the streets of Rome to the oppression of slavery. Over the next three decades, Whitney continued to make statues for social causes, including portrait busts and full-length sculptures of prominent political and historical figures who championed freedom. These works included suffragists like Lucy Stone, Frances Willard, and Harriet Martineau, as well as abolitionists like Harriet Beecher Stowe and William Lloyd Garrison.

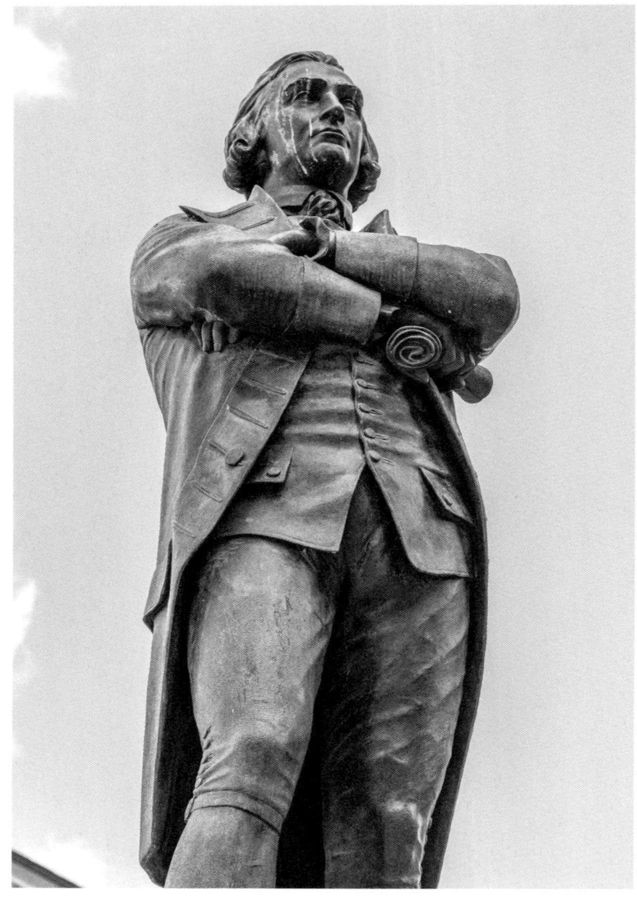

Samuel Adams, 1876

Samuel Adams (1722–1803) was an American statesman, politician, writer, and political philosopher, and one of the Founding Fathers of the United States. He protested unfair taxation on the residents of the colonies. His speeches and writings drew many American colonists into the fight for the end of British colonial rule.

Her works are in major museums throughout the United States and parks such as the Boston Common and the National Statuary Hall Collection in the United States Capitol building. The Wellesley College Archive holds Whitney's correspondence that consists of over 4,000 letters.

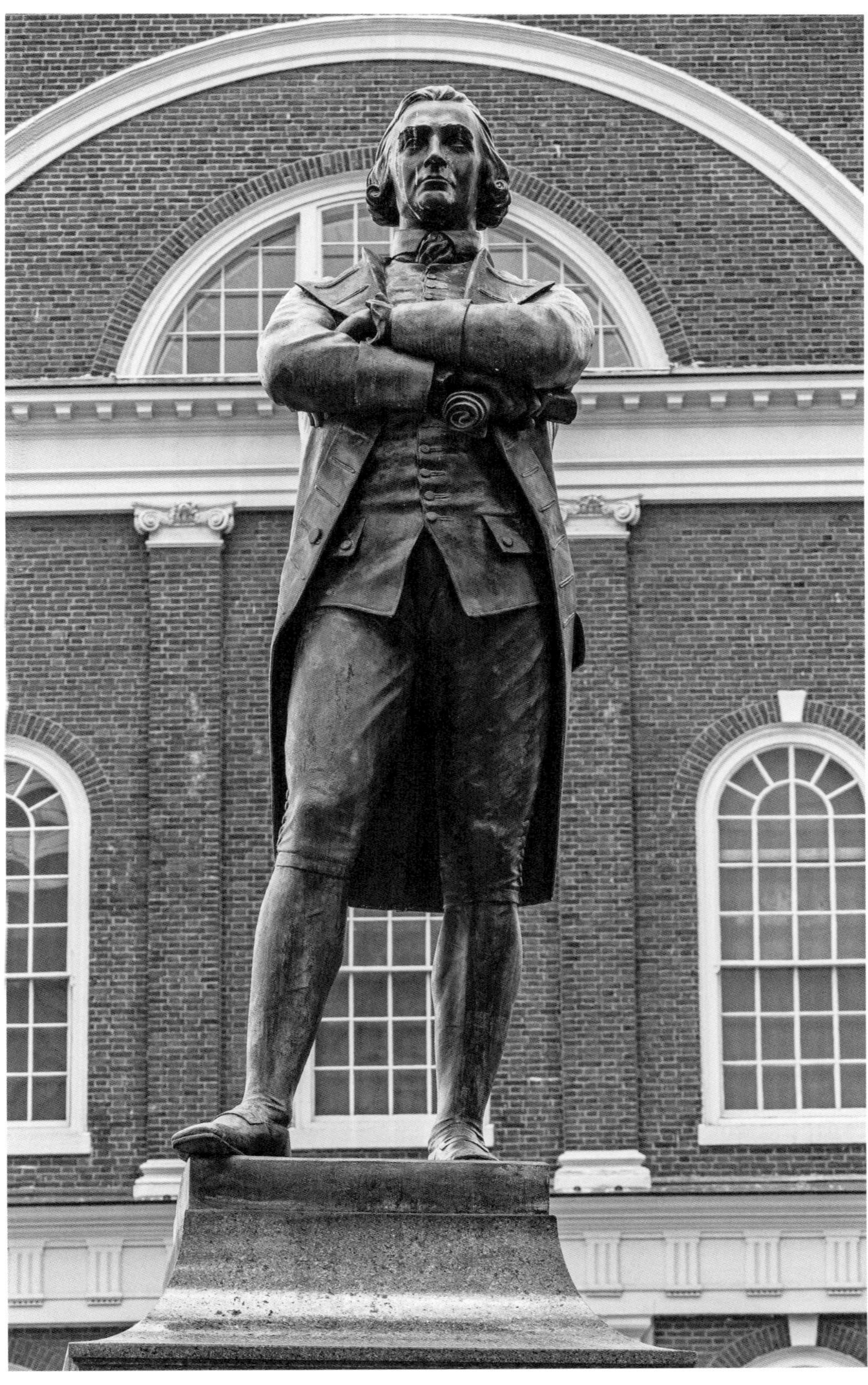

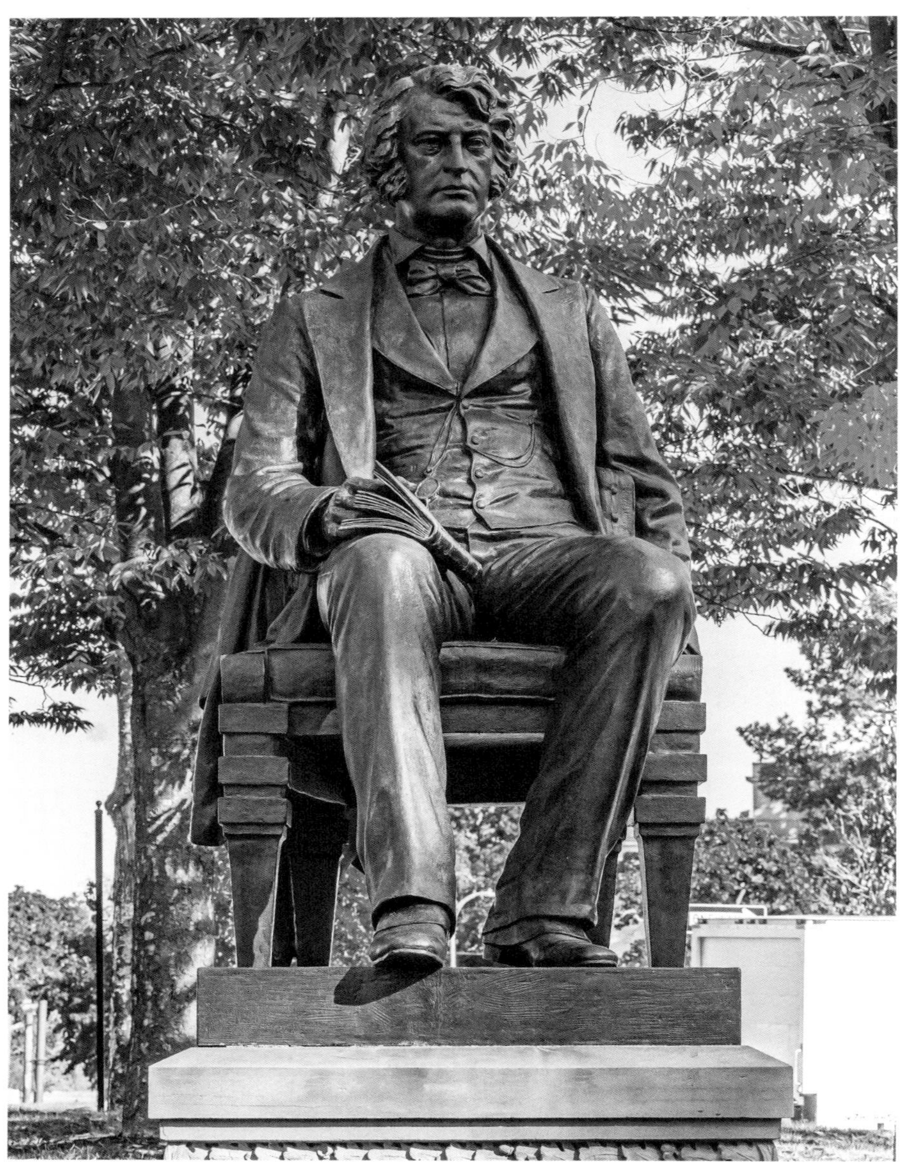

Charles Sumner, 1875

In 1856, American lawyer and politician Charles Sumner (1811–1874) was nearly killed by a South Carolina Congressman on the Senate floor two days after Sumner delivered an anti-slavery speech called "The Crime Against Kansas." Sumner fought hard to provide equal civil and voting rights for the freedmen.

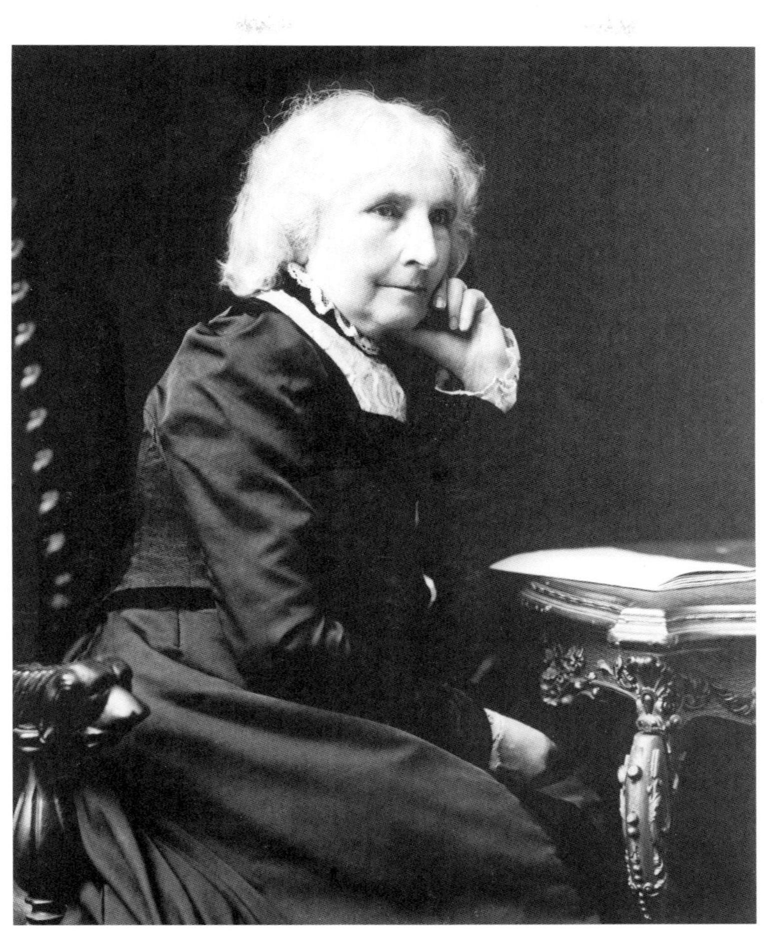

Anne Whitney

Anne Whitney was a passionate advocate for women's rights and social equality. "Bury your grievances. It will take more than a Boston Art Committee to quench me."[2]

At the age of ninety-three, Whitney died of cancer in Boston on January 23, 1915. Her ashes were buried in Cambridge at Mount Auburn Cemetery alongside those of Abby Adeline Manning under the same headstone.

3

Louisa Lander

(1826–1923)

LOUISA LANDER was born in Salem, Massachusetts, in 1826. At the age of six, she and her parents moved to her deceased grandmother's estate, where she was surrounded by art. Even as a child, she modeled heads for her dolls in clay and carved figures in stone with a penknife. Her mother died when she was in her early twenties. By then, she had already decided that she wanted to become a sculptor.

In 1855, Lander sailed to Italy and sought out famous American sculptor Thomas Crawford, whose work she had studied at the Boston Athenaeum. Impressed with her, Crawford would take her on as his one and only student until his untimely death from brain cancer in 1857. Rather than seek out a new mentor, Lander opened her own studio. During a trip to London, she visited the British Museum, where she became enamored of John White's sixteenth-century drawings of the New World. White's depiction of Virginia Dare, his granddaughter and the first child of English heritage born in America, inspired Lander to create a statue of her.

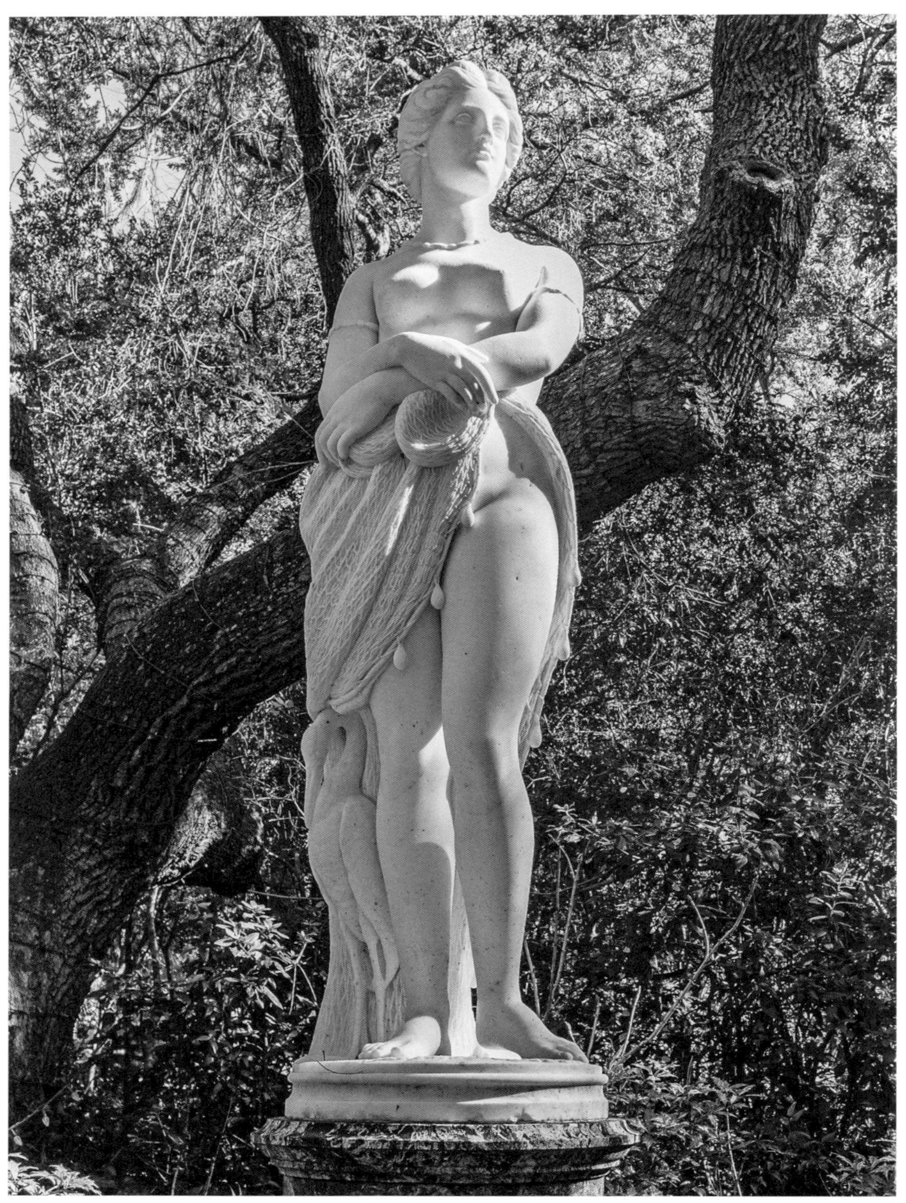

***Virginia Dare*, 1860**

Today the statue of *Virginia Dare* stands in the Elizabethan Gardens under a large live oak tree on the north end of Roanoke Island in Manteo, North Carolina, where she was born and subsequently vanished, along with every other member of what is now known as the "Lost Colony."

Virginia Dare's parents and grandfather were among the 117 settlers who left England in 1587 on an expedition sponsored by Sir Walter Raleigh. They landed on Roanoke Island, the site of an earlier unsuccessful attempt at a colony. Shortly after Virginia was born, John White, who was also the governor of the colony, returned to England for supplies. When he returned three years later with a relief expedition, the entire colony—including the Dare family—had vanished. Taking inspiration from one rumor that theorized the colony had been absorbed into a nearby Native American tribe, Louisa Lander created a statue of *Virginia Dare* as an adult Native American woman.

Lander invited author Nathaniel Hawthorne, a fellow Salemite, to sit for a bust while he was in Rome. He later wrote about his visit to her studio:

> (She) is from my own native town, and appears to have genuine talent, and spirit and independence enough to give it fair play. She is living here quite alone in delightful freedom and has sculpted two or three things that may probably make her favorably known. Virginia Dare is certainly very beautiful. During the sitting, I talked a good deal with Miss Lander, being a little inclined to take a similar freedom with her moral likeness to that which she was taking with my physical one.[3]

Lander was almost certainly the inspiration for the free-spirited woman artist Miriam in Hawthorne's novel, *The Marble Faun.*

Sadly, Lander was not immune to vicious sexist attacks by envious colleagues. William Wetmore Story, a male sculptor and jealous competitor, circulated a rumor that Lander had been overly familiar with a man and had posed nude for other artists. Male sculptors regularly used nude models in their studios, so this suggestion was not only sexist but ironic. The scandal hurt Lander's reputation and caused Hawthorne and others to shun her and her work. Although

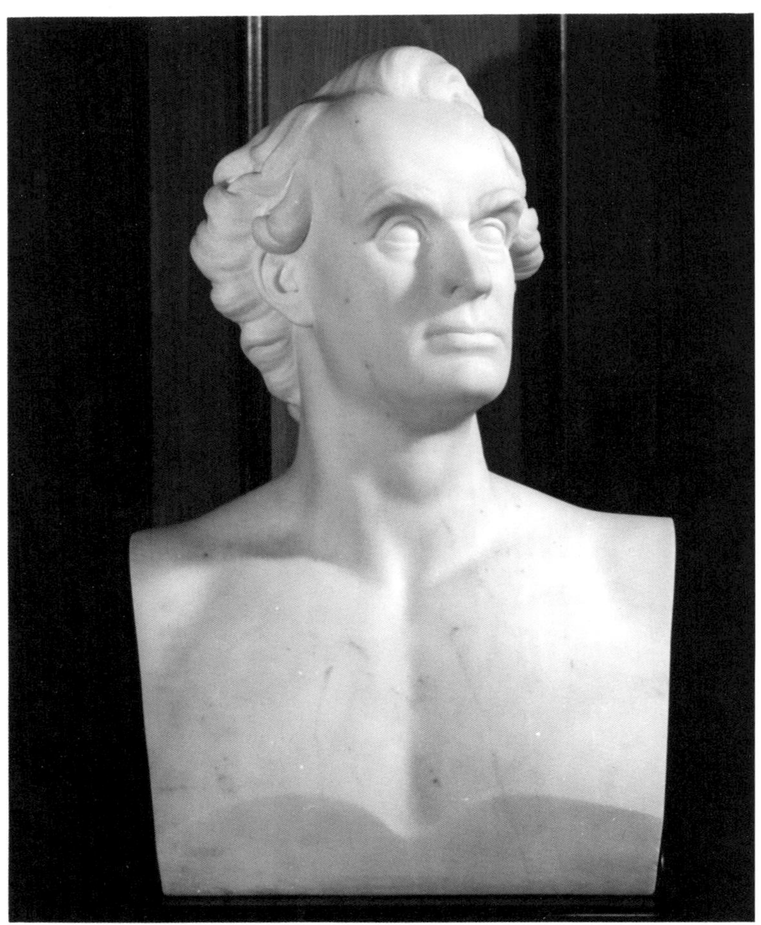

Nathanial Hawthorne, 1858

Lander called on the Hawthorne family five days after their arrival in Rome, and after seeing her work, Nathaniel Hawthorne agreed to sit and pay for a bust of himself.

she ignored the baseless charges, the slander caused permanent damage to her reputation and business.

Lander finally returned home to Salem in 1860, where she waited for the arrival of her life-sized Virginia Dare to be delivered by ship. Unfortunately, the ship carrying her masterpiece sank off the coast of Spain, and Lander had to pay to salvage it. It took two more years to reach America, and when it did, it was badly damaged. Although Lander was able to repair it, she was never able to sell the statue, so she kept Virginia Dare at her Washington, D.C. home until her death in 1923.

Lander's 1860 sculpture is unusual in the way the nude figure, loosely draped with fishing net that she holds with folded arms, stands proudly and boldly as a symbol of the new nation, the product of British culture and the noble American wilderness. She wears a necklace and arm bracelets of wampum beads, and her hair is bound with eagles' feathers. Caught between two worlds, her beautiful hair and regal stance suggest an elite and proper femininity. The semi-nude sculpture defied the standards of feminine decency, but only because the sculptor was a woman. Male sculptors such as Hiram Powers and Erastus Dow Palmer often created completely nude, docile female sculptures during the same time period, and they were well-received. Lander's *Virginia Dare*, in contrast, is a Native American princess, a nationalist image that had symbolized the North American continent since the eighteenth century. It was clearly ahead of its time, as was its creator, Louisa Lander.

4

Margaret Foley
(1827–1877)

MARGARET FOLEY was born in 1827 in Dorset, Vermont, where her father worked as a farmhand. She worked as a maid to pay for her room and board at school, where she trained to become a teacher. She had taught herself how to whittle and carve at an early age, and when she became a teacher, she often rewarded her students with prizes she'd made out of wood or clay.

At fourteen, Foley left her family to work as a mill girl for the Merrimak Corporation in Lowell, Massachusetts. She was one of the thousands of young, single women from New England farms who found employment in factories during the 1840s, hoping for educational opportunities. Foley attended lectures and evening classes after thirteen-hour workdays. In her spare time, she contributed poems and articles to a magazine called the *Lowell Offering*. Inspiring her co-workers to make their way as artists, she also carved figures and faces on wooden bobbins and taught drawing and painting to some of the other mill girls.

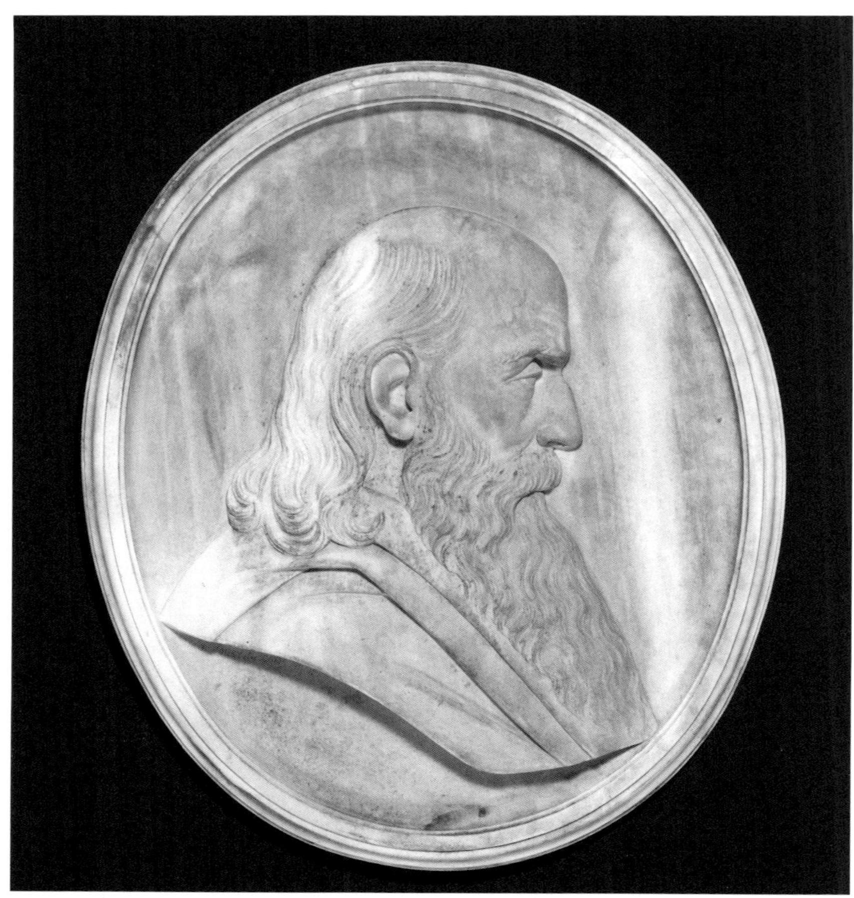

Head of Prophet Zephaniah, 1868

This large oval medallion with relief portrait is of an Israelite prophet, author of one of the Old Testament books. The elderly man seen in profile facing right has a long beard and wears a robe over his shoulder.

In 1848, Foley moved to Boston with the money she had saved from working one year at the mill, using her experience in Lowell as a springboard for her career as a sculptor. Two years later, she enrolled in the New England School of Design for Women, which offered classes in the "domestic arts," including textile and wallpaper design, wood engravings, and lithography. Here, Foley took classes in cameo carving.

In Boston, Foley made a living by restricting her work to cameos, or portraits of the head, since she had little training in anatomy. *The Boston Press* called her the most successful cameo cutter in the United States. She sold her cameos for $35 each, and many Boston reformers championed her work. Twenty of her miniature plaster medallions of famous people, mostly men, still survive today.

Foley dreamed of living in Rome but did not leave Boston for years due to illness and limited income. By 1861 she was finally able to travel and, along with Charlotte Cushman and Emma Stebbins, moved to Rome, where she connected with other expatriate women artists and rented a studio in the same building as painter Elihu Vedder and sculptors Randolph Rogers and Florence Freeman. Cushman helped Foley procure commissions, and in 1872, the struggling, hard-working artist earned an international reputation for her work and was finally able to afford her own house in Rome, where she managed two studios, one for work and the other for exhibitions. To support herself, Foley also wrote about art for the *Boston Evening Transcript* and *The Crayon*, an art journal. In order to assume authorial control over her work, much like Louisa Lander and Emma Stebbins, Foley insisted on carving her own marbles.

The profile medallions of the famous Swedish singer *Jenny Lind* (1865) and poet and journalist *William Cullen Bryant* (1867) are excellent examples of Foley's meticulously executed style as a cameo carver. She also completed medallions and busts featuring other literary and cultural celebrities of her time, including poet and journalist Henry Wadsworth Longfellow and abolitionist and poet Julia Ward Howe. Among her most well-known marble relief medallions is *Pascuccia* (1865), a famous Neopolitan model. The head, neck, and shoulders seen in profile are precisely rendered. She wears earrings, a necklace, and headscarf. The hair has deeply carved curls, and the facial features are highly specific rather than idealized, giving insight into her character.

Margaret Foley also created a Carrera marble bust of *Jessie White Mario* (1832–1906), an internationally acclaimed journalist who

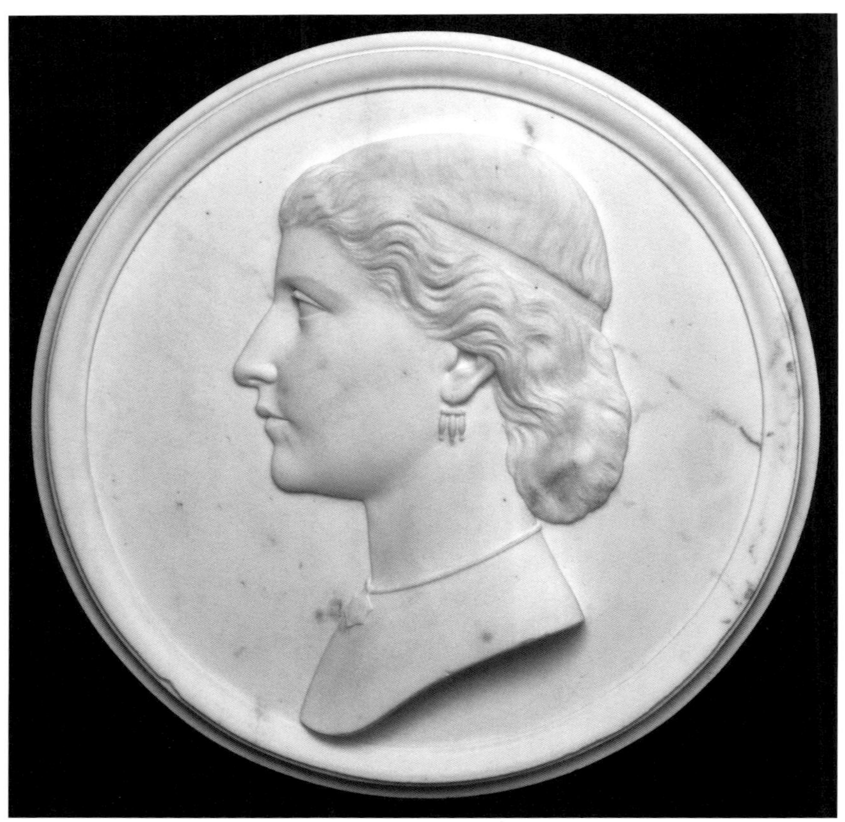

Jenny Lind, 1865

Foley carved this marble portrait of *Jenny Lind* (1820–1887) in profile in a low-relief tondo (round) setting, a format that was popular for depicting European nobility during the Renaissance. Known as "the Swedish Nightingale," Jenny Lind was a famous Swedish soprano whose international celebrity peaked following her 1850 American tour with entertainer P.T. Barnum.

protested against slavery and poverty and made a stand for women's rights in education. Mario was a loyal supporter and author of the biography of Italian revolutionary leader Giuseppe Garibaldi (1807–1882), who was committed to the Italian movement for unification and independence from foreign rule. Jessie White Mario and sculptor Margaret Foley were acquainted through connections in Rome.

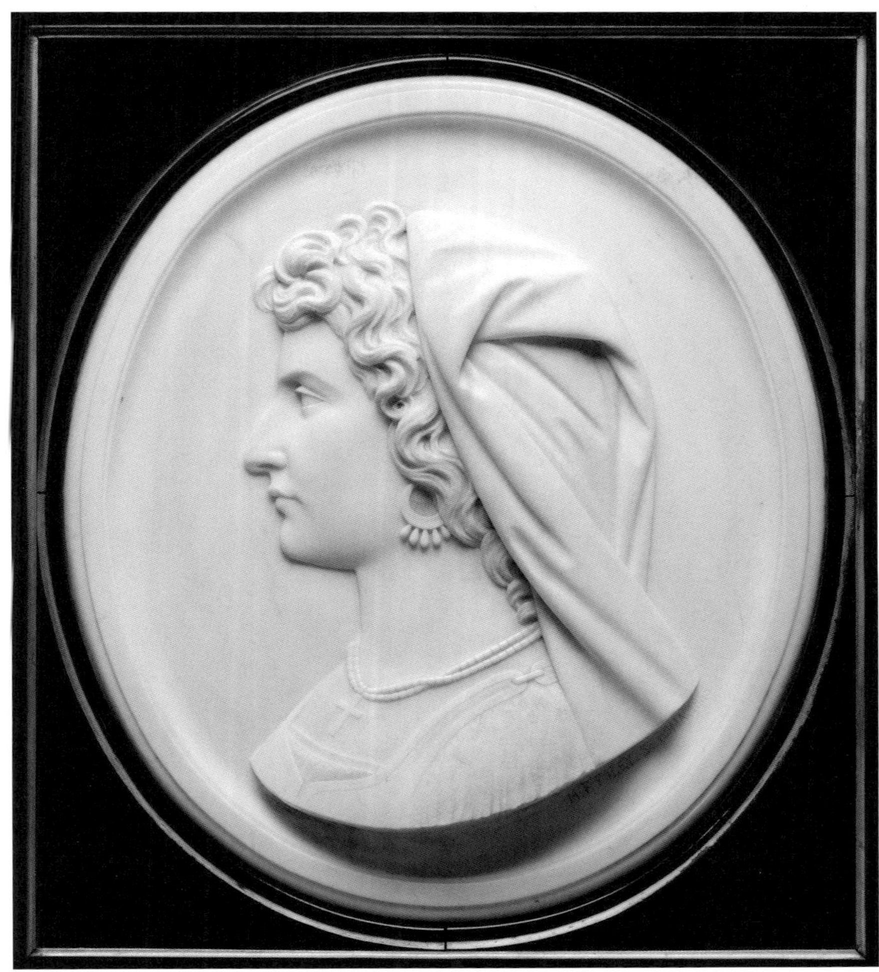

***Pascuccia*, 1865**

The marble relief depicts a well-known local artist's model *Pascuccia*. Carved in Rome in 1865, the sculpture was purchased there by an American collector.

In 1876, Foley began sculpting more ambitious, larger pieces, such as the life-sized head and shoulders of Cleopatra wearing a crown adorned with an asp. The *Cleopatra* statue was exhibited at the 1876 Philadelphia Centennial Exposition along with Foley's major opus, an eight-foot fountain (1874–76) showing three children

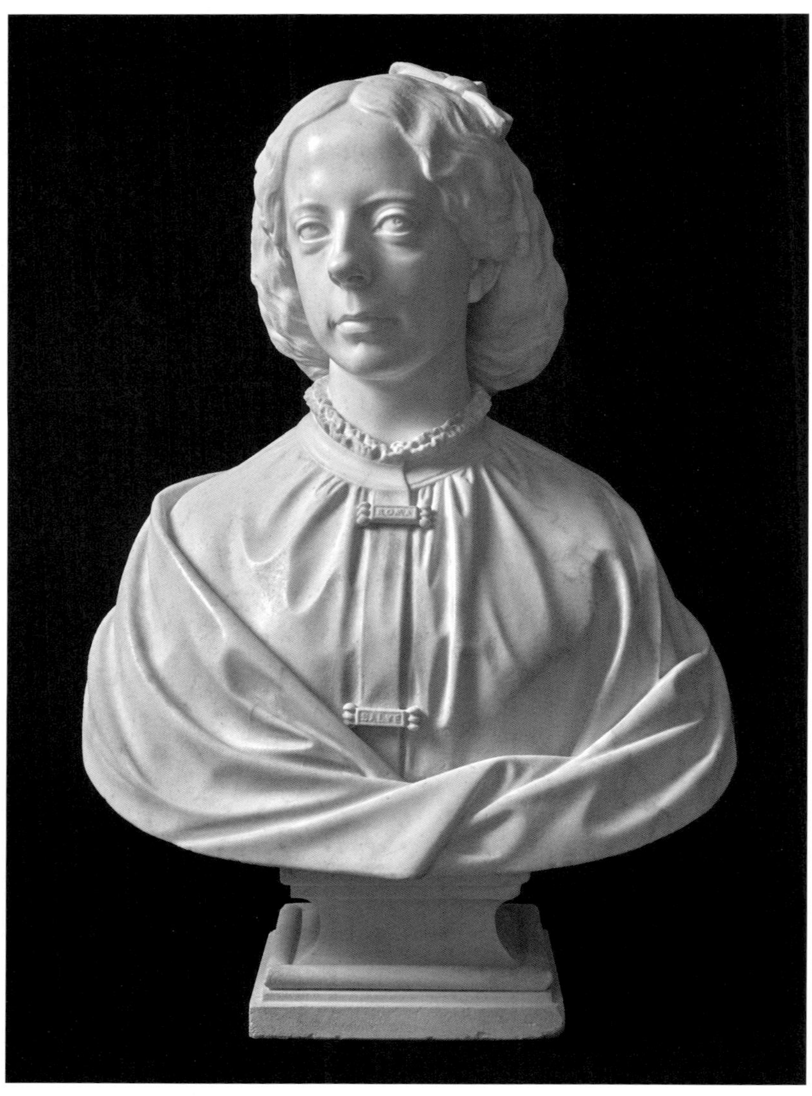

Jessie White Mario, 1867–68

Jessie White Mario (1832–1906), activist, journalist, war correspondent, nurse, and biographer of *Garibaldi,* was known by the Italian press as "Hurricane Jessie" for her commitment to social and economic equality. Confronting senators of slave-owning states in America, she said: "I would not dare to ask support in this great country for the oppressed Italians without strong faith in the right of every nation, of every race, of every man to his liberty… For whites and blacks, for everyone together."[4]

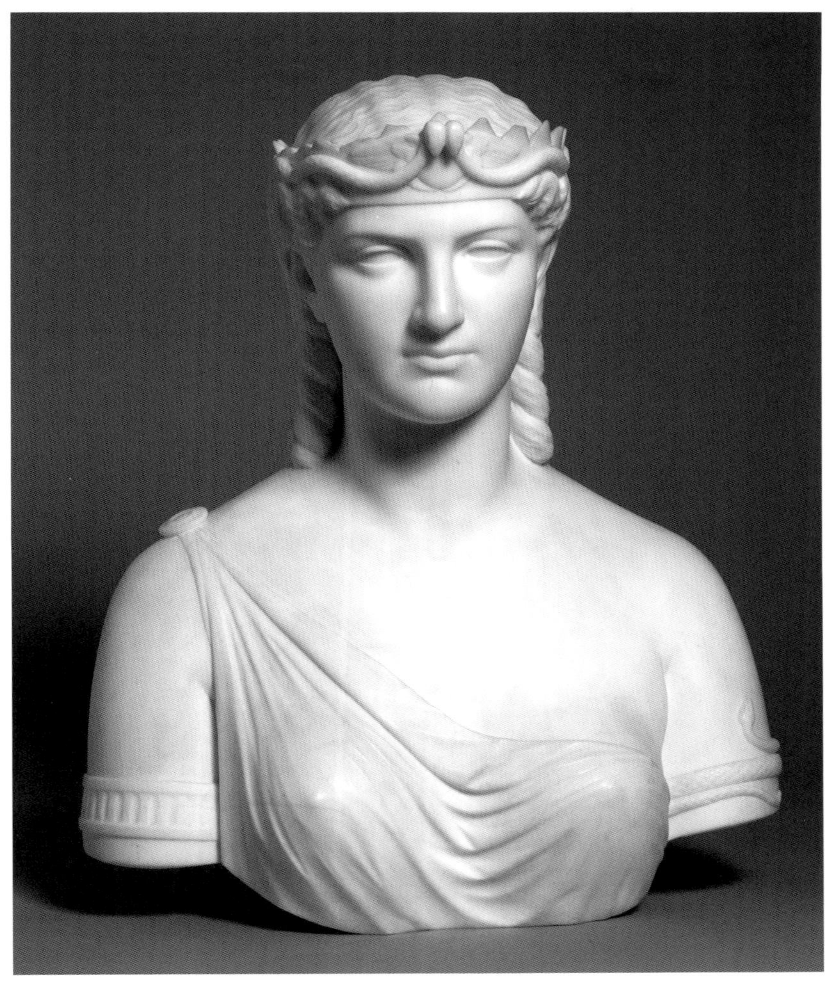

Cleopatra, 1876

Cleopatra, the powerful queen of Egypt, was one of many works that Foley completed while suffering symptoms of a brain illness. The snakes on Cleopatra's crown evoke the kingdoms of Egypt as well as the queen's suicidal death from a poisonous snake bite.

supporting a basin, as well as a statue of Jeremiah, and several medallions. The fountain is located in the Fairmount Park Horticultural Center in Philadelphia. The *Cleopatra* statue is now part of the Smithsonian Institution's American Art Collection.

Foley's lifelong bouts of ill health increased in the 1870s, and in 1877, at the age of fifty, she had a fatal stroke while in Austria, where she had traveled with friends.

As someone who became a successful and internationally acclaimed artist, Foley inspired generations of working women and artists throughout her life.

> This world is our home for a little time, its inhabitants are our brothers and sisters, bound to us 'by one holy tie.' We are all travelers here, destined to meet 'thorns and quicksands in life's way,' that depend much for their mitigation on mutual kind offices.[5]
>
> —MARGARET FOLEY
> The *Lowell Offering*, 1842

Harriet Goodhue Hosmer

(1830–1908)

HARRIET HOSMER was born in 1830 in Watertown, Massachusetts, near the intellectual hubs of Boston, Cambridge, Concord, and Salem. Her mother, Sara Grant, as well as her three siblings, all died of tuberculosis during Harriet's childhood. Her father, Hiram Hosmer, was a physician, and to save Harriet from succumbing to the same fate as her mother and siblings, he encouraged her to pursue physical activity. She quickly became skilled in rowing, swimming, skating, and riding. Her family had a private boathouse where she kept a gondola she used to explore the Charles River. Her father also encouraged her artistic talents. From a clay pit in her home's garden, she modeled people, horses, dogs, and sheep based on the stuffed animals she kept in her bedroom, as well as the animals she came into contact with in the fields and forests around her home.

When Harriet, who was called "Hatty," was sixteen, she was sent to Mrs. Charles Sedgewick's school for girls in Lenox, Massachusetts, where she met literary figures such as Ralph Waldo Emerson, Nathaniel Hawthorne, William Cullen Bryant, and Fanny Kemble. The school was perfect for her temperament and intellectual gifts and proved to be a critical turning point for her future. Elizabeth Sedgewick called Hosmer "the most difficult pupil to manage that I ever saw, but I think I never saw one in whom I took so deep an interest and whom I learned to love so well."[6]

After three years of schooling, Hosmer returned home, where she built a studio on the family grounds and began to study with Boston sculptor Peter Stephenson. Since no medical school in Boston would admit women to anatomy classes, Hosmer studied under the private tutelage of Dr. Joseph McDowell at Missouri Medical College in St. Louis, which later became the Washington University School of Medicine. Hosmer took her lessons privately in the doctor's office while the rest of the all-male class met as a group.

After returning home to Watertown, Hosmer created her first major sculpture: a marble bust of *Hesper* (1852) based on an Alfred, Lord Tennyson poem. Receiving praise for this work from famous Boston actress Charlotte Cushman, Hosmer was encouraged to study in Rome with British sculptor John Gibson. Cushman became a pivotal figure for Hosmer, providing her with rent-free lodging for the next seven years.

With a studio in Gibson's garden, Hosmer's patrons soon included queens, princes, and other members of royalty from various European nations. Hosmer was the first woman artist to go to Rome, and she executed almost all of her most important work during her first decade there. She was one of the many Neoclassical sculptors who traveled to Rome in search of good marble and skilled carvers, historical collections of classical sculpture, and an inexpensive and congenial environment. The first of a group of seven American women sculptors active in the 1850s and 1860s, Hosmer was part of what Henry James described as "a strange sisterhood of American

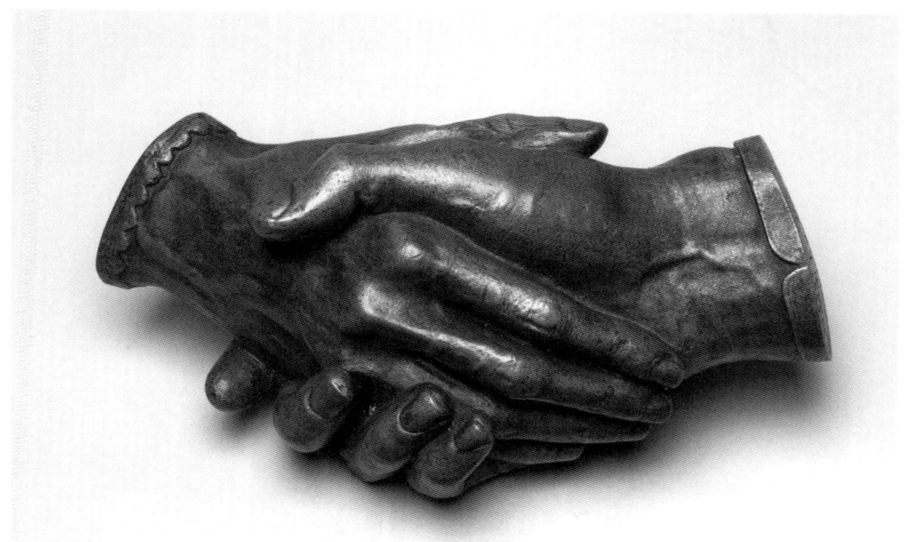

Clasped Hands of Robert and Elizabeth Barret Browning, 1853

Hosmer arranged the two right hands, one lightly clasped by the other. Elizabeth's hand is delicately outlined in a thin border of embroidery while Robert's hand is delineated by a narrow cuff. The *Clasped Hands* sent a sensual message in the nineteenth-century world, where the touch of a hand hinted at a great deal more.

lady sculptors who at one time settled upon the hills in a white marmorean (resembling marble) flock,"[7] in an attempt to link the women with the marble with which they worked.

In 1853, Hosmer met well-known English poets Robert and Elizabeth Barrett Browning, who had eloped to Italy seven years earlier. Hosmer approached them about modeling their hands, and Elizabeth consented on the condition that Hosmer do the casting herself. Hosmer created a bronze cast of their joined hands to symbolize the deep devotion that the couple felt for each other.

In 1854, Hosmer completed *Daphne*, a Victorian symbol of purity and chastity based on Greek mythology. Daphne was a nymph who was saved from Apollo's unwanted advances by being turned into a laurel tree. Rather than depicting the more common, dramatic

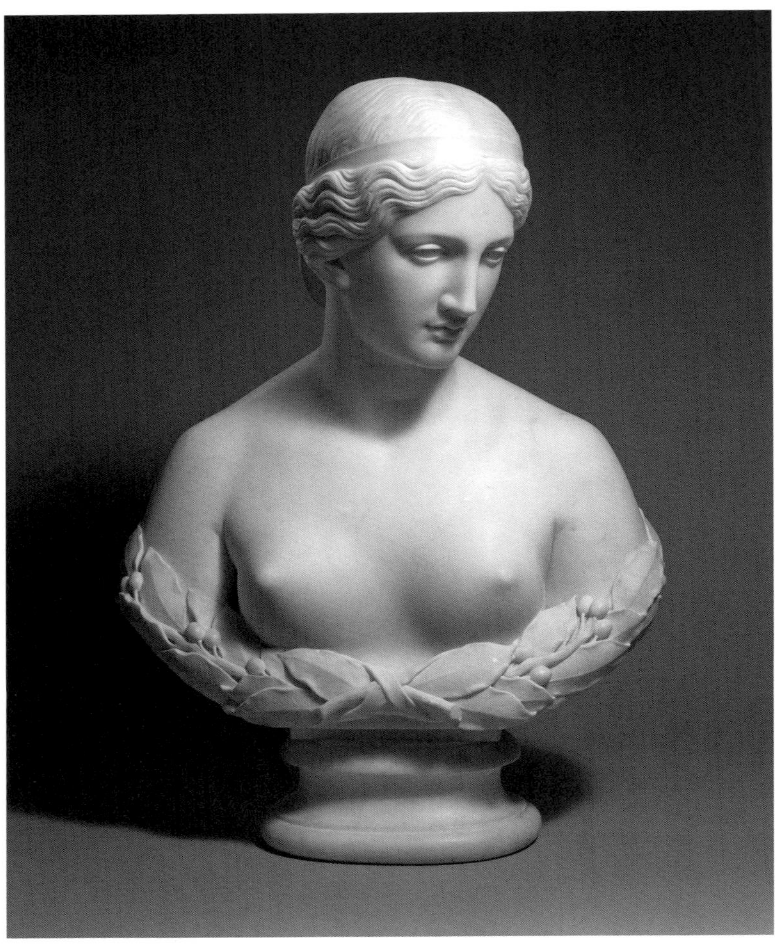

***Daphne*, 1854**

Daphne was a natural choice for Hosmer. Greek myths were popular among Victorians, and expatriate sculptors in Rome drew heavily on antique sources for their themes. In Victorian literature, as seen here, metamorphosis is perceived as the transformation of the human character towards perfection; in this case, a laurel tree.

moment of her escape, Hosmer's bust sits serenely on a wreath of laurel branches, which symbolize her transformation.

Hosmer often chose to model strong, active females who did not need to depend on a man for their livelihood. Calling her sculptures

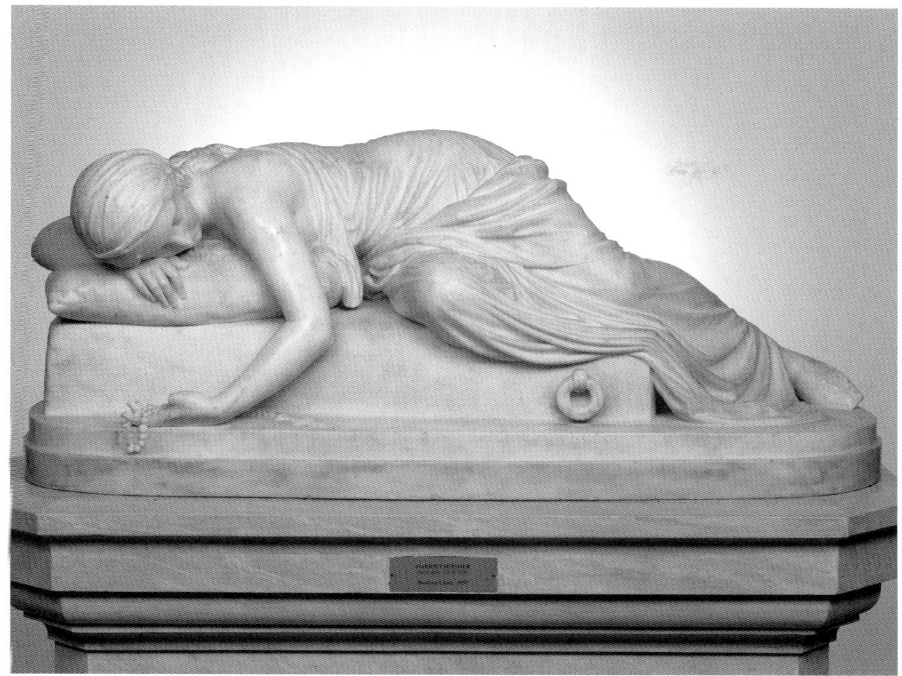

Beatrice Cenci, 1857

Hosmer chose a subject which conformed to traditional images and expectations of women even as she offered a different interpretation of the powerless female. Asleep in her prison cell on the eve of her execution, Beatrice Cenci is at her most vulnerable and innocent.

her "children," she herself remained single, exchanging marriage and domesticity for a professional career.

> An artist has no business to marry. For a man, it may be well enough, but for a woman, on whom matrimonial duties and cares weigh more heavily, it is a moral wrong, I think, for she must either neglect her profession or her family[8] ...

Hosmer's productive career, threatened when her father wrote that he could no longer support her, improved when she sized up

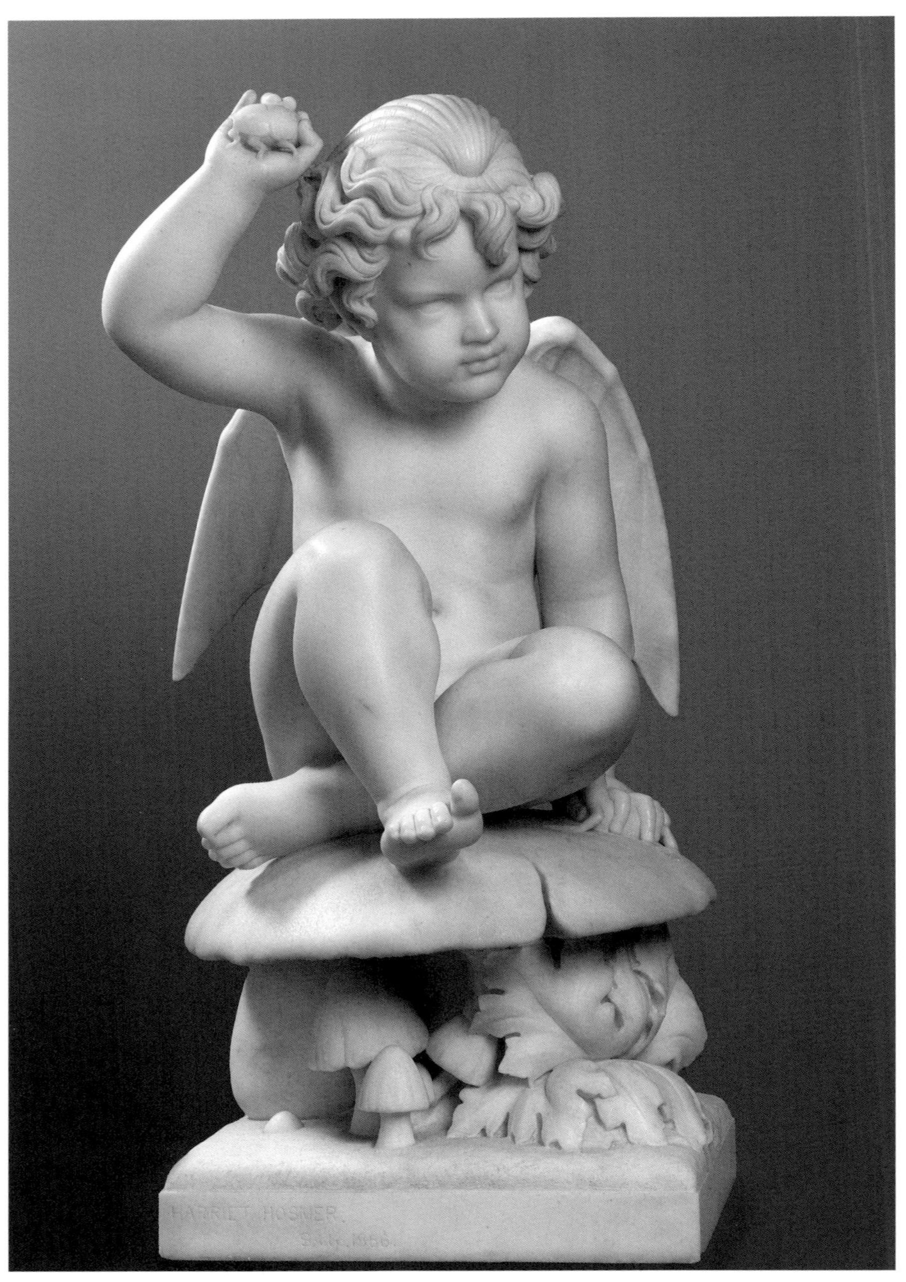

Puck on a Toadstool, 1856

"I have another order for Puck; he has already brought me his weight in silver."[9] —HARRIET HOSMER

her market and created a purely commercial sculpture with great popular appeal. Unlike her other sculptures, Puck's popularity among the English aristocracy and wealthy Americans visiting Rome showed little concern for social issues. *Puck on a Toadstool* (1856), the shrewd little forest elf who causes confusion in Shakespeare's *A Midsummer Night's Dream*, earned her $50,000 and ensured her financial independence, fame, and the ability to remain in Rome as long as she wanted.

One of Hosmer's finest works is *Beatrice Cenci* (1857). The sleeping figure of Beatrice is shown at the moment in poet Percy Bysshe Shelley's drama and in a seventeenth-century Guido Reni painting when she can temporarily escape the horror of having murdered her hateful, incestuous father. One arm hangs down, holding a rosary and cross, symbols of her purity and faith, despite her crime. Hosmer based the statue's pose and facial expression on the poet Percy Shelley's description: "How gently slumber rests upon her face, / Like the last thoughts of some day sweetly spent, / Closing in night and dreams, and so prolonged ..."[10]

By this time, Hosmer had many commissions, and she admitted that she was busier than a hornet. Moving into her own studio to make room for her next work of art, Hosmer commenced a seven-foot statue of *Zenobia*, the third-century queen of Palmyra known for her courage, intellect, and beauty who led her country in war against imperial Rome but was captured.

Hosmer's depiction of this famed warrior conveys her as stoic and regal. It was well-received when exhibited in the United States because it embodied a new, stronger, more courageous ideal of womanhood.

Although *Zenobia* (1859) was the peak of Hosmer's career, slander against the well-known sculptor in the British press caused her to spend much time defending herself. For years she had been aware of jealous male sculptors spreading rumors about her, but she could hardly believe it when she saw the accusations in print. She sued for libel and forced the guilty authors of the publications to print

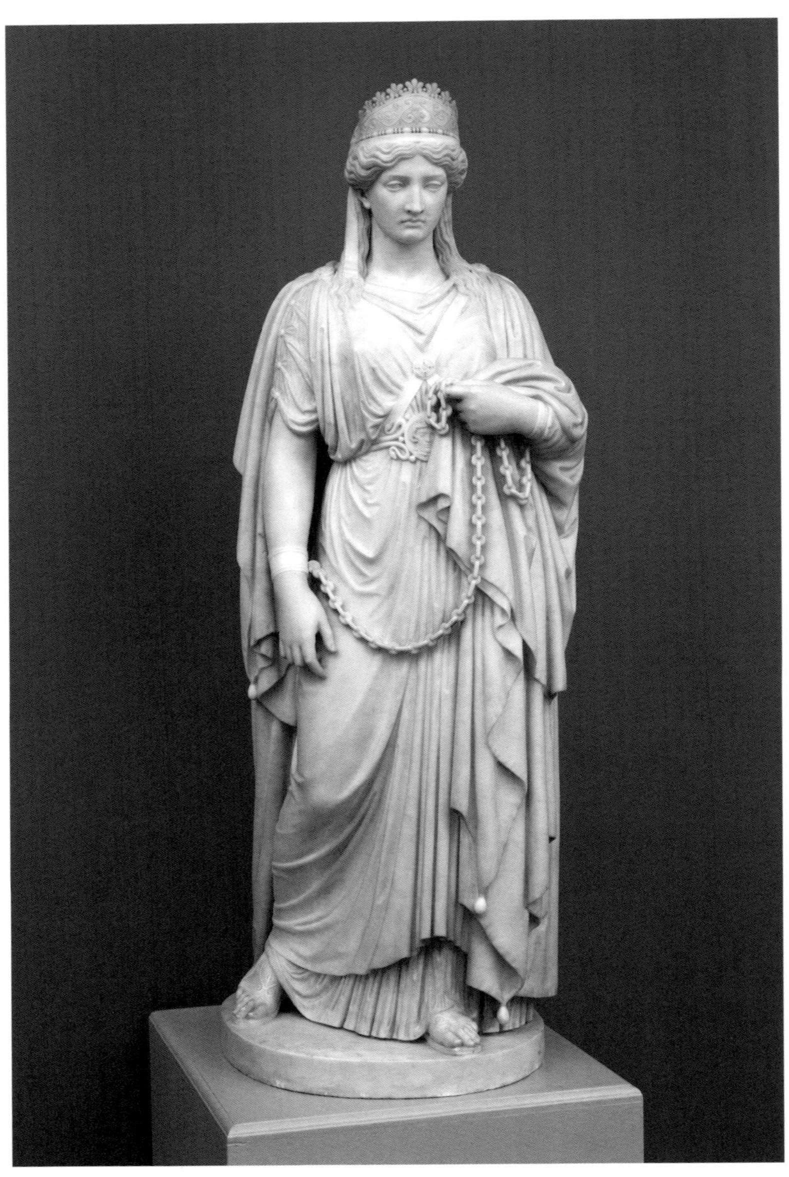

Zenobia, 1859

Although Zenobia, a powerful leader who conquered Egypt and parts of Asia Minor, was marched in chains through the streets of Rome following the defeat of her army, Hosmer presents her as a noble captive who accepts her defeat with dignity and reserve. The statue was praised in newspaper articles and seen by more than 15,000 people in Boston.

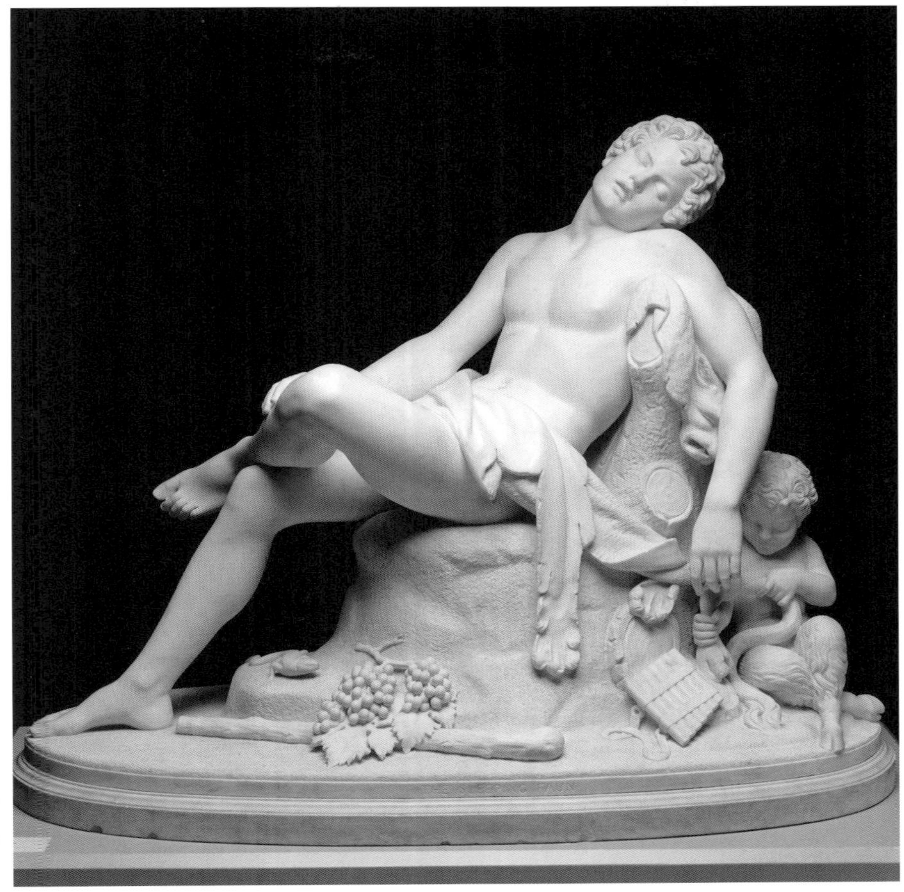

The Sleeping Faun, 1870

The Sleeping Faun was Hosmer's first rendering of the life-size adult male form. While this break in progression of female figures may have been arbitrary, the faun may have been attractive to Hosmer because he was an androgynous creature who was familiar with childlike deeds.

retractions. In spite of these distractions, Hosmer remained successful, busy with commissions from many wealthy patrons, and was the owner of one of the most beautiful, frequently visited studios in Rome.

One of Hosmer's later works of art, *The Sleeping Faun* (1870), playfully depicts an inebriated faun with pointed ears slumped

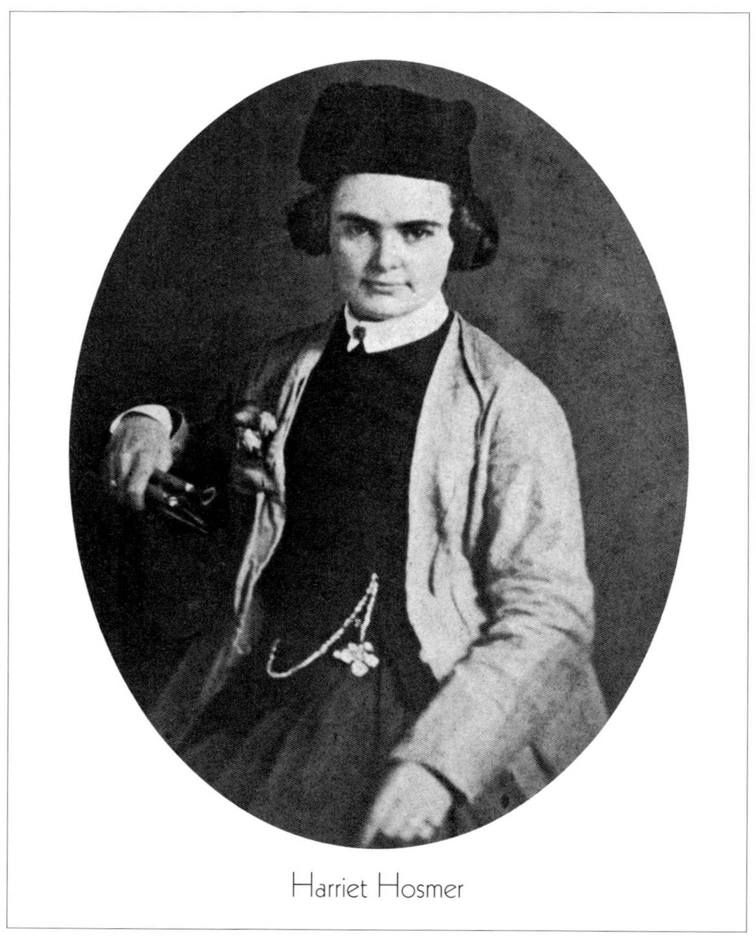

Harriet Hosmer

Challenging nineteenth-century expectations of women, Hosmer became the foremost woman sculptor of her time. She was internationally known for her willful independence as well as for her accomplishments as an artist. "I honor every woman who has strength enough to step outside the beaten path when she feels that her walk lies in another; strength enough to stand up and be laughed at, if necessary."[11]

against a tree stump. A mischievous half-human, half-goat satyr ties the faun's tiger-skin garment to the tree while he sleeps. Inspired by ancient Greek and Roman art, this sculpture was one of Hosmer's most acclaimed works.

Hosmer's finest works were created during the first ten years after her arrival in Rome, but she stopped producing in her later years. Always interested in technology, she invented an imitation marble that could be cast like plaster and patented plans for a motion machine. She returned to Watertown in 1900 where, eight years later, she died of pneumonia at the age of seventy-seven.

The best-known woman sculptor of her day, Hosmer challenged nineteenth-century expectations of women and helped to make Rome especially attractive to her fellow American women sculptors. Specializing in studies of heroic historical and mythological women whose victimization ultimately rendered them wronged by patriarchal oppression, Hosmer was an inspiration to more than two generations of women sculptors, most of whom came from liberal families where female independence was valued.

6

Edmonia Lewis
(1844–1907)

BORN IN Rensselaer, New York, around 1844 to a Native American mother and an African American father from Haiti, Edmonia Lewis was orphaned at an early age and raised by her mother's family. In 1861, she attended Oberlin College in Ohio, a private, coeducational liberal arts college that had been admitting African Americans since 1835. While in school, Lewis lived at the home of Reverend John Keep, a white supporter of women's rights and abolitionism. Nonetheless, she was not immune from ongoing racism and discrimination. Accused of poisoning two classmates, she was attacked by unknown assailants, who beat her and left her for dead. But she recovered, and the charges against her were eventually dropped.

Lewis left school in 1863 without graduating, hoping to become an artist. She went to Boston, the center of liberal thought, carrying a letter of introduction from the Keeps to the abolitionist leader William Lloyd Garrison. As she said:

> I had heard a great deal about Boston, and I thought if I went there, I should perhaps find means to learn what I wanted to know. So we came here, and my brother hired a little room in the Studio Building (a well-known hive for artists' studios and theater companies) for me.[12]

Garrison introduced Lewis to neoclassical sculptor Edward Brackett, who offered criticism and encouraged her work with clay. She also asked sculptor Anne Whitney, another resident of the building, for some informal lessons. As was common for budding female artists of the time, this was the extent of her training. Yet, in Boston, Lewis was able to cultivate the white liberal community and modeled portrait busts and medallions of anti-slavery leaders and Civil War heroes like Garrison, John Brown, Charles Sumner, and Wendell Phillips.

Among her early works is a posthumous bust of Colonel Robert Gould Shaw, leader of a troop of African American soldiers in the Civil War. Lewis had seen Shaw on the day he marched out of the city and proposed to make a portrait bust of him. When it was completed, the bust was shown at the Soldier's Relief Fair of 1864, and about one hundred plaster copies were eventually sold. With this money, Lewis bought a boat ticket to Rome the following year, knowing that Rome was considered the international center of sculpture.

In Rome, Lewis joined Harriet Hosmer's circle of abolition-minded intellectuals and received instruction from John Gibson. She experienced racism and sexism in Rome as well, but she had more opportunities there than in the U.S. For example, author Henry James wrote in his biography of sculptor William Wetmore Story that "... one of the sisterhood, if I am not mistaken, was a negress whose

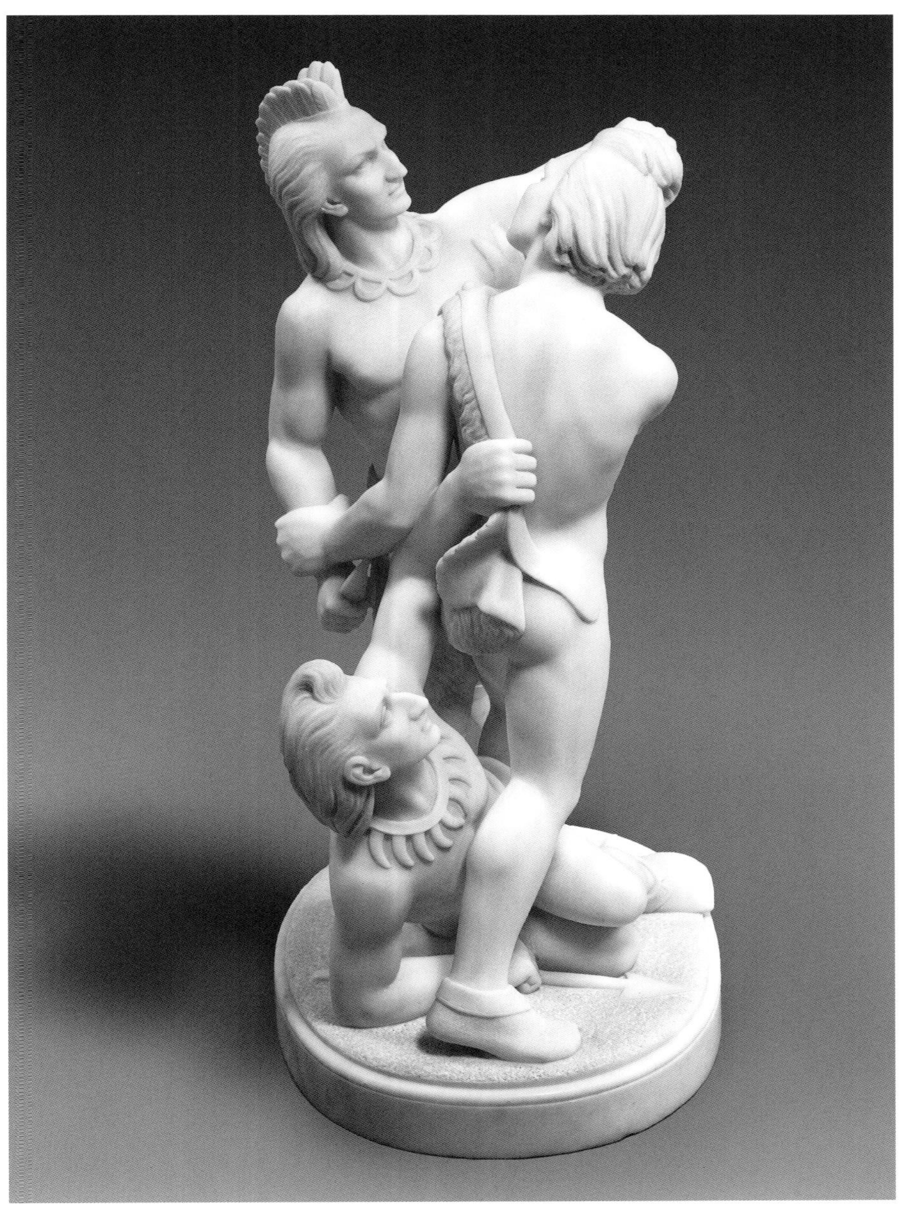

Indian Combat*, *1868

Three Native American men are engaged in combat. This complex integration of multiple protagonists was unusual at the time. Lewis carved the marble herself without the help of assistants. A wide variety of textures is seen in the moccasins, animal hides, and loin cloths.

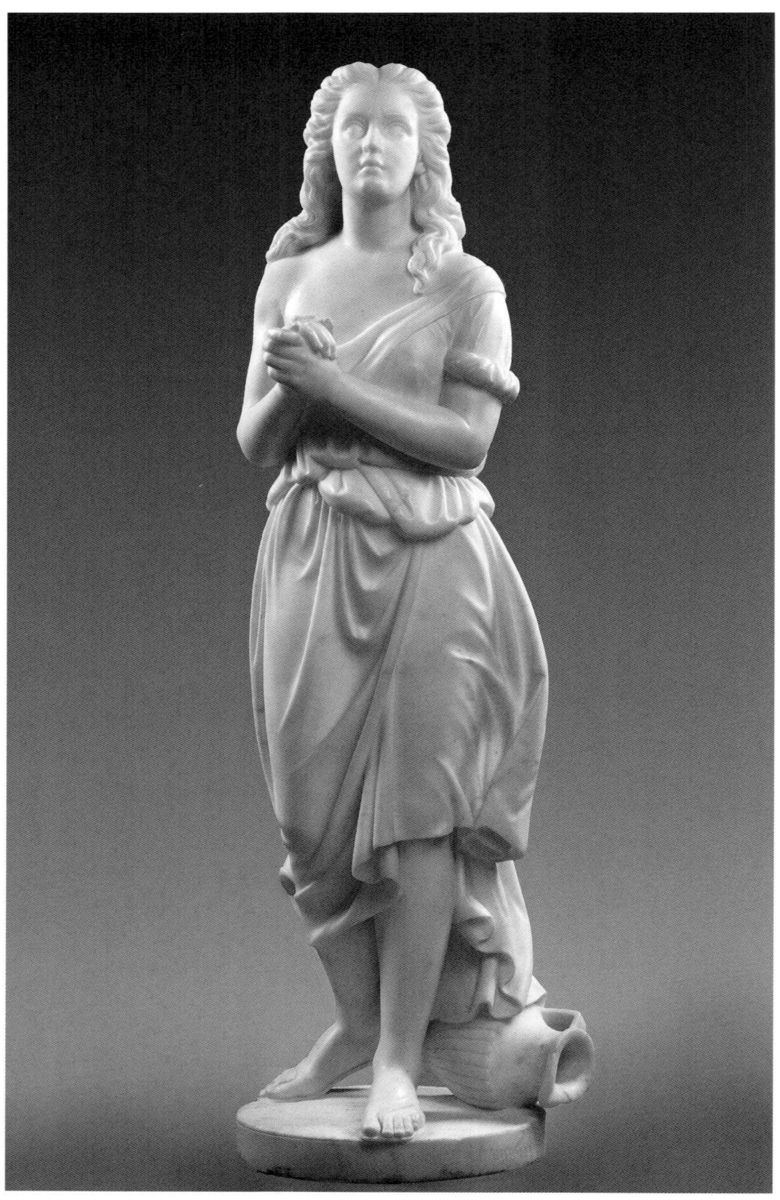

Hagar, 1875

The Old Testament Egyptian slave Hagar is portrayed after being ejected from Abraham and Sarah's home. In Lewis's sculpture, Egypt represents black Africa, and Hagar is a symbol of courage and the mother of a long line of African kings.

color picturesquely contrasting with that of her plaster material was the pleading agent of her fame."[13]

It is not surprising that Lewis carved all her own work, unlike most foreign sculptors in Italy who hired native artisans to enlarge their clay and wax models in marble. Although this hands-on approach was impressive, it was primarily because Lewis feared accusations that others were doing her work. She was even afraid to study with artists in the city for this same reason. She understood the racial and sexual barriers confronting her and her colleagues and was determined to achieve legitimacy on her own terms.

Lewis's work reflects either her own experiences or the experiences of heroines with whom she identified. In *Forever Free* (1867), an African man has broken the chains of slavery while an African woman kneels at his side in prayerful gratitude for her long-awaited freedom.

One of Lewis's finest works, her life-sized statue of *Hagar* (1875), is based on the Biblical story of Abraham's Egyptian maidservant who bore him his first child, Ishmael, and then was cast out by Abraham's jealous wife, Sarah, to wander in the wilderness. Lewis depicts Hagar looking upward with her hands clasped in prayer. Lewis said she was expressing her sympathy for all suffering women. Symbolizing Africa, Hagar, in her despair, represents the plight of the African American people during Reconstruction, the disappointing post-Civil War era when racism was still rampant.

Another reminder of the pain caused to African Americans by discrimination, and one of Lewis's most famous works, is her statue of the Egyptian queen *Cleopatra*, depicted after being bitten by an asp. It was shown at the Philadelphia Exposition in 1876, a time when women represented one-fifth of the American labor force. The Exposition showed more than six hundred exhibits displaying women's achievements.

Lewis drew from her Native American heritage in several works based on Henry Wadsworth Longfellow's popular narrative poem *The Song of Hiawatha* (1855). She also made a bust of Longfellow

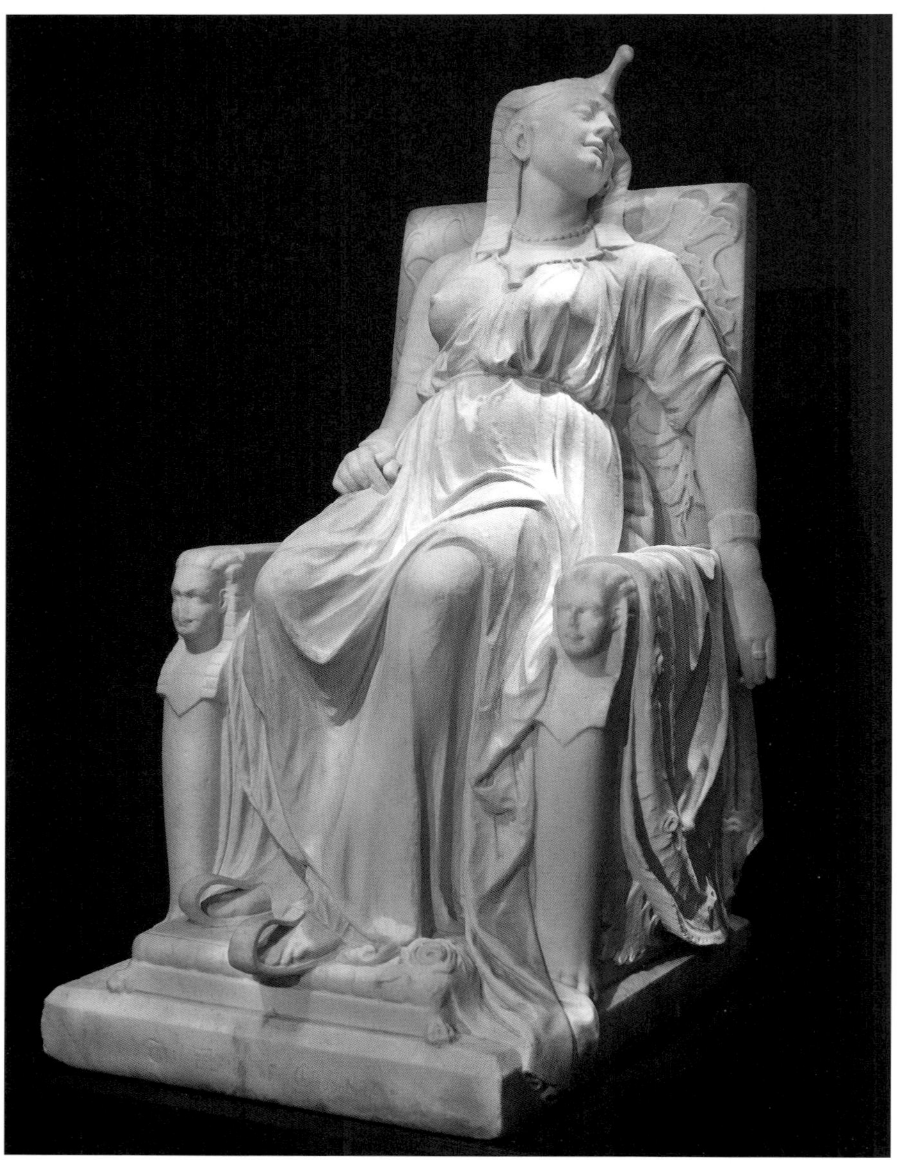

The Death of Cleopatra, 1876

Lewis shows the legendary queen of ancient Egypt on her throne. The lifeless body with head tilting back and arms splayed open portrays a vivid realism uncharacteristic of the late nineteenth century. Committing suicide, we see that Cleopatra had the last word on how she would be recorded in history.

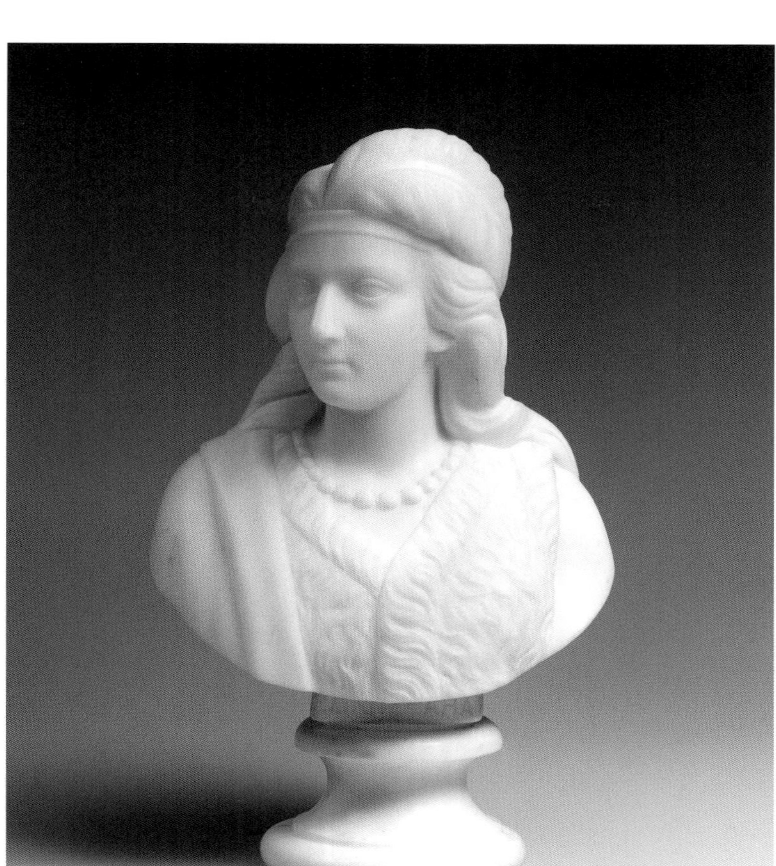

***Minnehaha*, 1868**

Lewis greatly admired the poetry of Henry Wadsworth Longfellow. Her sculpture of *Minnehaha* is based on Longfellow's poem "The Song of Hiawatha." The woman depicted here was a member of the nation of the Dakotas. In the poem, an Ojibwe Native American leader wins her love, even though she is a member of a rival nation.

himself sometime between 1869 and 1871. At the height of her career, Lewis received many commissions from prominent Americans and British royalty. In spite of her success and fame, however, Lewis disappeared around 1880, and it is believed that she died in London

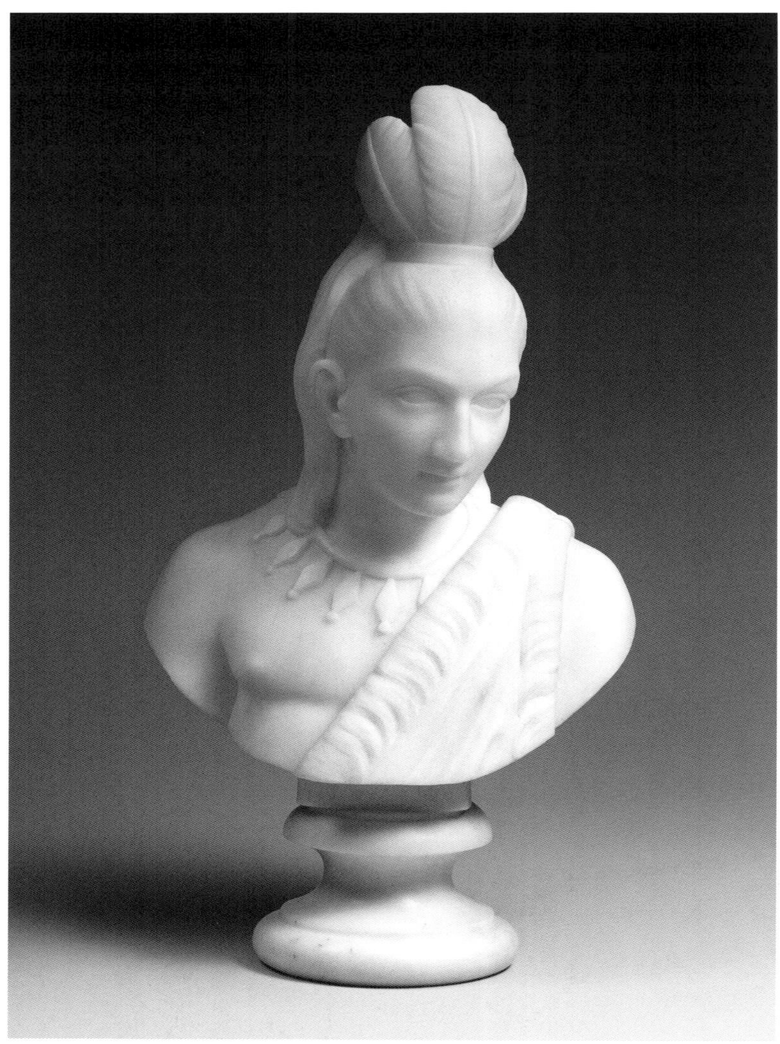

***Hiawatha*, 1868**

This sculpture of Hiawatha blends an idealized form with Native American dress and accessories, such as the feathers in his hair and his necklace.

in 1907. Nonetheless, her work dealing with her Native American heritage and the oppression of black people is popular today, and she is known as the first African American artist to receive international fame as a sculptor.

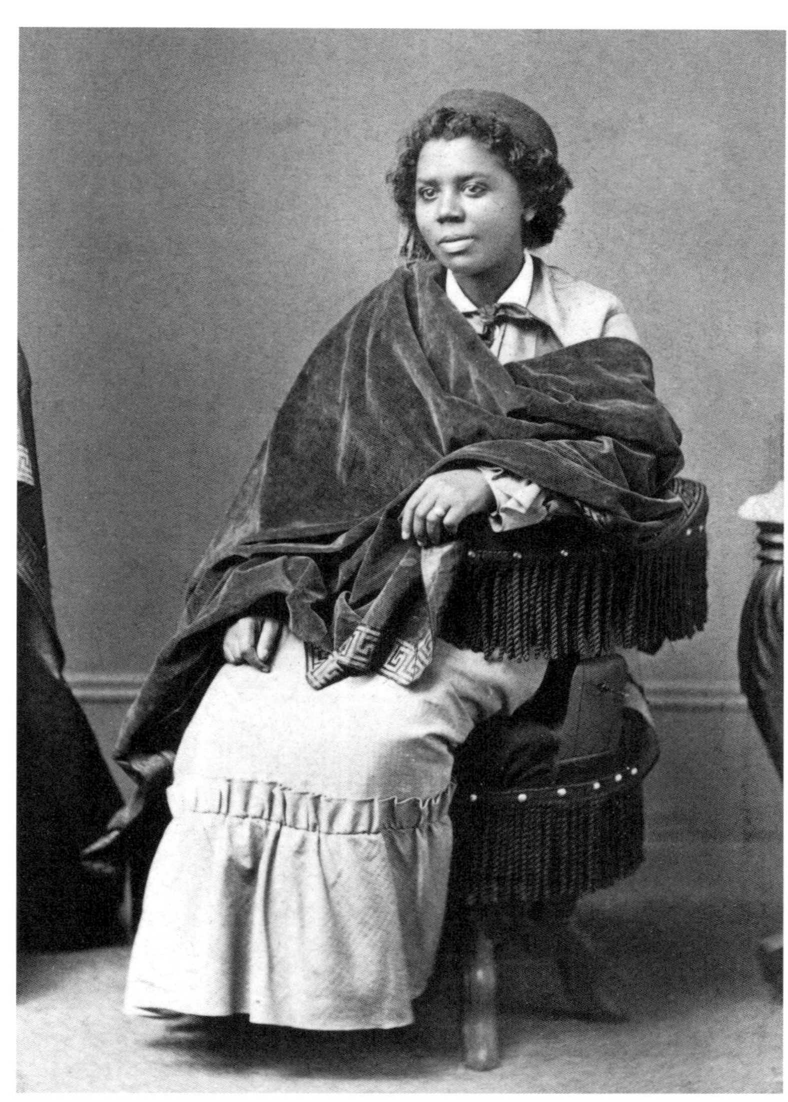

Edmonia Lewis

"There is nothing so beautiful as the free forest. To catch a fish when you are hungry, cut the boughs of a tree, make a fire to roast it, and eat it in the open air, is the greatest of all luxuries. I would not stay a week pent up in cities, if it were not my passion for art."[14]

7

Vinnie Ream
(1847–1914)

THE YOUNGEST of three children of Robert and Lavinia Ream, Vinnie Ream was born in 1847 in a log cabin near Madison, Wisconsin. She was raised on the Midwestern frontier, on the edge of territory belonging to Native Americans. Her father was employed by the United States Surveyor General to map the wilderness, so the family moved frequently and lived in several western and southern states.

As a young child, Ream learned to play musical instruments and sang at church. When she was nine, she was sent to school in Missouri, where it was discovered that she was good at poetry and art as well as music. At the beginning of the Civil War, the family settled in Washington, D.C., where Ream worked as a clerk in the Dead Letter Office of the U.S. Post Office. She also became reacquainted with James Rollins, a Missouri lawyer and politician who had been a supporter of Ream's school and had recognized her talents. He was now a U.S. Representative, and it was Rollins who introduced Ream to prominent sculptor Clark Mills.

In 1864, at age seventeen, Ream became an apprentice in Mills's Washington, D.C. studio. With help from Rollins, the female prodigy gained permission to visit the White House every day for months in order to model a bust of *Abraham Lincoln* as he worked at his desk. She completed it but was then deeply saddened to learn of his assassination. When a competition was announced for a Lincoln memorial, the eighteen-year-old showed her recently completed bust and was awarded the commission, but her young age, inexperience, origins as a Midwesterner, friendships with members of Congress, and the general sexism of the time caused controversy. Some saw Ream as an untutored genius who, like Lincoln himself, proved that privilege and social refinement were not requirements for success in America. Others saw her as an opportunist who used her youth and good looks to manipulate powerful middle-aged men. In June 1869, her plaster model was approved, but, as was typical for women artists at the time, Ream was accused of plagiarism. The rumor spread that Clark Mills had actually done the work, which forced him to write a letter denying his involvement.

With the money she received for the *Lincoln* memorial, Ream and her parents, who were dependent on her earnings, traveled to Europe for sixteen months. After four months of studying drawing and sculpture in Paris, she and her family moved to Rome, where she would have her plaster model of *Lincoln* carved in marble. They were warmly greeted by the American expatriate community of sculptors, including William Wetmore Story, Charlotte Cushman, Harriet Hosmer, Edmonia Lewis, Margaret Foley, Anne Whitney, and Emma Stebbins, whose studio was next to Ream's. In addition to the Lincoln sculpture, Ream completed at least four major works and several commissioned portrait busts and medallions. She understood the need for good public relations and regularly entertained visitors and held Wednesday evening salons in her studio filled with flowers, cooing doves, an American flag, and a portrait of Lincoln.

While the workmen carved the marble statue of *Lincoln* from the plaster model, Ream worked on a life-sized figure of the Greek poet *Sappho* (1865–70). Then she returned to Washington, D.C., for the unveiling of *Lincoln* at the Capitol Rotunda, a circular room beneath the dome at the center of the Capitol building. Standing and gazing downward contemplatively, *Lincoln* hands the Emancipation Proclamation directly to the viewer. His gesture and solemn gaze urge every viewer to assume the position of a slave about to be freed. Women's rights activists suggested a link between the monument and the battle for women's rights because the image encouraged citizens to embrace a more egalitarian consciousness necessary for accomplishing the goals of Reconstruction, which were suffrage and citizenship. Ream noted:

> I think history is particularly correct in writing Lincoln down as a man of sorrow. The one great, lasting, all-dominating impression that I have always carried of Lincoln has been that of unfathomable sorrow, and it was this that I tried to put into my statue.[15]

In 1875, a few years after settling into her home on Pennsylvania Avenue in Washington, D.C. Ream won a commission for a bronze statue of Admiral David G. Farragut, the Civil War naval hero who had led his fleet to victory at Mobile Bay in Alabama. Lieutenant Richard Hoxie, an army engineer, fell in love with Ream while she was at work on the ten-foot-high statue and asked for her hand in marriage. The couple married and moved to a house on Farragut Square, where the monument would stand in line with the White House.

Farragut would be Ream's last major work for many years. She stopped working because her husband felt it was improper for a married Victorian woman of her social status to earn money. In 1883, the couple had a son who suffered a brain injury as a child and died as a young man. Ream continued to entertain at their home, gave

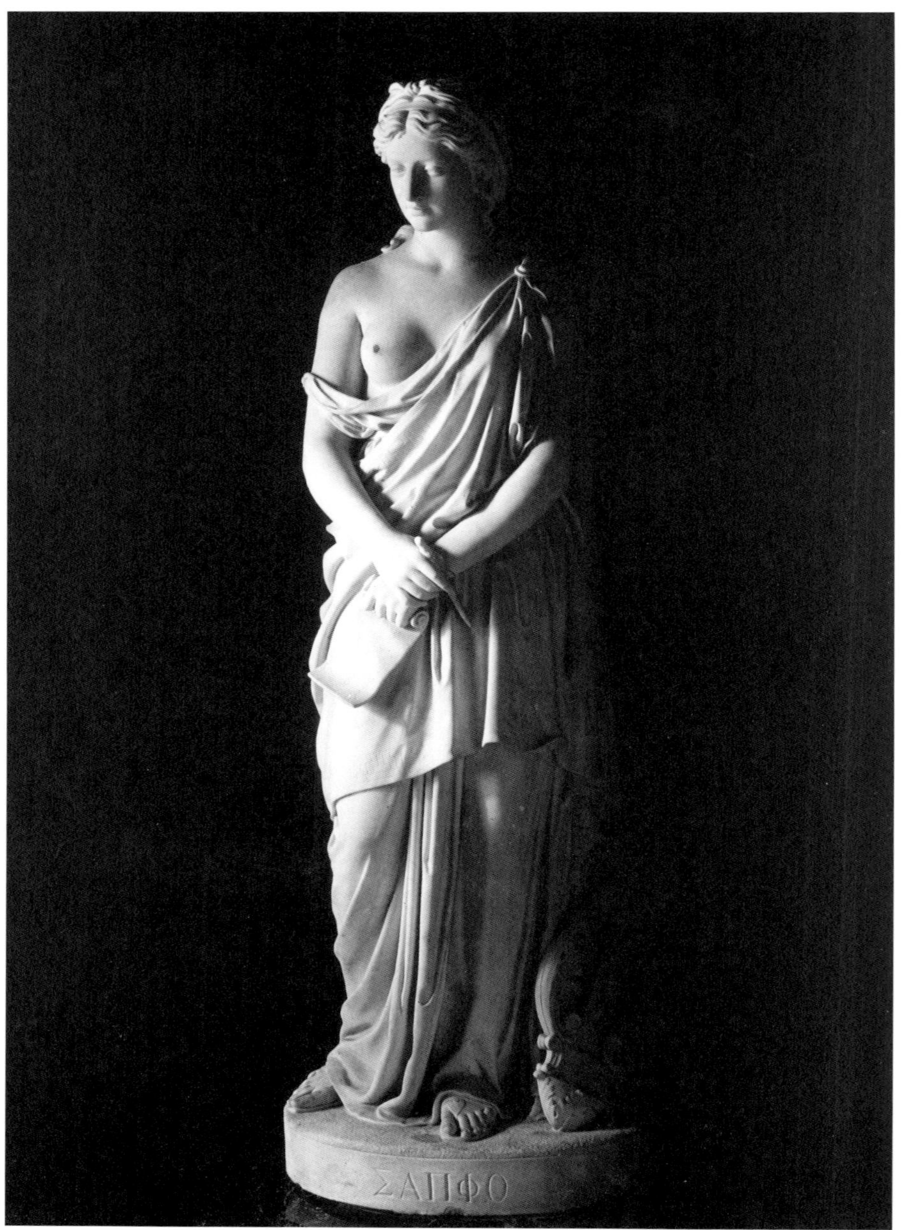

Sappho, 1865–70

Sappho was one of the only sculptures of a female figure that Ream ever created. The preeminent female poet of ancient Greece was admired for the beauty of her writing.

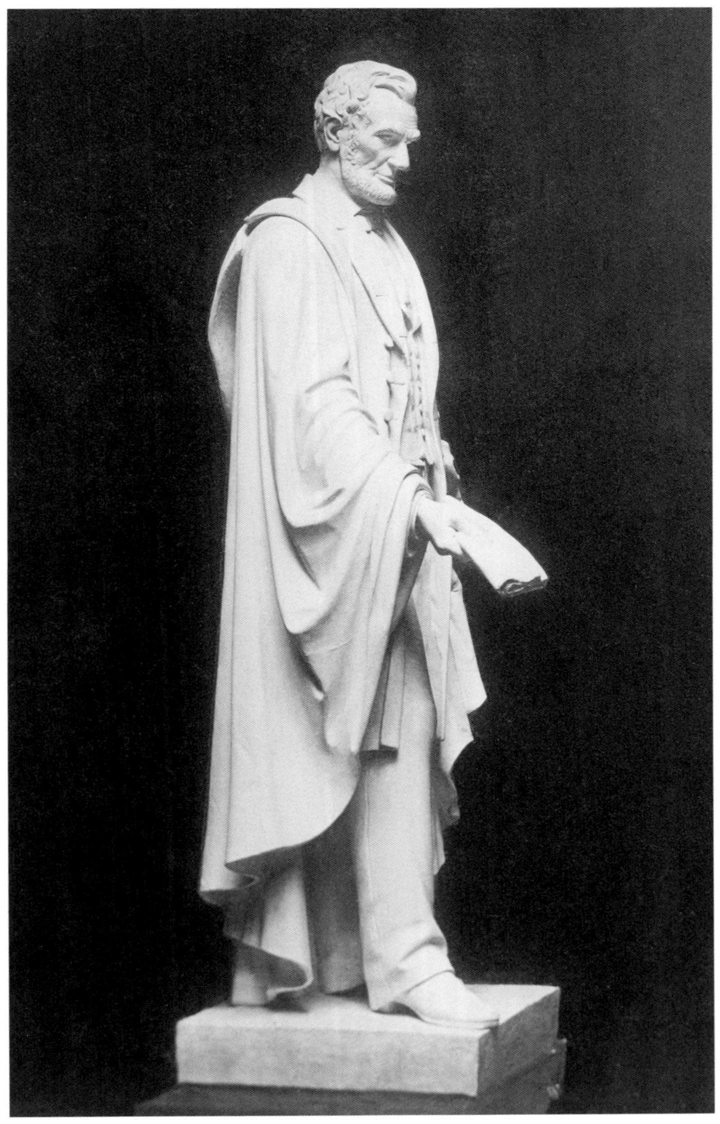

***Lincoln*, 1870**

Ream's statue of *Lincoln* was a big departure from American sculpture that portrayed leaders as larger than life. Her version, showing Lincoln deep in thought, was more realistic. As she explained, "So lately had I seen and known President Lincoln that I was still under the spell of his kind eyes and genial presence when the terrible blow of his assassination came and shook the civilized world."[16]

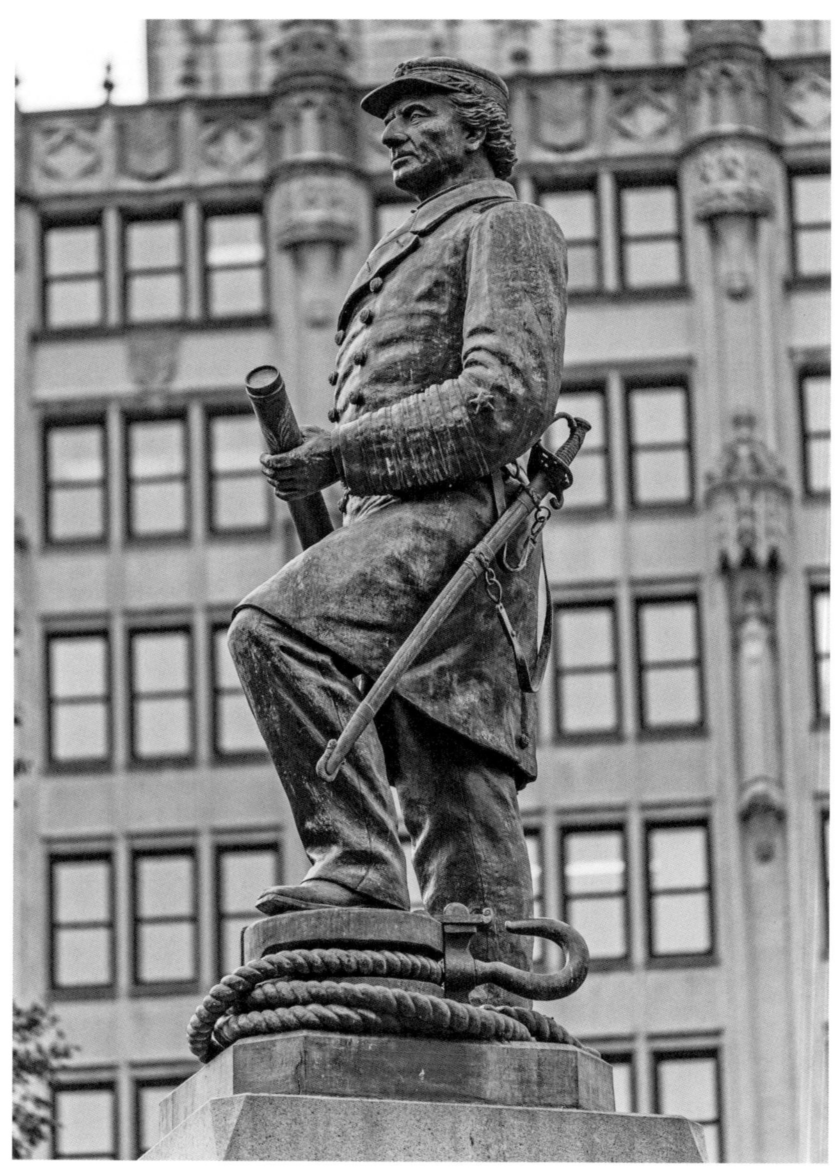

***Farragut*, 1875**

On the heels of her great success with the *Lincoln* statue, Ream began to work on the *Farragut* statue in 1872. The first monument erected in Washington, D.C., in honor of a naval war hero, the *Farragut* statue was made from the melted-down bronze propeller of the ship he commanded during the Civil War.

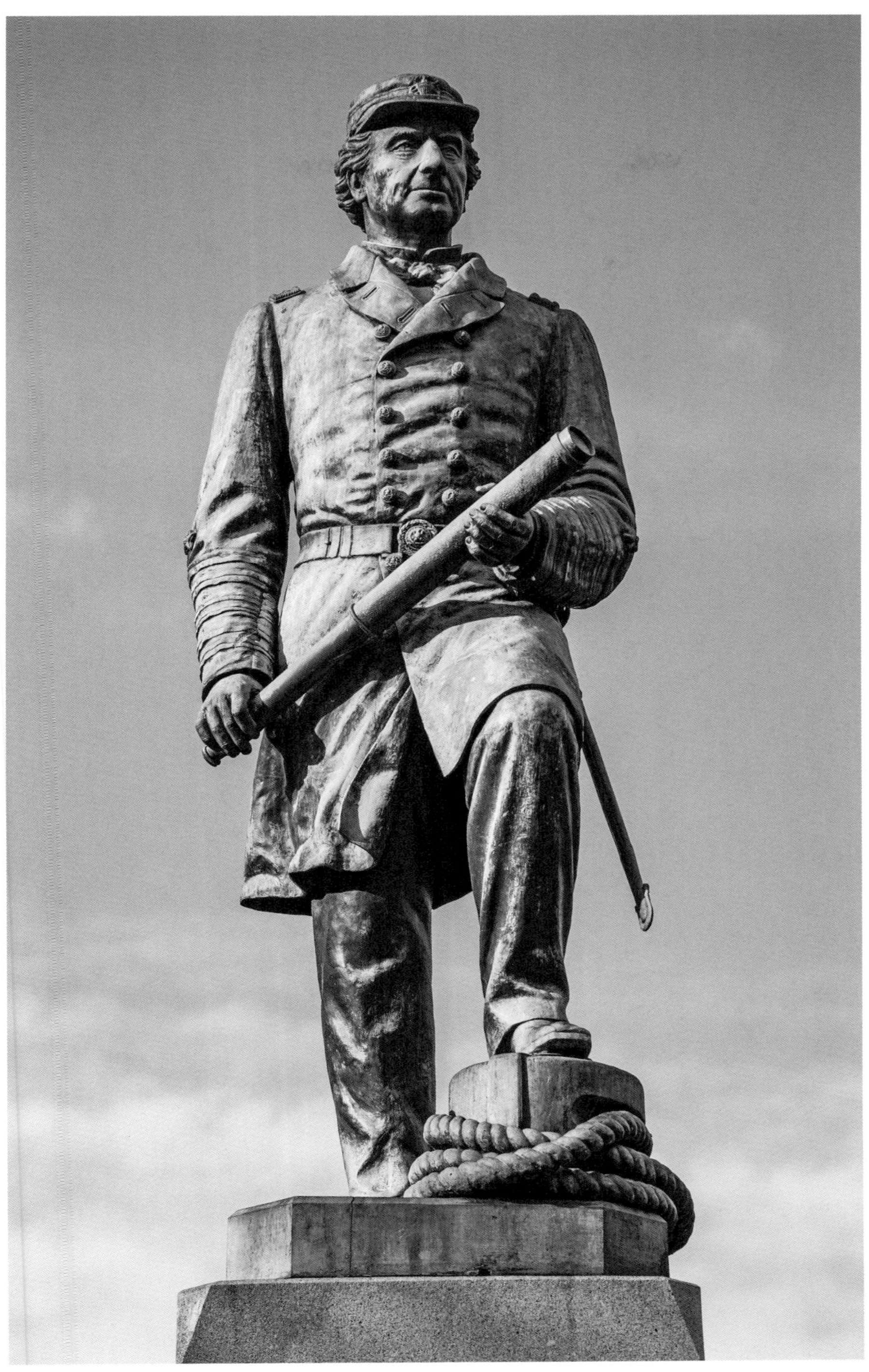

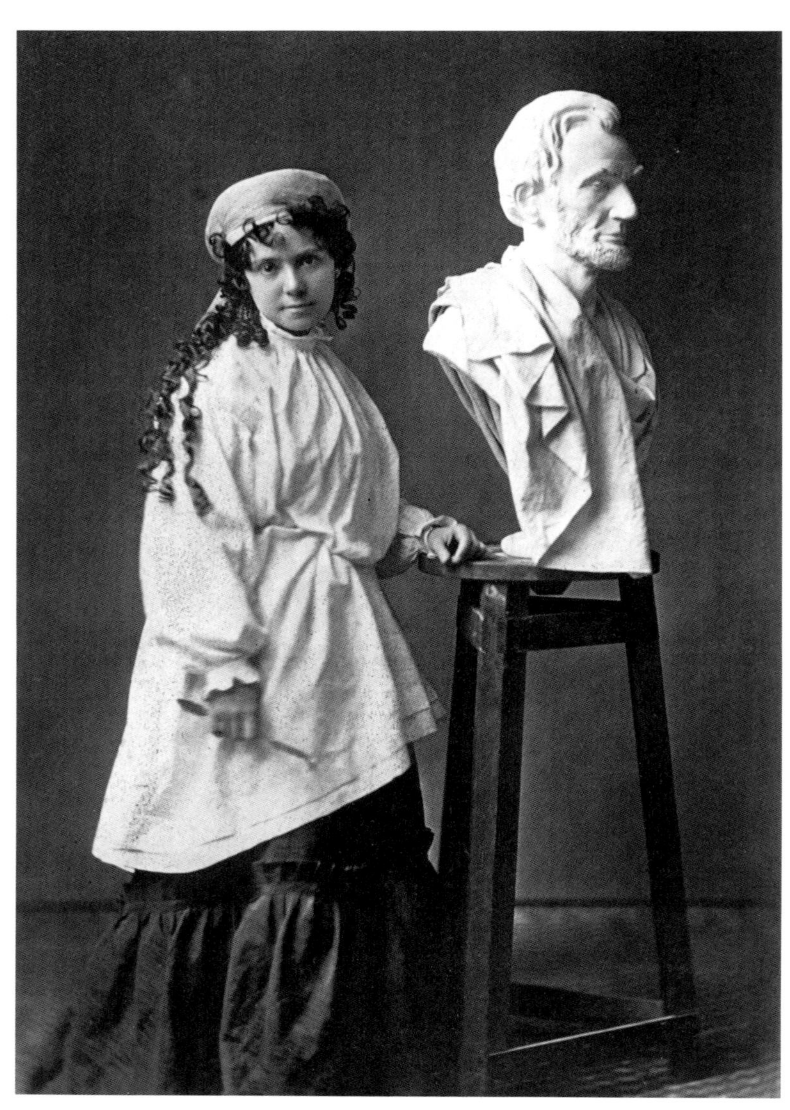

Vinnie Ream

Vinnie Ream was the first woman—and the youngest artist—to get a commission from the United States Congress for a statue. The child prodigy with remarkable talent is best remembered for her sculpture of *Abraham Lincoln* in the rotunda of the Capitol in Washington, D.C.

sculpture classes for young people, and raised money for charities. The couple moved often as her husband advanced to become a general.

After a twenty-five-year hiatus, Ream returned to her career in 1906. Although she had a kidney ailment, she worked on a statue of Cherokee leader Sequoya, inventor of the written alphabet for the Cherokee language. Ream died of uremic poisoning in 1914, at the age of sixty-seven, and was buried in Arlington Cemetery, marked by a replica of her sculpture *Sappho*. Forty years later, two bronze statues by Ream were placed in the U.S. Capitol, those of *Samuel Jordan Kirkwood* (1906) and *Sequoya* (1912).

Stung by critics who disapproved of her successful career and fearful of losing commissions, Ream remained neutral in the suffrage debates. But she had an impressive career and is known as the first woman and youngest artist ever to receive a commission for the United States government. She noted, "I have worked in my studio not envying kings in their splendor, my mind to me was my kingdom and my work more than diamonds and rubies."[17]

Janet Scudder

(1869–1940)

NETTA DEWEZE FRAZEE SCUDDER, who later changed her name to Janet, was born in 1869 in Terre Haute, Indiana, the fifth of seven children. Her mother died when she was five, so she spent much of her youth with her blind grandmother. She enjoyed copying the illustrations from the books her grandmother gave her. At a county fair, she was awarded a medal for her hammered brass tray that depicted the head of Medusa. On Saturdays, Scudder took drawing classes where the director, impressed with her work, suggested she attend the Cincinnati Academy of Art. At the academy, Scudder studied anatomy, drawing, and modeling before deciding to specialize in wood carving. She helped to support herself by taking a job as a woodcarver, and carved decorative grapes and acanthus leaves on furniture and mantelpieces for the elegant homes in Cincinnati.

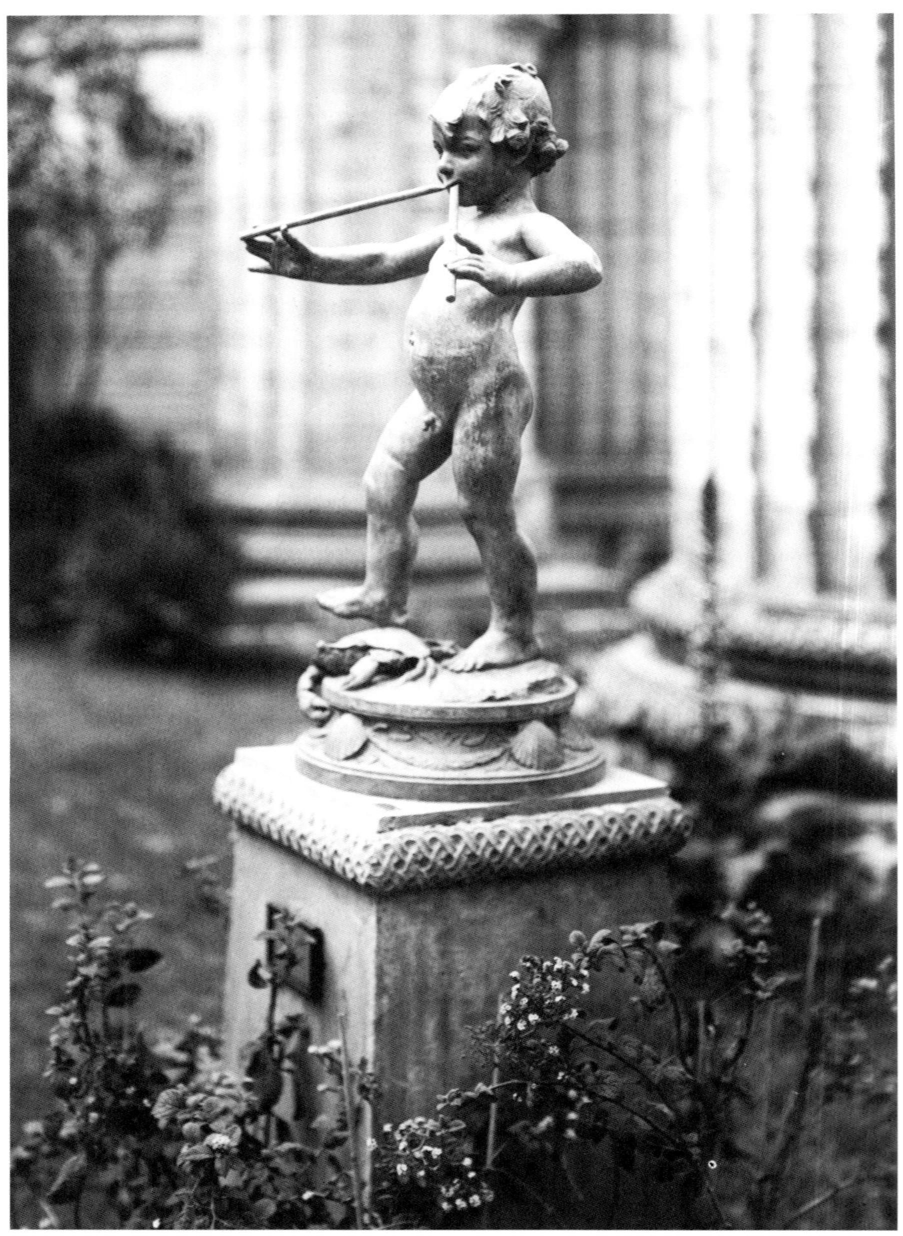

***Pan Playing Pipe*, 1916**

A common subject in ancient art, Pan is a Greek god associated with fertility. He was a piper and shepherd concerned with flocks and herds of both tame and wild animals.

Scudder's father died while she was still at the academy, but with help from her older brother and her woodcarving job, she was able to complete her studies. In 1891, she moved to Chicago to live with her brother and his wife and briefly became a furniture carver in a factory. She quickly lost this job because the union did not permit women to become members, but then found work as a studio assistant to sculptor Lorado Taft joining a group of women sculptors nicknamed the "White Rabbits," who made sculptures for the 1893 Chicago World's Columbian Exposition. According to Scudder, when Taft asked the director of the fair if he could hire women, the director told him "to employ anyone who could do the work of white rabbits if they would help out." The assistants became known as "White Rabbits," a name made more appropriate by the fact that they usually were covered by plaster dust. With Taft's support, Scudder also worked independently on commissions for the fair, creating the figure of *Justice* for the Illinois Building and the *Nymph of Wabash* for the Indiana building.

Having saved the money she earned from the Exposition, Scudder moved to Paris, where she worked for two years in American sculptor Frederick MacMonnies's all-male studio. During her second visit to Paris, she also studied drawing at the Academy Colarossi.

Upon her return to New York City, Scudder had difficulty finding work, but eventually, she received an important commission to design the seal for the New York State Bar Association. This led to orders for architectural decorations, memorial tablets, and portrait medallions. With the support of Frederick MacMonnies, Scudder sold several of her sculptures to the Luxembourg Museum in Paris—the Museum's first acquisitions of sculpture by an American woman. The Indianapolis Museum of Art followed suit, acquiring fourteen of her sculptures.

Influenced by Italian Renaissance artists, Donatello and Verrocchio, Scudder decided to make ornamental sculpture. Her work was admired by Beaux-Arts architects McKim, Mead, and White, a renowned American firm. Stanford White even ordered *Frog Fountain*

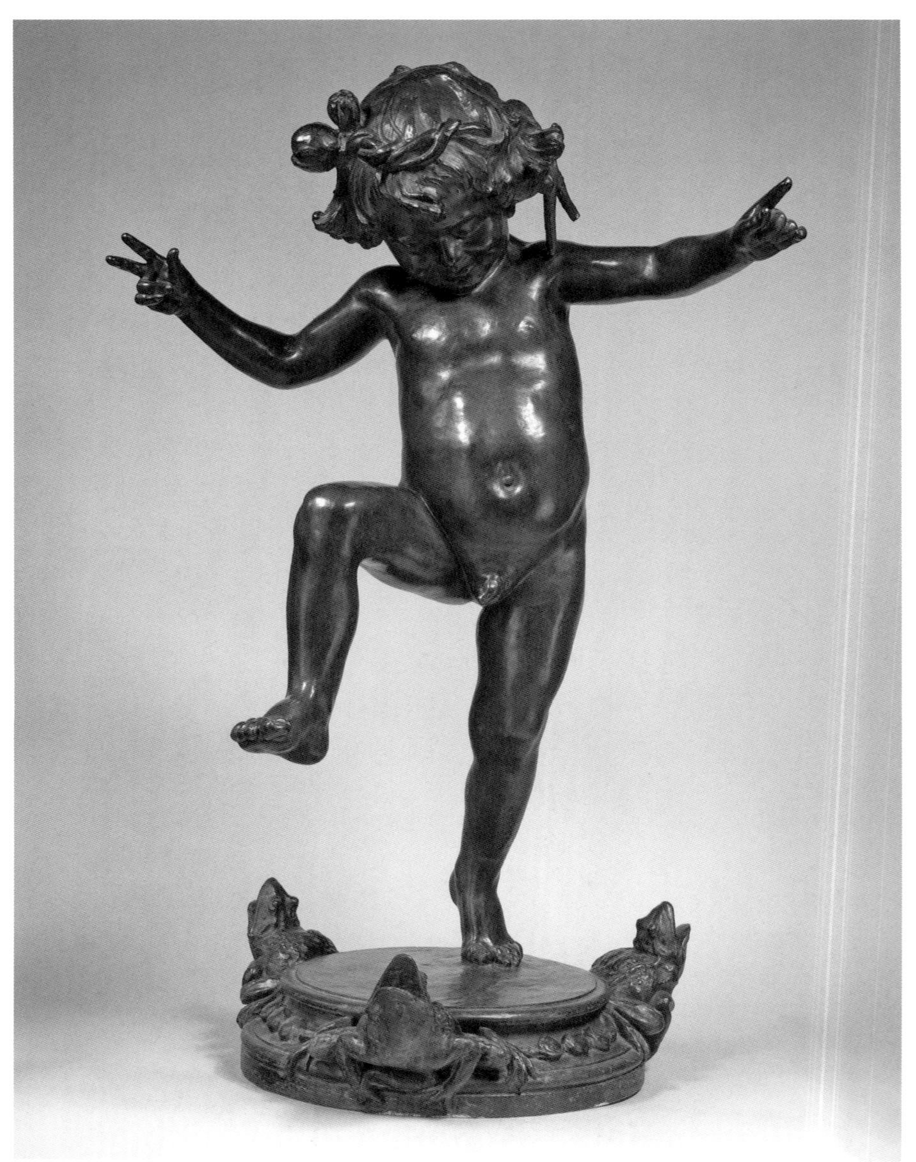

Frog Fountain*, *1901

Influenced by Renaissance sculptures, Scudder modeled *Frog Fountain* in Paris in 1901 and brought it to New York to attract commissions. Architect Stanford White (1853–1906) purchased a cast for his Saint James, Long Island estate. He recommended Scudder to his clients, initiating a productive working relationship that lasted until White's death in 1906.

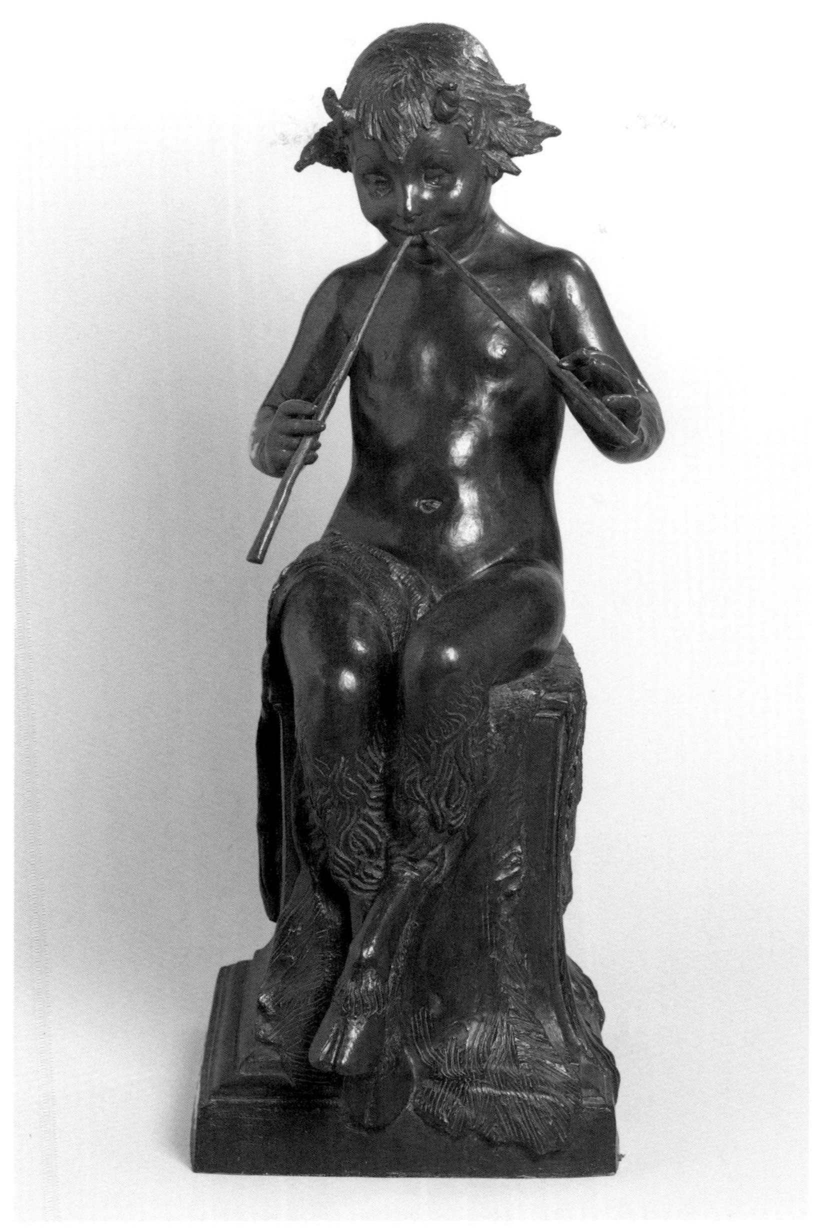

***Seated Faun*, 1924**

In *Seated Faun,* Scudder took as inspiration the part-human, part-goat figure found in classical mythology.

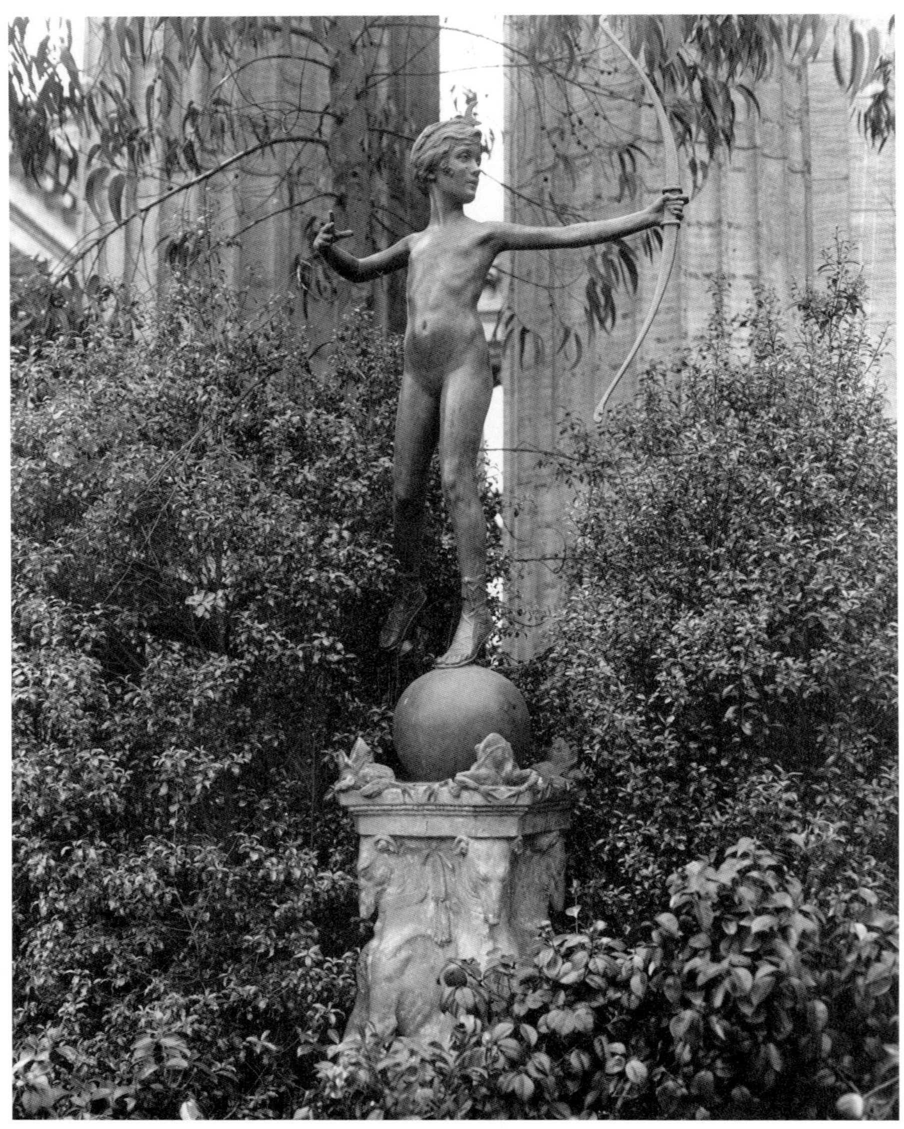

Young Diana in Garden, 1918

This sculpture, photographed by Frances Benjamin Johnston (1864–1952), was originally located at "Welwyn," the gardens of the Harold Pratt House in Glen Cove, New York. One of Janet Scudder's most famous works, Young Diana was shown at the American Pavilion of the Rome Exposition, and a year later won an honorable mention at the Paris Salon.

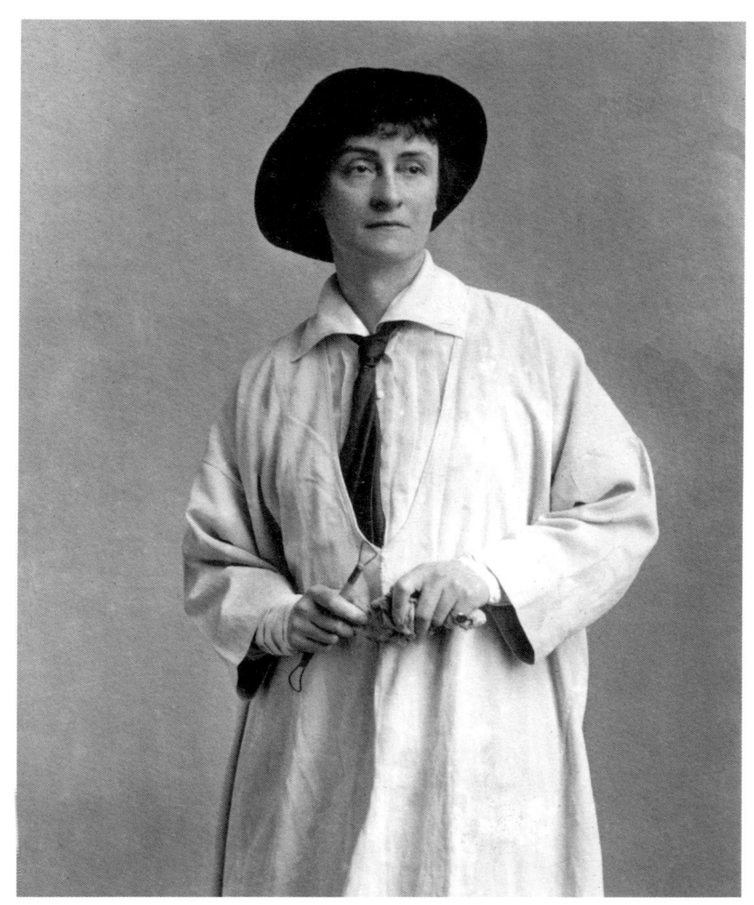

Janet Scudder, c. 1910–1915

Janet Scudder is best known for her ornamental garden sculptures sought by wealthy Americans for the landscaped grounds of their lavish estates.

(1901) to be installed at one of his estates, which depicts a joyful urchin dancing on a base surrounded by three frogs. The Metropolitan Museum of Art also purchased this fountain. Scudder then made *Tortoise Fountain* (1908), a winged cupid on a turtle that sprays water from its mouth. Soon Janet Scudder became one of the most successful American sculptors of her day.

In 1913, Scudder bought a house outside Paris that she lent the Red Cross and the YMCA for the duration of World War I. At this house, she could view her sculpture in a garden and worked there for the next twenty-five years, making garden fountains for estates of the wealthy. Although at first she wanted to complete large public commissions, she later decided that she preferred making small sculptures rather than the memorials that were being erected in American cities after the World Wars. As she wrote in her autobiography, *Modeling My Life* (1925):

> I won't do it! I won't add to this obsession of male egotism that is ruining every city in the United States with rows of hideous statues of men-men-men-men-men, each one uglier than the others ... My work was going to make people feel cheerful and gay, nothing more![18]

After World War II, Scudder began to paint. She died of pneumonia in 1940 while on vacation in Rockport, Maine, at the age of seventy. Today she is recognized as a trendsetter who helped popularize bronze fountain figures of small children and elves for gardens of wealthy clients. She is one of the most successful women sculptors of the early twentieth century. She received several medals for her work, including at the 1893 World's Columbian Exposition in Chicago, the St. Louis World's Fair in 1904, and the Panama-Pacific International Exhibition in San Francisco in 1915. In 1920, she was elected an associate of the National Academy of Design. Her first solo show was held in 1913 in New York City, and her work was also included in the art competition of the 1928 Summer Olympics. Her bronzes are in more than fourteen museums throughout the United States.

9

Bessie Potter Vonnoh

(1872–1955)

BESSIE POTTER VONNOH was born in St. Louis, Missouri, in 1872, the only child of Alexander and Mary McKenney Potter. When she was two years old, her father was killed in a railroad accident. It is now believed that her subsequent paralysis, until she was ten, was the result of the shock brought on by her father's death.

Shortly after her father died, Vonnoh's family moved to Chicago to live with her mother's family. By the time she was fourteen years old, Vonnoh knew she wanted to be a sculptor. She admitted that the "touch of clay and the joy of creating gave me a sense of deep contentment."[19] She enrolled at the Art Institute of Chicago in 1886, taking painting and drawing classes, but in 1890 took modeling classes with renowned Paris-trained sculptor Lorado Taft. Taft would become a lifelong friend, hiring Vonnoh to work as a studio assistant, where she joined other talented women apprentices. The group of women known as the "White Rabbits" helped Taft make sculptures

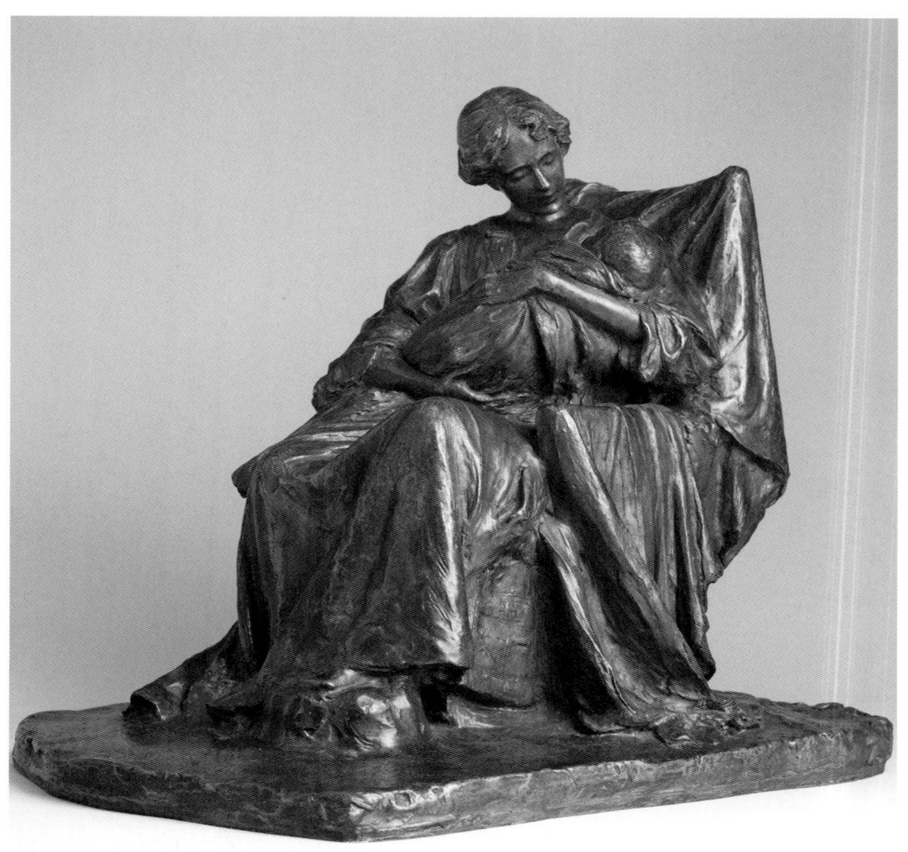

A Young Mother, 1896

In one of the most sensitive studies of the mother-and-child theme in American sculpture, Vonnoh uses abundant fabric to soften the mother's figure. Her gaze upon her child conveys the intimacy of their relationship.

for the Horticultural Building at the 1893 World's Columbian Exposition. At the Fair, Vonnoh was inspired by the work of Russian sculptor Paul Troubetzkoy to create small intimate statues.

Vonnoh set up her own studio in Chicago when she was twenty-two. With the money she saved from selling small statues of society women who were her friends, she traveled to Florence and Paris with her mother, along with Lorado Taft and his artist sister. In Paris, she visited the studio of Auguste Rodin (1840–1917), who became an important influence. When she returned home to Chicago, she created her most successful statue, *A Young Mother* (1896). The small bronze became so popular, it made her name as a sculptor of motherhood scenes, not unlike Impressionist painter Mary Cassatt or photographer Gertrude Käsebier. The sculpture of the seated mother cradling an infant in her arms was made in a loose, curving, fluid manner. As Vonnoh would later say, "What I wanted was to look for beauty in the everyday world, to catch the joy and swing of modern American life."

With a major commission of a bust of *Major-General Samuel W. Crawford* scheduled for Fairmount Park in Philadelphia, Vonnoh decided to move to New York. In 1899, she married American Impressionist painter Robert Vonnoh who had met her in Taft's Chicago studio.

During this era, most women artists gave up their careers to become homemakers. Cecilia Beaux and Mary Cassatt, the two most famous American women painters who were Vonnoh's contemporaries, stayed single to concentrate on their careers. Robert Vonnoh supported his wife's career. In fact, the couple's careers became closely linked. They worked and exhibited together in many cities while living in a New York City apartment studio, as well as at their summer home near the art colony of Lyme, Connecticut, and in southern France. Vonnoh earned many medals, had two important solo shows, and in 1921 became the first woman sculptor to become elected a full academician at the National Academy of Design, and earned its Elizabeth N. Watrous Gold Medal for *Allegresse* (1921).

Beginning in the 1920s, Vonnoh made larger, life-sized public works, such as a fountain for the Theodore Roosevelt Memorial Bird Sanctuary in Oyster Bay, Long Island, which depicts two children and swallows. Vonnoh's sculpture for the *Burnett Memorial Fountain*, the centerpiece of an English garden located between 103rd and 106th Streets along the eastern perimeter of Fifth Avenue in

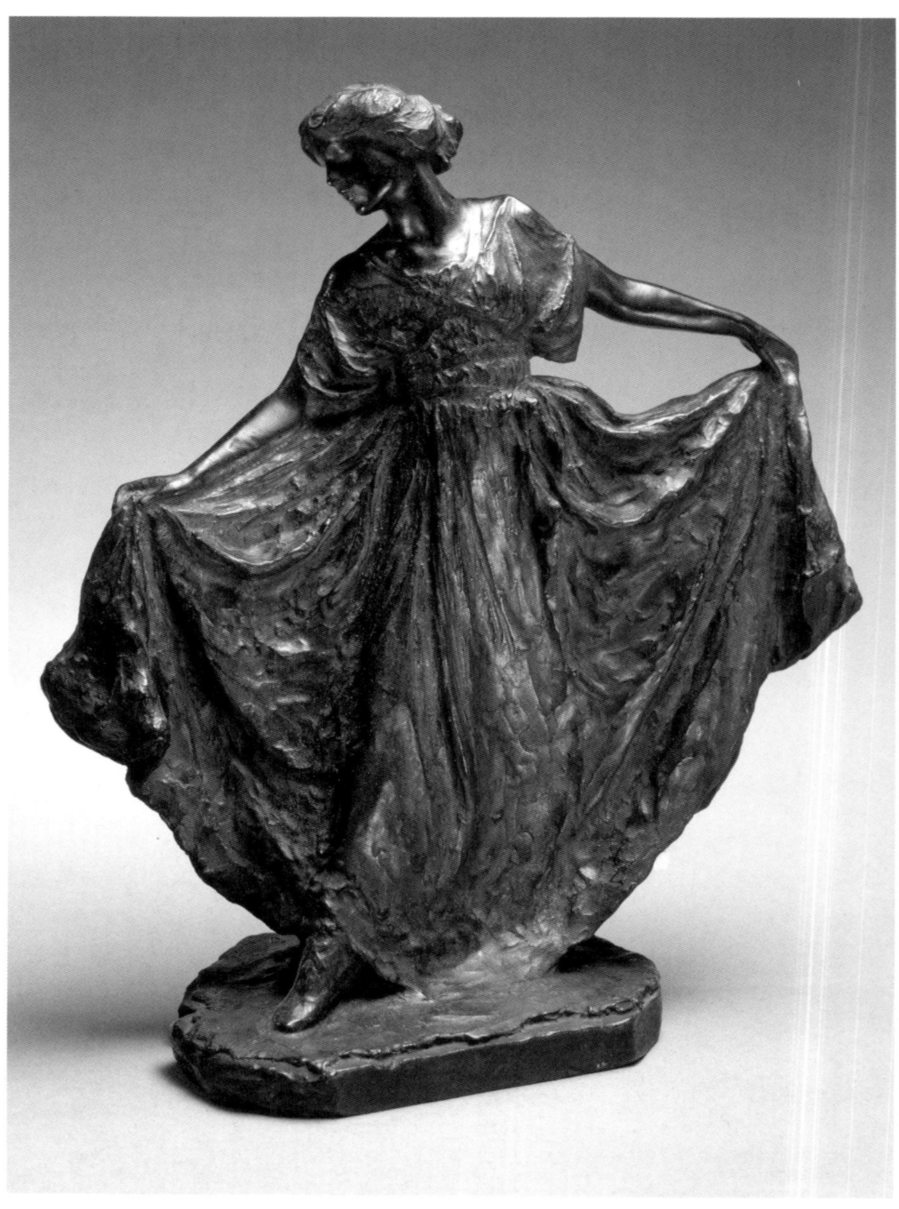

The Dance, 1897

Vonnoh explores rhythm of movement and the play of drapery over the figure in this portrayal of a fashionable young woman in a high-waisted gown. The dancer could be part of a quadrille, a dance popular in the nineteenth century performed by couples in a square formation.

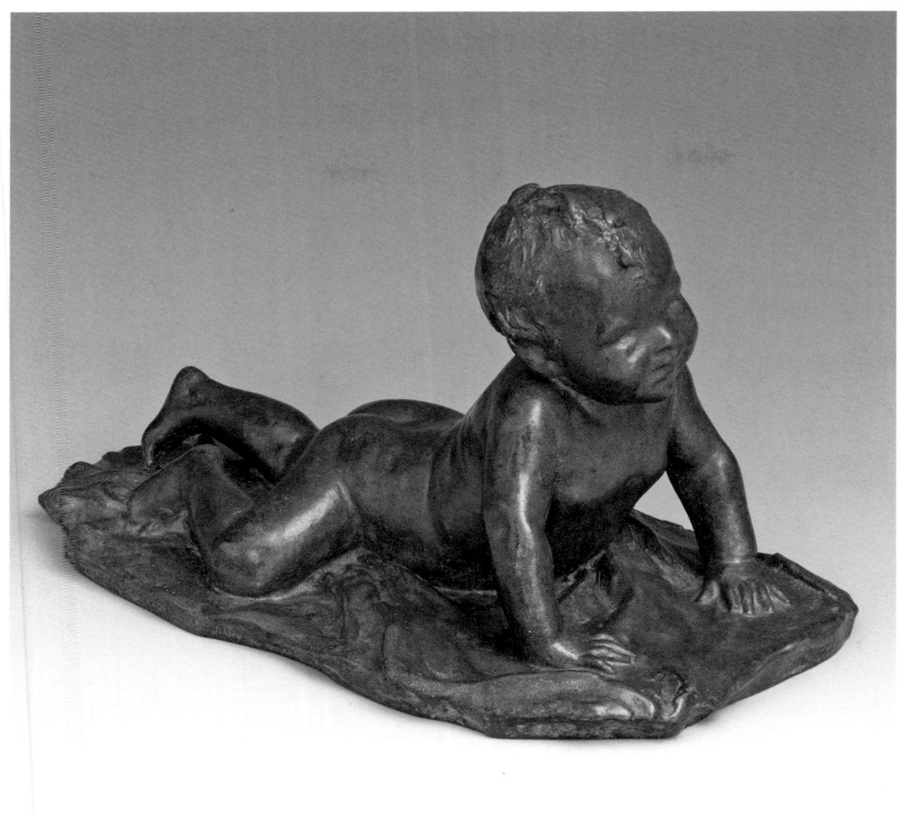

***His First Journey*, 1901**

Vonnoh captures the moment a baby learns to crawl. He glances upward and grins as he pushes himself up on his hands to make his way across a blanket. This statuette was one of Vonnoh's most popular interpretations of childhood.

Central Park, New York, depicts a girl holding a bowl and a boy below her playing the flute. The sculpture group in a lily pond is based on the characters of Mary and Dickon from *The Secret Garden* (1910), a classic written by well-known English-born author of novels and children's books, Frances Eliza Hodgson Burnett (1849–1924).

In Burnett's story, the two children find a secret garden and bring it back to life. Burnett wrote the children's book in Long

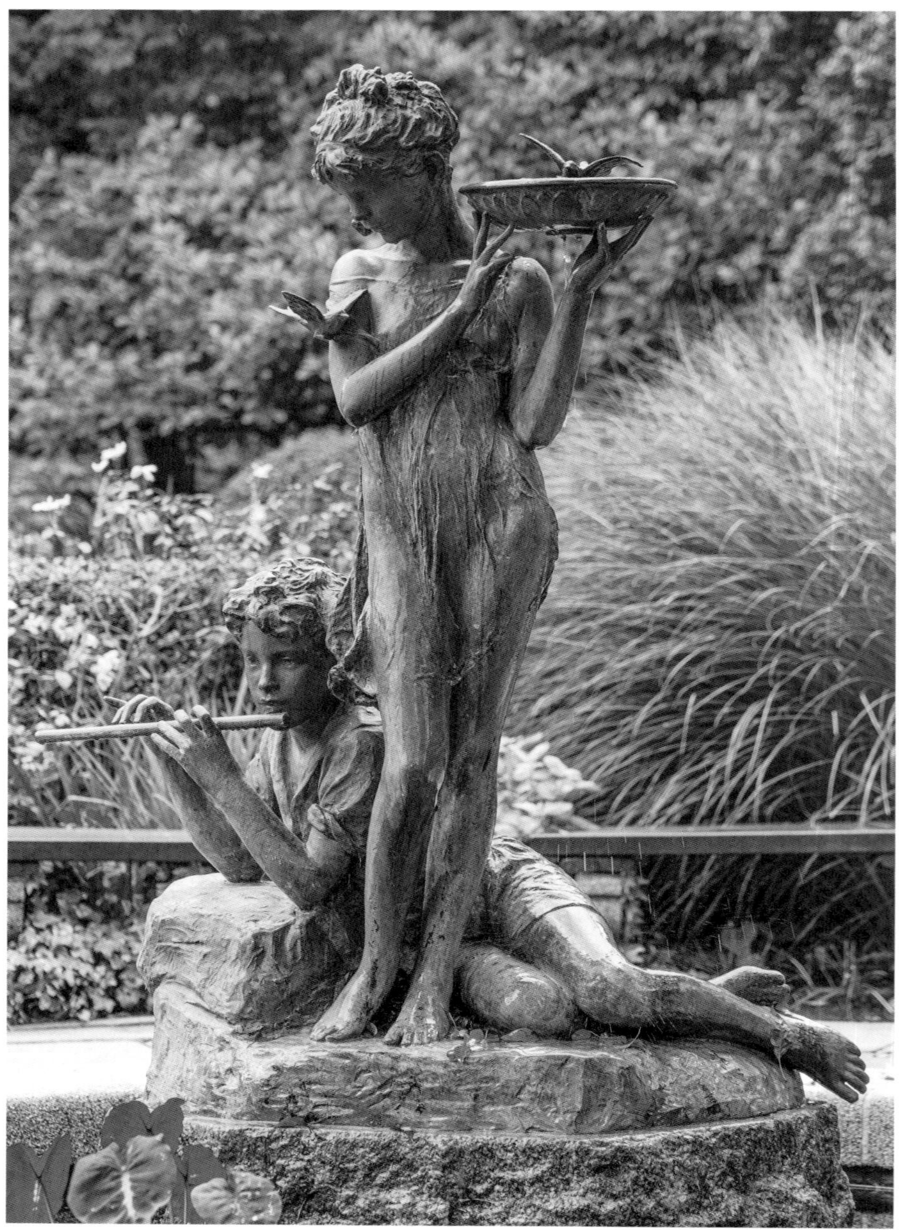

Burnett Memorial Fountain, 1936

Bessie Potter Vonnoh dedicated the memorial fountain to the literary genius of Frances Hodgson Burnett. The centerpiece for an English garden is based on the famous author's 1910 classic.

Island, where she lived at the end of her life. Within a few years, her fans raised funds for a tribute in Central Park. The memorial was completed in less than a decade.

After her husband's death in 1933, Vonnoh worked less often. She remarried in 1948, but her husband, Dr. Edward L. Keyes, died only nine months later, and she died six years after him in New York City at the age of eighty-two. One of the most successful women artists of her generation, Vonnoh enjoyed a long career at a time when it was still unusual for an American woman to be a professional sculptor.

Gertrude Vanderbilt Whitney

(1875–1942)

GERTRUDE VANDERBILT WHITNEY was born in 1875 to Cornelius Vanderbilt II and Alice Claypoole Gwynne. Her great grandfather was shipping and railroad tycoon Cornelius Vanderbilt, and the Vanderbilt family was one of the wealthiest and most prominent American families at the turn of the twentieth century. Raised in a Fifth Avenue mansion in New York City with several brothers and one sister, Gertrude attended Brearley School where she showed an early interest in art. She and her siblings posed for John Everett Millais. Her diaries were filled with drawings and watercolors.

In 1896, she married Harry Payne Whitney, the boy who hailed from a family of similar wealth and status and lived across the street, but the young couple soon grew apart. Mrs. Whitney was not destined to settle into the life of the Fifth Avenue socialite. She broke the rules of her elite caste and chose to live independently. Encouraged by artist Howard Cushing, Whitney began to study sculpture.

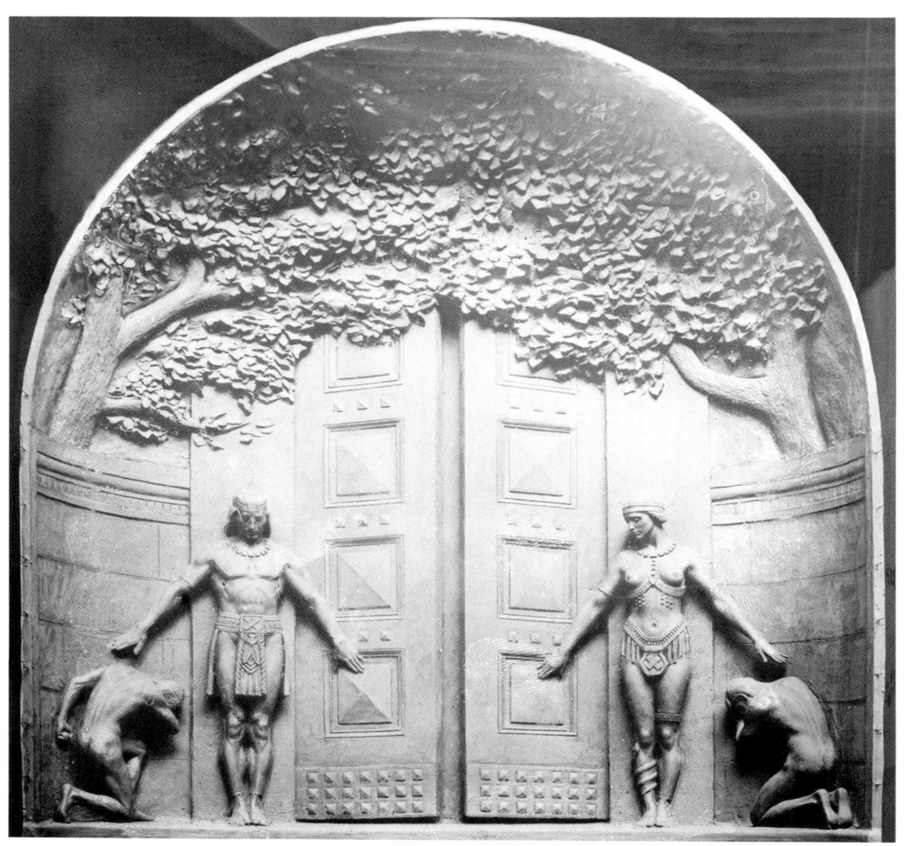

Fountain of El Dorado, c. 1915

The El Dorado Fountain was exhibited in San Francisco for the Panama-Pacific Exposition. The stated purpose of this world's fair was to celebrate the completion of the Panama Canal.

In 1900, she began her studies with sculptor Hendrik Christian Anderson, and her plaster sculpture *Aspiration,* a life-sized male nude, was accepted one year later at the 1901 Pan-American Exposition in Buffalo.

Back in New York City, Whitney studied at the prestigious Art Students League where she acquired connections with the contemporary art world. In 1907 she opened a studio on MacDougal Alley in Greenwich Village, the heart of the artists' neighborhood.

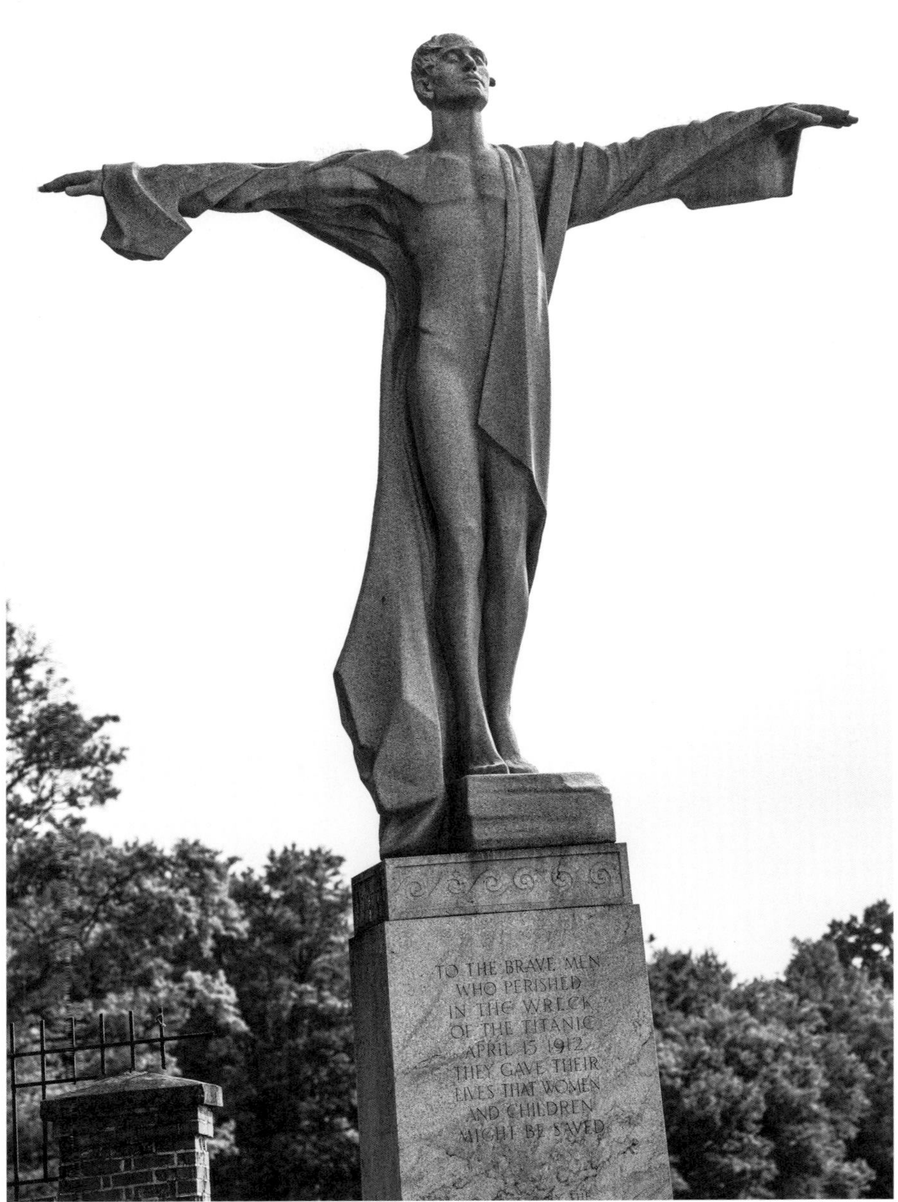

***Titanic*, c. 1915–1920**

This photograph shows a model figure for the Titanic Memorial in Washington, D.C. It was made to honor those who gave their lives during the disaster so that others might be saved.

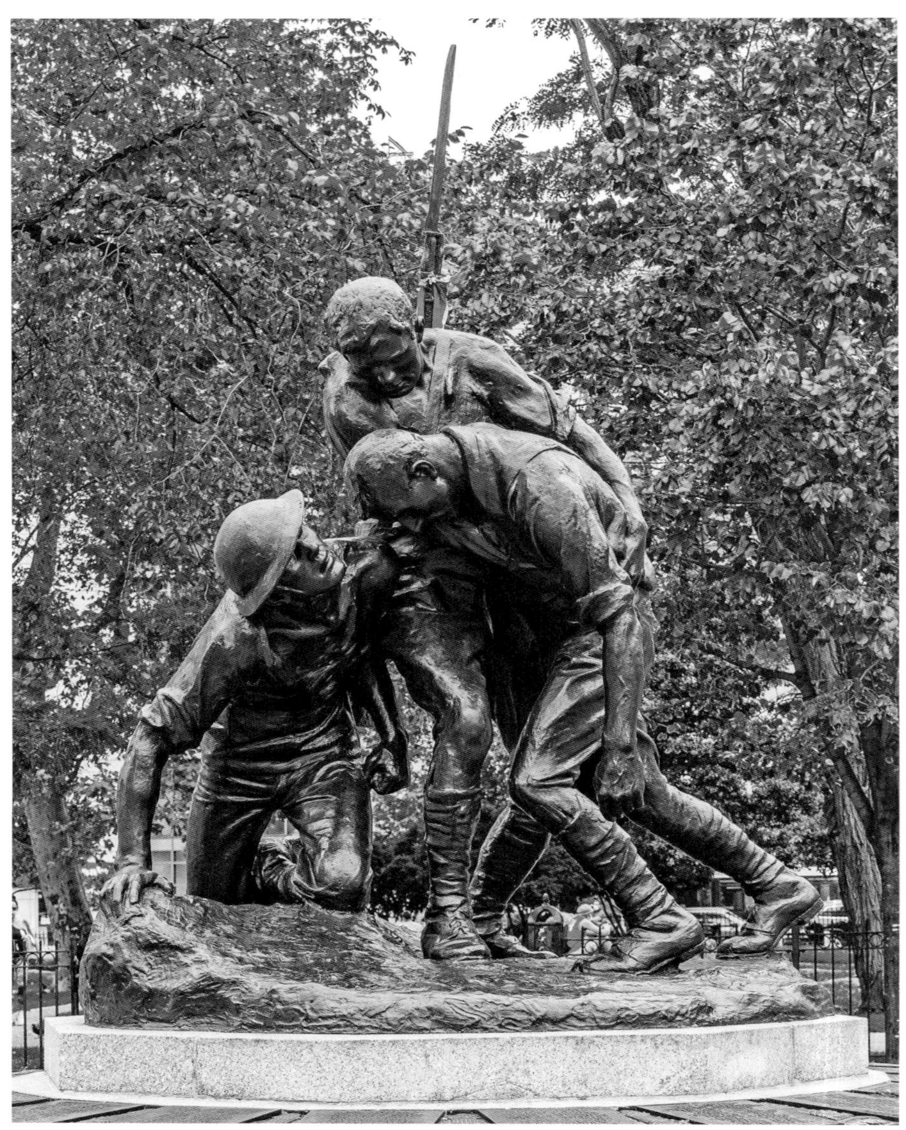

Washington Heights-Inwood War Memorial, 1922

Commemorating servicemen from three military branches: the Navy, Army, and Marine Corps, the figures of Whitney's memorial are derived from original wartime sketches she made while in France, where she traveled to start a hospital to help wounded soldiers. The sculpture began with two figures, but a third was later added during the design process.

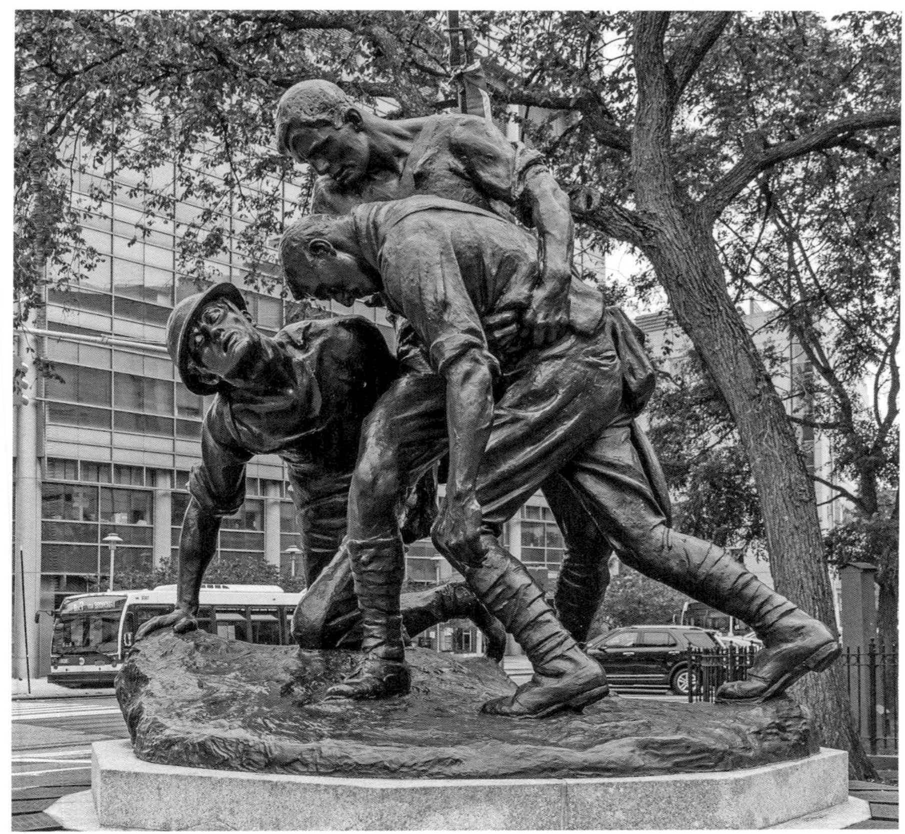

One year later, under an assumed name, she won a prize from the Architectural League for her depiction of Pan. After one of her marble statues was received well at the National Academy of Design in 1910, Whitney began to exhibit under her own name.

Whitney's career as a sculptor took off in the 1910s. She made the Aztec Fountain for the Pan American Union Building in Washington, D.C., the Fountain of El Dorado for the 1915 Panama-Pacific Exposition in San Francisco, and two reliefs for Madison Square Park's Victory Arch in New York City. She also created a memorial for the sinking of the Titanic in Washington, D.C.

She was very active in relief efforts during World War I, and after the war, sculpted a memorial monument known as the *Washington Heights-Inwood War Memorial* which depicts the realities of war.

Erected on Memorial Day in 1922 at the intersection of Broadway and St. Nicolas Avenue at Mitchel Square Park, the statue honors men from northern Manhattan who fought and died during World War I. There are twenty star-shaped plaques made of bronze and set into a flagstone paving surrounding the monument and its base, which symbolize the fatalities of 357 local men. The dedication ceremony coincided with parades and military demonstrations throughout the five New York City boroughs.

Though a relatively traditional sculptor, Whitney was a strong patron of modern American art. In 1908, she opened the Whitney Studio Gallery in the same building as her Greenwich studio and welcomed many young artists, such as Robert Henri, William Glackens, and John Sloan, to showcase their works, often purchasing them. She also supported the exhibitions of women artists such as Peggy Bacon and Mabel Dwight.

As a patron of American artists, Whitney helped many who were starting their careers, including Charles Sheeler, Reginald Marsh, Edward Hopper, Stuart Davis, and countless others. Six years after she opened the gallery, she launched the Whitney Studio Club, where artists could meet and socialize, attend programming, and debut new pieces. In a magazine article, Whitney argued that American art was no longer going to be the provincial stepchild of Europe. According to art critic Henry McBride, "there was not a contemporary artist of note in America who has not been helped by Mrs. Whitney."[20]

Eventually, Whitney offered to donate her growing collection of contemporary American art to the Metropolitan Museum of Art with an endowment to support the construction of a new wing. Her offer was refused because the Museum would not take American art at that time, so Whitney opened the Whitney Museum of American Art in Greenwich Village in 1931. The Museum moved to West 54th Street in 1954 and again relocated in 1966 to West 75th Street and Madison Avenue. In 2015, The Whitney Museum moved to its current location at 99 Gansevoort Street. Whitney also helped fund the Whitney wing of the American Museum of Natural History in New York City.

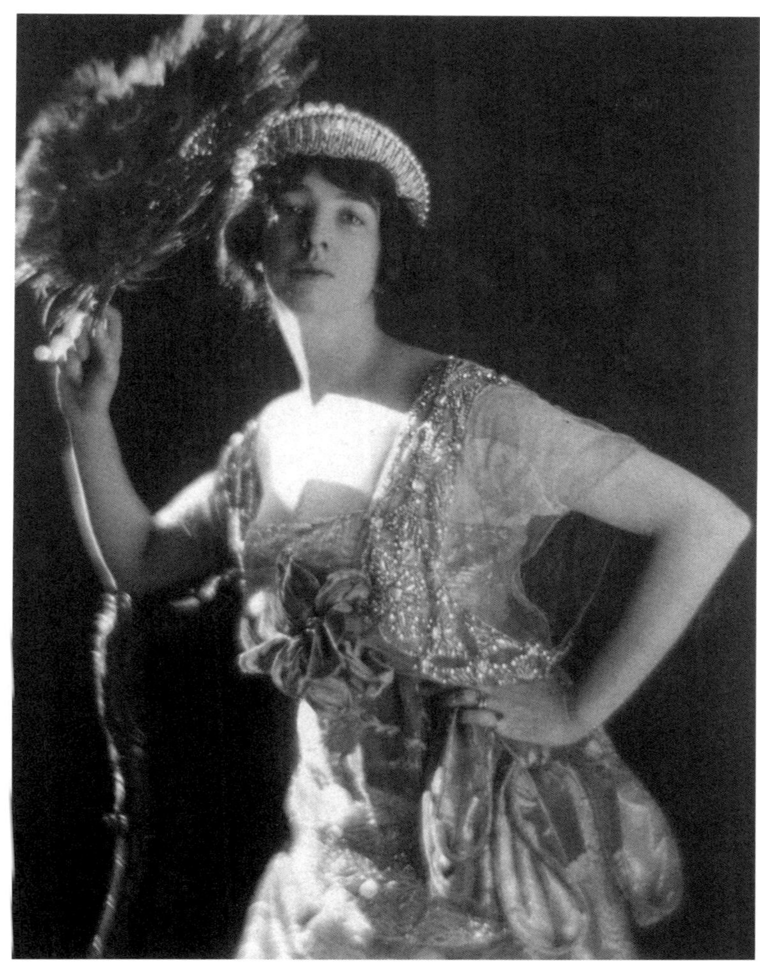

Gertrude Vanderbilt Whitney, 1920

The life that Gertrude Vanderbilt Whitney chose for herself had a huge impact on the art world. Her work can be seen in France, Spain, and Canada. Remembered not only as a sculptor but also as a leading patron and collector of American art created during her lifetime, Whitney is also known for founding the Whitney Museum of American Art.

Anna Hyatt Huntington

(1876–1973)

ANNA HYATT HUNTINGTON was born in Cambridge, Massachusetts in 1876, the youngest of three children. Her mother, an amateur landscape artist, and her father, a professor of paleontology and zoology at Harvard University and the Massachusetts Institute of Technology, encouraged her interest in animals and made sure she was surrounded by animals, both living and dead. Before Anna could even read, she could distinguish over one hundred thoroughbred horses simply based on pictures.

Huntington spent much of her childhood sketching and recording animals in movement and developed a great affection for horses, making her first clay models of horses, dogs, and other domestic animals. She spent several years training to become a concert violinist, but when her sister Harriet, who also enjoyed sculpting, asked for

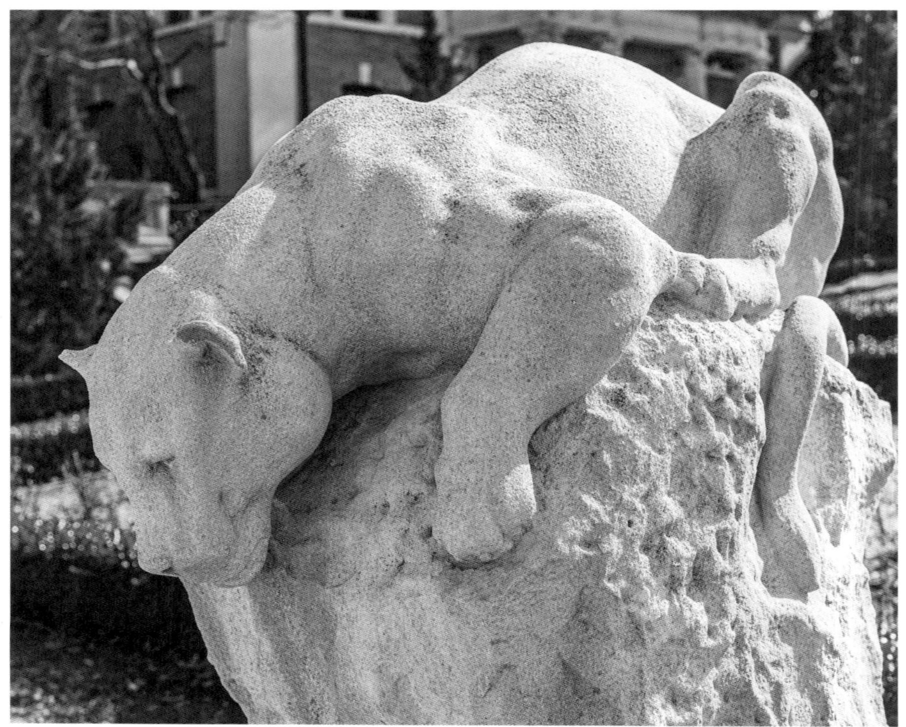

***Reaching Jaguar*, 1906**

Reaching Jaguar and its companion piece, Jaguar, were based on Huntington's studies of Señor Lopez, a *jaguar* from Paraguay who was the first feline occupant at the Lion House of the Bronx Zoo. These sculptures can be viewed at the Metropolitan Museum of Art in New York City. Stone versions are installed as gateposts at the zoo.

her help to mend a broken foot on a piece she had created, Harriet was so pleased with the results that she asked Anna to collaborate on another sculpture, which was then exhibited and purchased. The sisters began dreaming of opening an art academy, but their father's death and Harriet's marriage in 1902 derailed their plans.

Anna began studying sculpture with Boston portrait sculptor Henry Hudson Kitson, and in 1900 held her first solo exhibition, consisting of forty animal sculptures, at the Boston Arts Club. In 1903, she moved to New York City where she briefly attended the

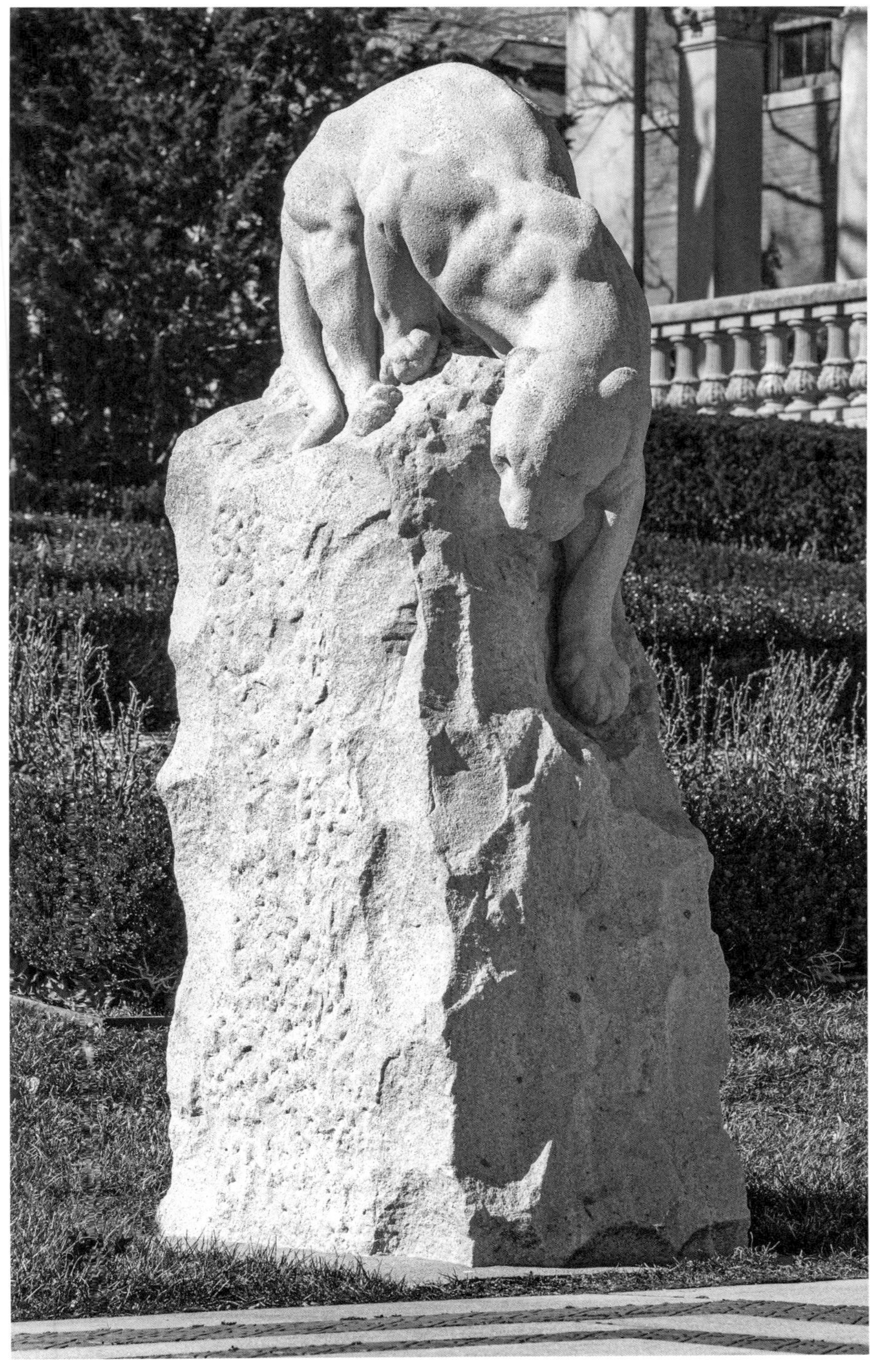

Art Students League and studied with sculptors Hermon Atkins MacNeil and Gutzon Borglum before deciding that she preferred to work independently and study from direct observation. She spent long hours at the Bronx Zoo where she completed *Reaching Jaguar* (1906), one of her first major works.

In 1907, Huntington moved to Paris, the center of the art world, and worked on small pieces which she exhibited at the 1908 Paris Salon. She then left France for Naples, Italy, to work on an enormous bronze lion that had been commissioned by a high school in Dayton, Ohio. When she had completed this piece, she returned to France to work on her first major equestrian statue, *Joan of Arc.* Huntington had long dreamed of creating this statue. She rented the former studio of French sculptor Jules Dalou and researched Joan of Arc by reading about her life and traveling to places where the saint had lived. Then she found a horse and brought it to her studio. She worked ten-hour days for four months to complete her model, using three and a half tons of clay.

Although Huntington carried out the project with one female assistant, the Paris Salon jury had doubts that she could have made the life-sized sculpture by herself. Nevertheless, it won an honorable mention at the 1910 Paris Salon, which led to a New York City commission of a bronze version to mark the saint's 500th anniversary. Huntington concentrated on the saint's spiritual intensity. "I thought of her before her first battle, speaking to her soldiers, holding up the ancient sword."[21] The statue, unveiled in 1915 at Riverside Drive and 93rd Street, received worldwide praise. It was the city's first public monument outside Central Park made by a woman, as well as the city's first monument to honor a real woman. This event led to more commissions and awards. Huntington became one of the highest-paid female entrepreneurs in the United States and had a long and illustrious career as an artist.

While serving on a committee to plan a sculpture exhibition at the Hispanic Museum, Anna met Archer Huntington, railroad heir, scholar, poet, philanthropist, and the founder of the museum. They married on March 10, 1923, Anna's forty-seventh birthday, a birthday the couple shared. Archer's love of Spanish culture would have the greatest impact on Anna's future work. After their honeymoon in 1927, she completed her second major equestrian statue, that of El Cid Campeador, the medieval Spanish warrior. In fact, Archer had just translated the epic poem, *The Song of El Cid.* The seven-meter high statue exists today in five versions.

In 1927, Huntington was stricken with tuberculosis and worked less often as she battled the disease. Nevertheless, she was able to complete a number of sculptures for the grounds of New York City's Hispanic Society of America, which Archer had established in 1904 as a public library, museum, and educational institution to study Spanish and Portuguese literature, history, and languages. Anna and her husband were dedicated to designing the layout of the courtyard, the space surrounded by Beaux-Arts buildings at Broadway and 155th Street.

After Anna recovered from her illness in the 1930s, Archer bought an estate outside the city where she could keep a full zoo of animals that served as models. The couple also bought 10,000 acres in Murrells Inlet, South Carolina, the site of four old plantations, and transformed it into a sculpture garden and wildlife preserve. Brookgreen Gardens is today a National Historic Landmark and the largest sculpture garden in the United States, consisting of more than 1,400 sculptures from both nineteenth- and twentieth-century artists.

When Archer became ill, Anna devoted herself to his care. After his death in 1955, she returned to her work, though she was eighty years old. She received a commission to honor Cuba and chose as her subject the Cuban patriot, *Jose Marti* (1965). Her work depicts him falling from a rearing horse hit by Spanish bullets. Though finished in 1959, the monument wasn't unveiled until 1965, delayed by the fear of violence between pro- and anti-Castro supporters. This was one of Anna Hyatt Huntington's final works.

In her final years, Huntington was dismayed by modern abstract art, which she called "an overwhelming flood of degenerate trash

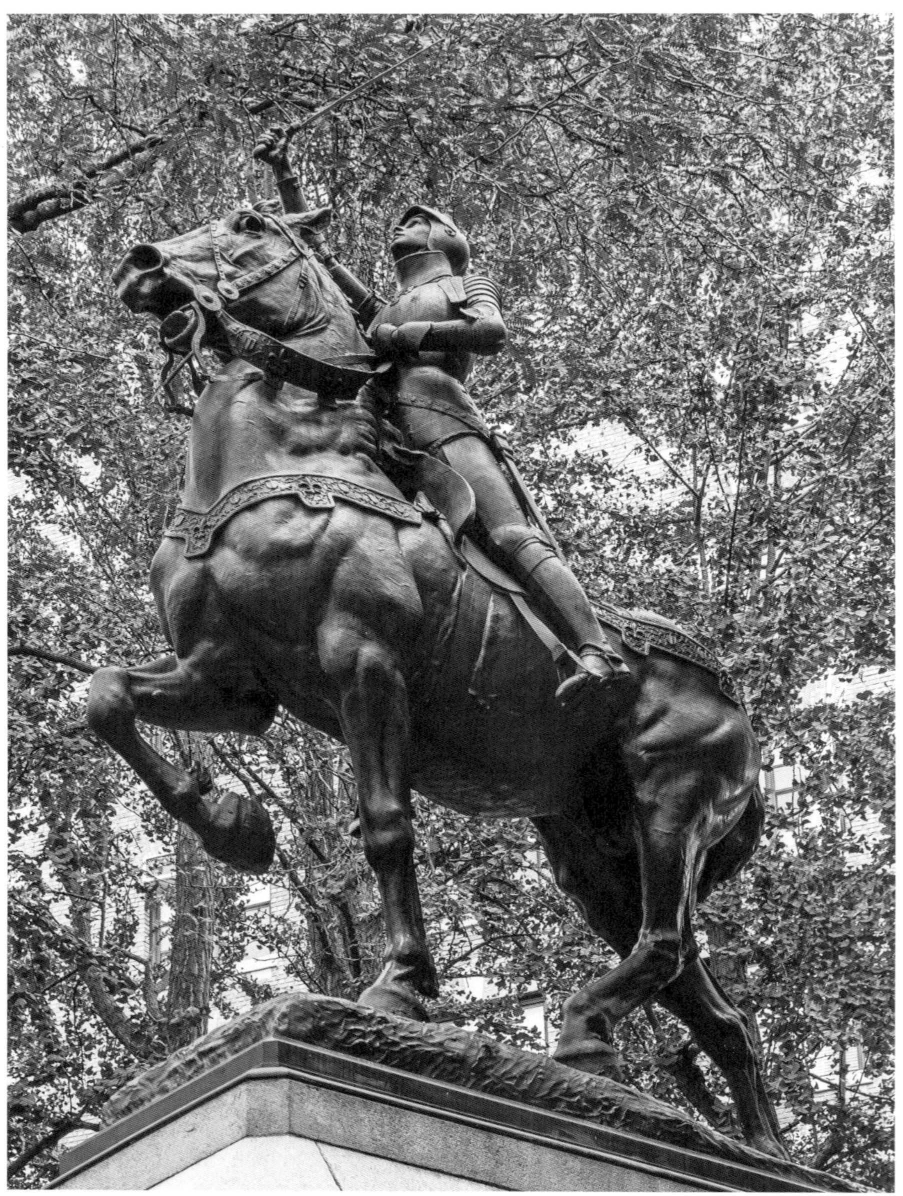

St. Joan of Arc, 1915

St. Joan of Arc is a national heroine of France. The peasant girl, believing she was acting under divine guidance, led the French army to victory in 1429 that repulsed an English attempt to conquer France during the Hundred Years' War.

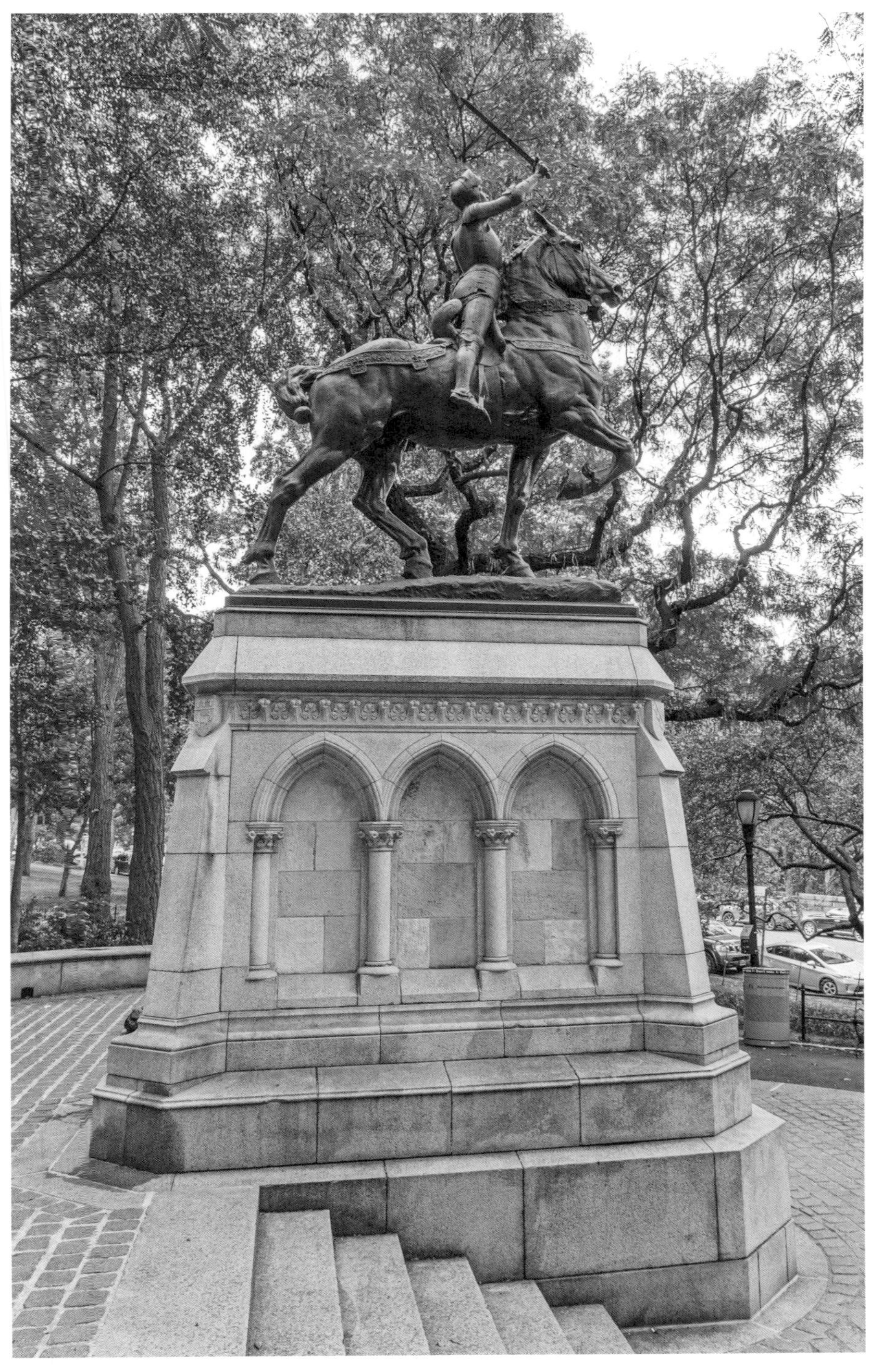

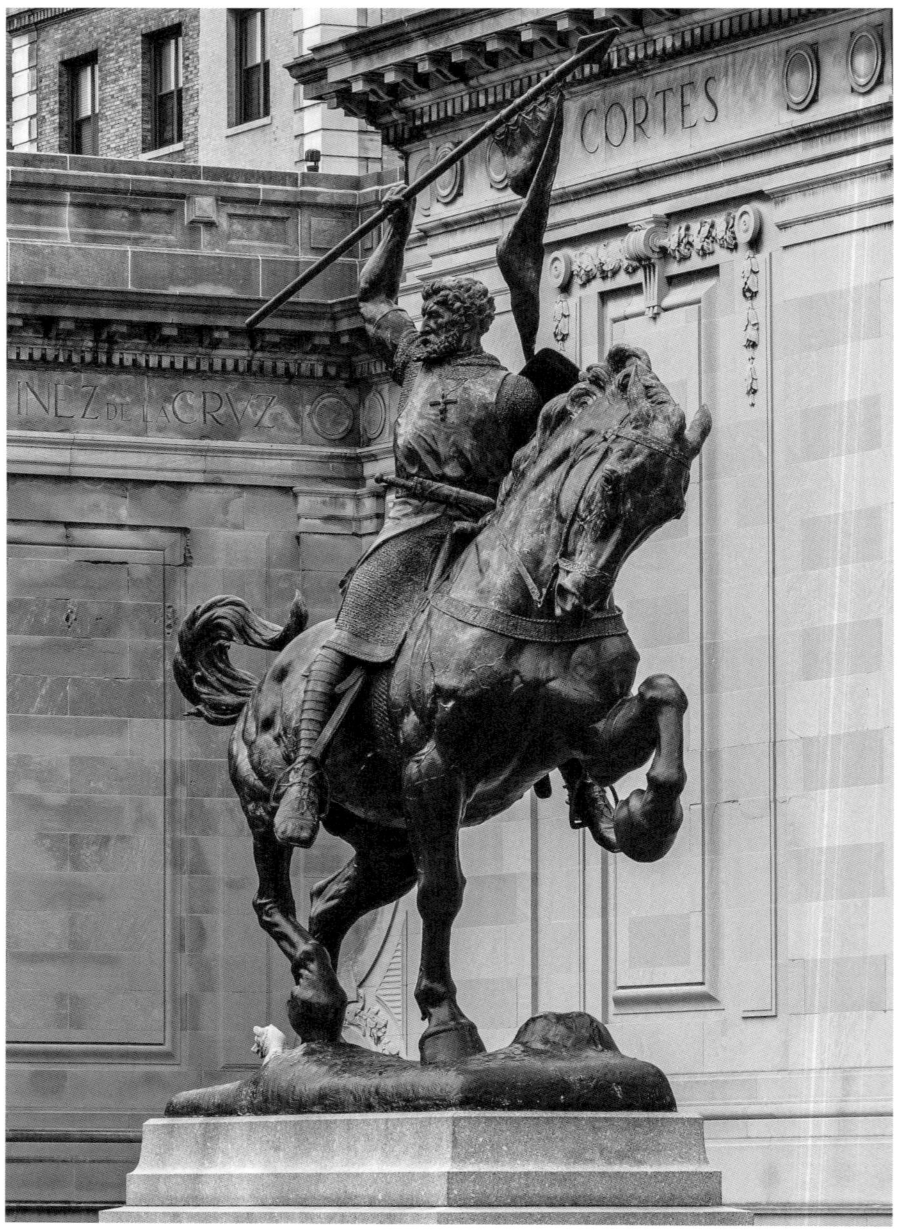

El Cid, 1927

The statue of the legendary hero of Spain (1043–1099), mounted on his horse and holding a spear and shield, is located at the Audubon Terrace in New York City.

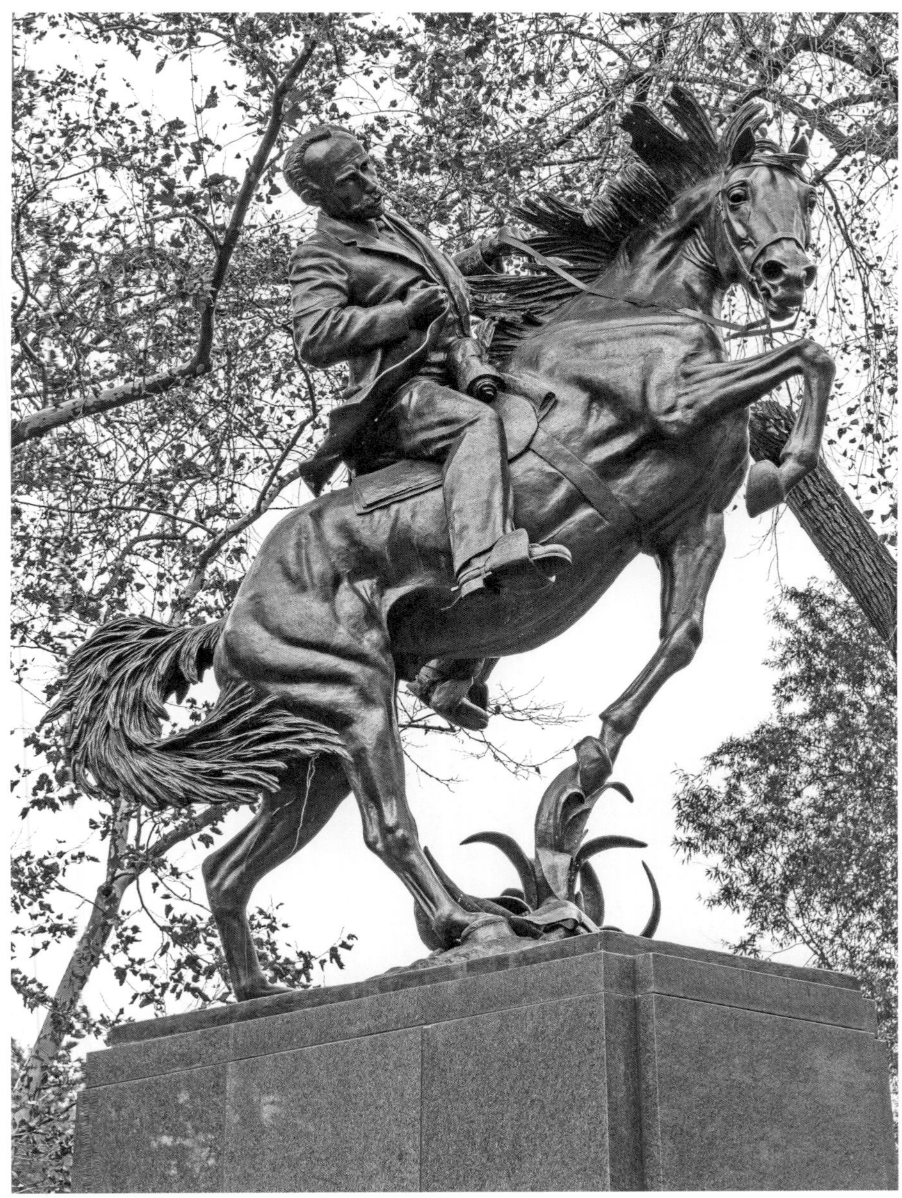

***Jose Marti*, 1965**

At the entrance to Central Park in New York City, located at 59th Street and Avenue of the Americas, the statue of Jose Marti was one of the last works of Huntington. So strongly did she believe in Cuban independence that she created the statue for free.

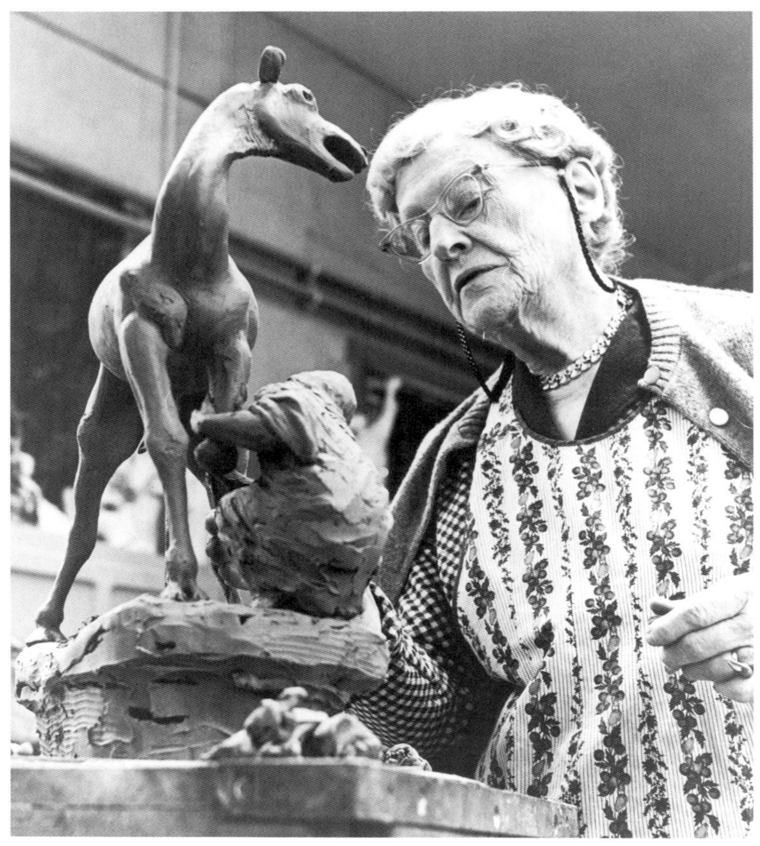

Anna Hyatt Huntington

The famous American sculptor is remembered for being the first woman to create a public monument in New York City.

drowning sincere and conservative workers in all the arts."[22] Ironically, though, her naturalistic works helped to bridge the gap between traditional styles of the 1800s and modern abstract art. She continued to work and win awards until she died in 1973 at the age of ninety-seven, and is buried with her husband in the Huntington Family Tomb at Woodlawn Cemetery in The Bronx, New York City.

The Anna Huntington Papers Special Collection is located at the Syracuse University Library. Along with her husband, Archer Milton Huntington (1870–1955), Anna Huntington was responsible for founding fourteen museums, several wildlife preserves, and America's first sculpture garden. The couple also donated 800 acres for the Collis P. Huntington State Park in Redding, Connecticut. Anna Huntington's greatest gift lay in her portrayal of animals, in the way she combined her acute observation as a naturalist with a sense of artistic design and rhythm. Her small bronze statues and larger-scaled statues can be found in museums around the world, and she continues to be an inspiration to other female artists today.

Malvina Hoffman

(1885–1966)

MALVINA HOFFMAN was the fourth of six children born to Richard Hoffman, a concert pianist and composer, and Fidelia Marshall Hoffman, also a pianist. She grew up in Brooklyn, New York City, and was educated by her mother at home until she was ten years old. While attending Brearley School, Hoffman took evening classes at the Women's School for Applied Design as well as the Art Students League of New York.

Hoffman studied painting with John White Alexander and sculpture with Herbert Adams, George Gray Barnard, and Gutzon Borglum, the sculptor of Mount Rushmore, as well as a family friend. Her first finished sculpture was a bust of her father, made in 1909 just two weeks prior to his death. When she finished it, her father looked at her and said. "My child, I'm afraid you are going to be an artist."[23] Borglum praised the piece and encouraged Hoffman to present it at the 1910 National Academy Exhibition. After her father's death, Hoffman and her mother traveled to France where she hoped to study with the world-famous sculptor Auguste Rodin. Al-

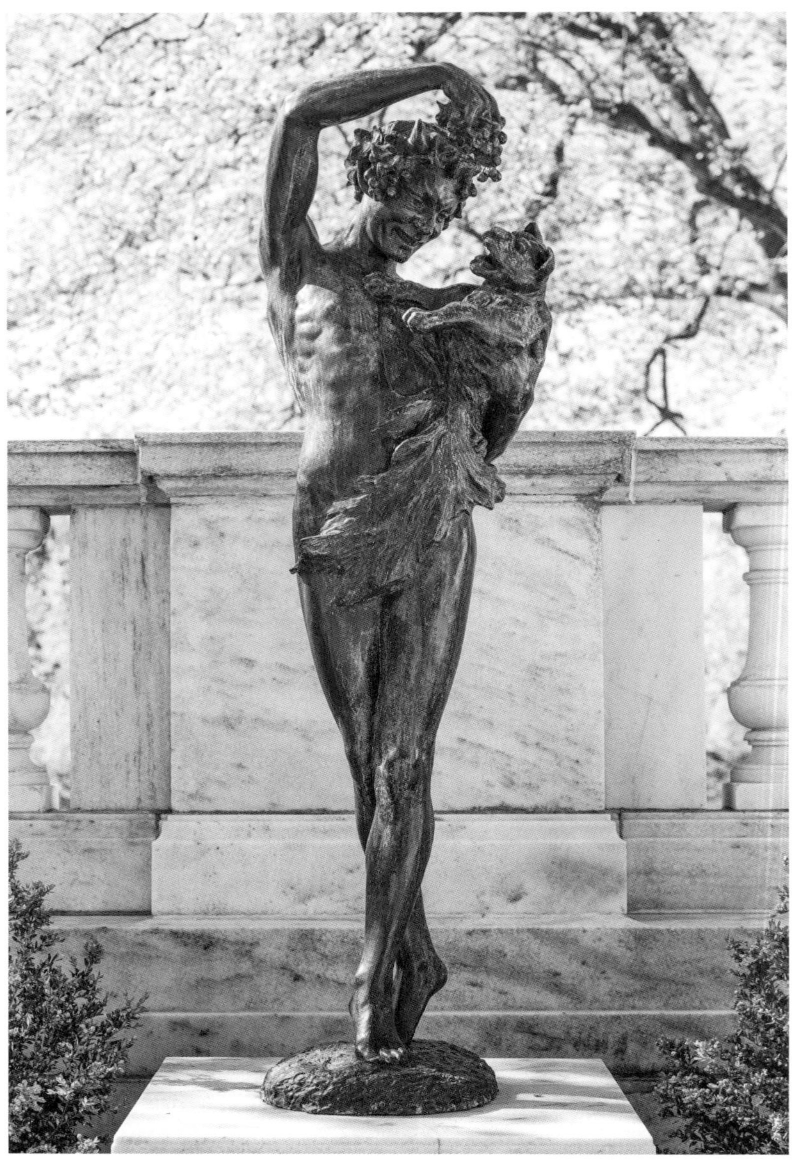

Boy and Panther Cub, 1915

Malvina Hoffman created this garden sculpture showing a young boy holding a small panther cub with his left arm while dangling a bunch of grapes over its mouth. Commissioned by Cleveland industrialist John L. Severance, the sculpture depicting tenderness that the boy has for the cub suggests harmony between humans and nature.

though she had a letter of recommendation from Borglum, she was turned away at Rodin's door five times before he finally accepted her as one of his students and then as his assistant. It was from Rodin that she learned a more naturalistic approach to form. Hoffman worked with Rodin until the beginning of World War I in 1914, when she returned to New York City on Rodin's advice to study anatomy at the Cornell University College of Physicians and Surgeons.

Seeing world-famous Russian ballerina Anna Pavlova perform in London in 1910 had a profound effect on Hoffman, and the two women later became close friends. "Fireworks were set off in my mind ... impressions of ... dazzling vivacity and spontaneity ... the incomparable Anna cast her spell over me."[24] Even before meeting Pavlova in person, Hoffman created many sculptures inspired by her, such as *Russian Dancers*, which won a prize in the 1911 Paris Salon, and *Bacchanale Russe* (1912), which depicts dancers rushing forward while holding fluttering drapery over their heads.

Hoffman finally met Pavlova in 1914, and Pavlova often posed for her in her studio, allowing Hoffman to create such works as *La Gavotte* (1915), *Les Orientales*, and *La Peri* (1921). For Pavlova's birthday, Hoffman threw a masked costume ball for two hundred people. At midnight, Pavlova posed with her hands together in prayer. Hoffman preserved this image in sculpture, naming it *Byzantine Madonna* (1924).

In 1929, Hoffman received a commission from the Chicago Field Museum of Natural History to create more than 105 life-size figures for their Hall of Man. She traveled all over the globe to study people from diverse cultures, and at the end of this project she felt "this collection of bronze figures and heads is a sculptor's interpretation of Humanity, studied from three angles—Art, Science, and Psychology."[25] Her sculptures were featured at the Century of Progress International Exposition at the Chicago World's Fair of 1933.

Well-known for her life-sized sculptures of notable people, such as friends Gertrude Stein and Henry Clay Frick, Hoffman received countless awards for her work, including a gold medal from the

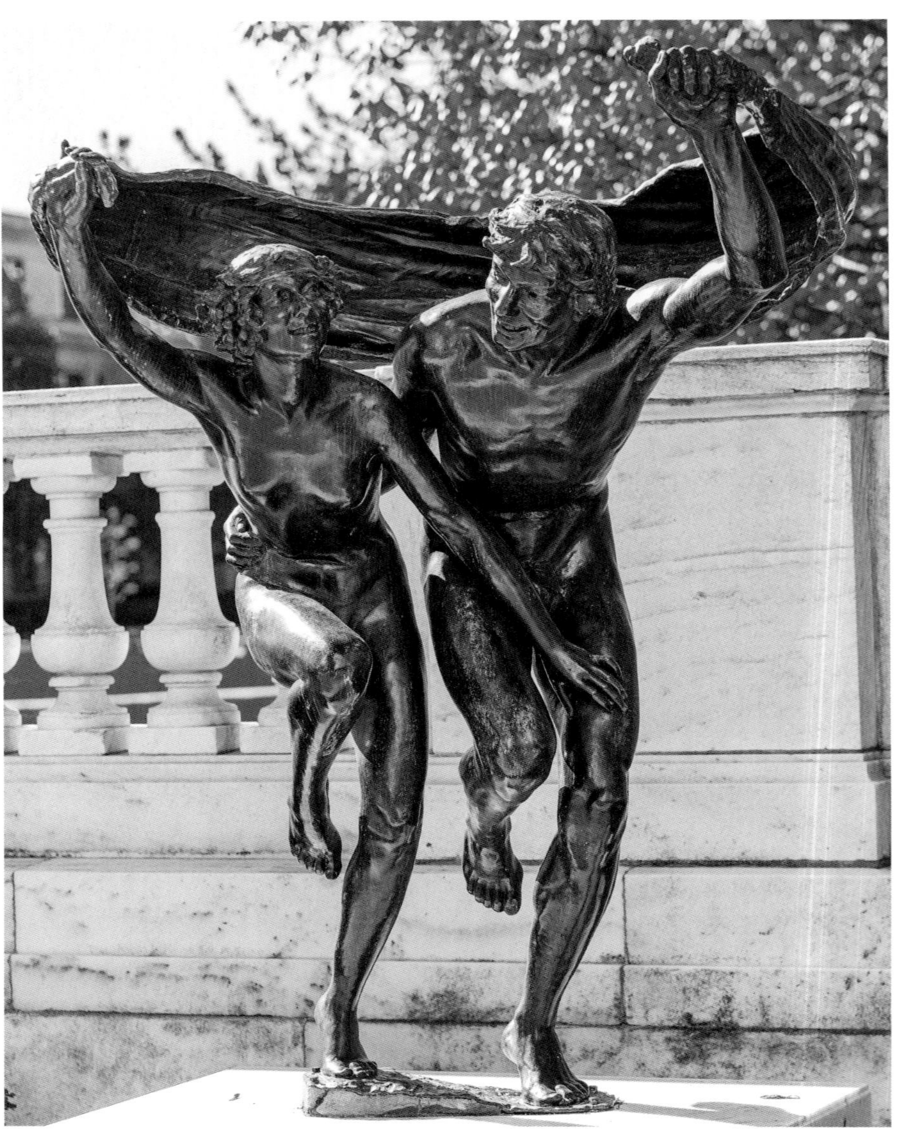

***Bacchanale Russe*, 1912**

The graceful elegance of the figures on the marble promenade that lines the southern entrance outside the Cleveland Museum of Art reflects Hoffman's ability to capture the beauty of movement and the human form. The two lovers are engaged in the pleasantries of a Bacchanal festival, the Roman feast in honor of the god Bacchus, god of wine and revelry.

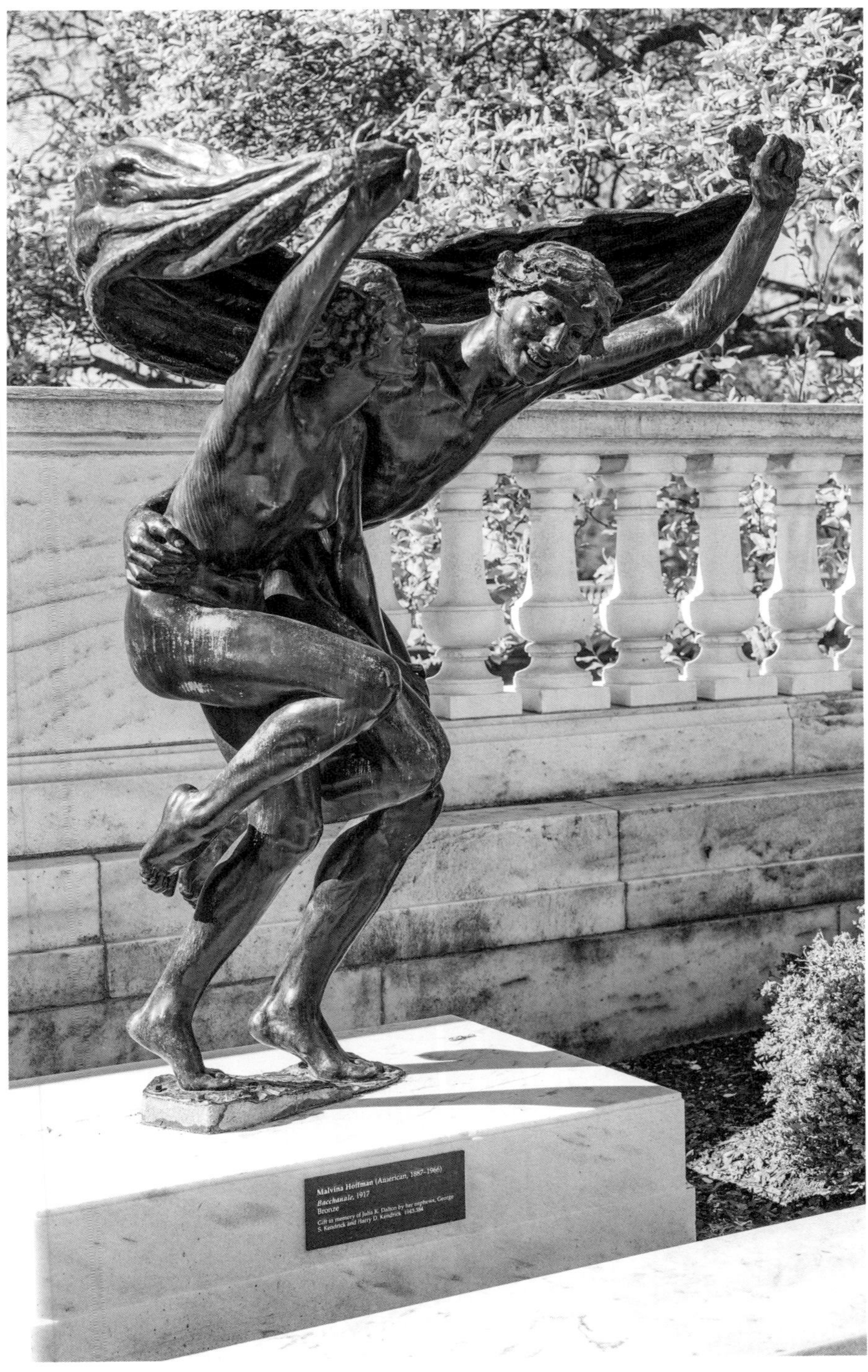
Malvina Hoffman (American, 1887–1966)
Bacchanale, 1917
Bronze
Gift in memory of Julia K. Dalton by her nephews, George
S. Kendrick and Harry D. Kendrick 1943.384

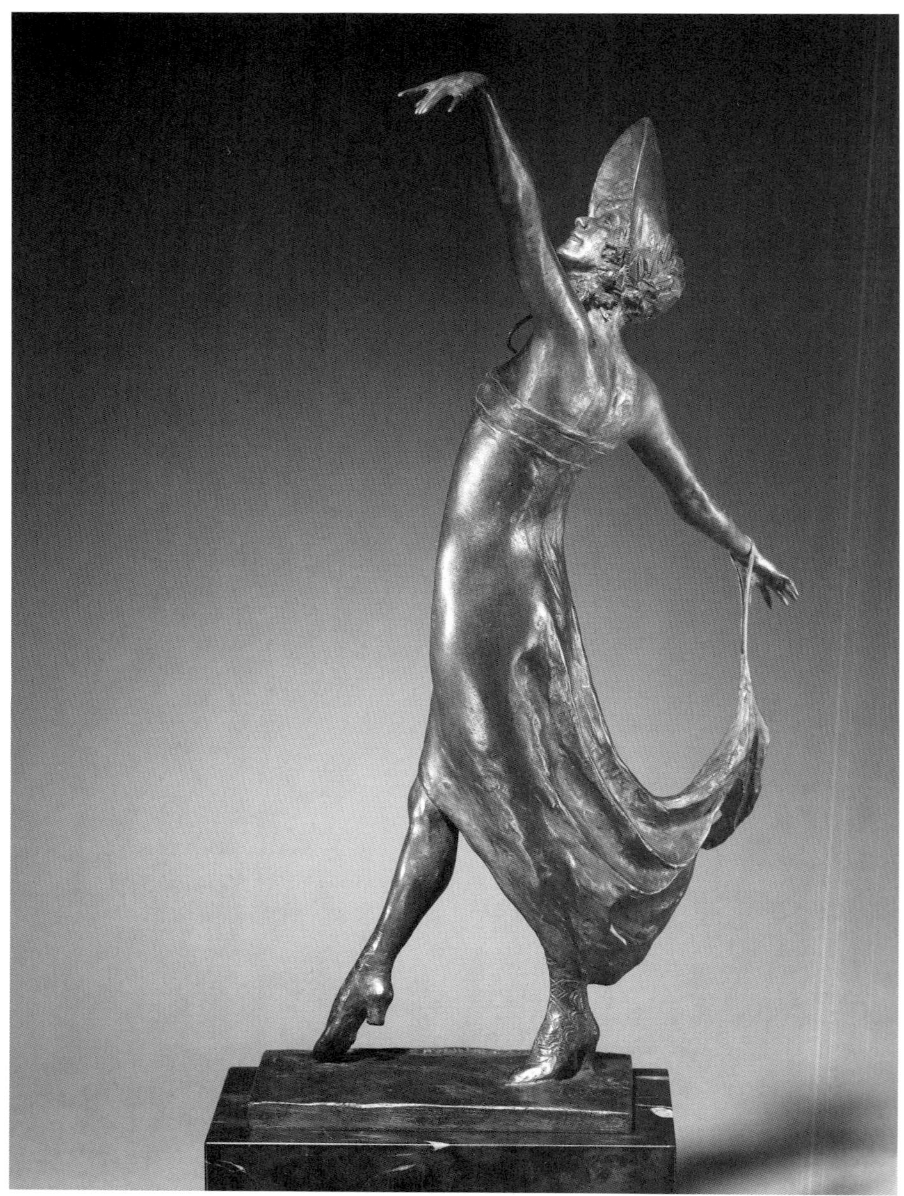

La Gavotte, 1915

The dance that inspired this statue was performed to music by German composer Paul Lincke (1866–1946). Hoffman's statue features Pavlova's exquisite form—the ease of her movements, the perfect positioning of her feet, and the broad sweep of her arms.

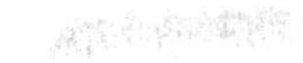

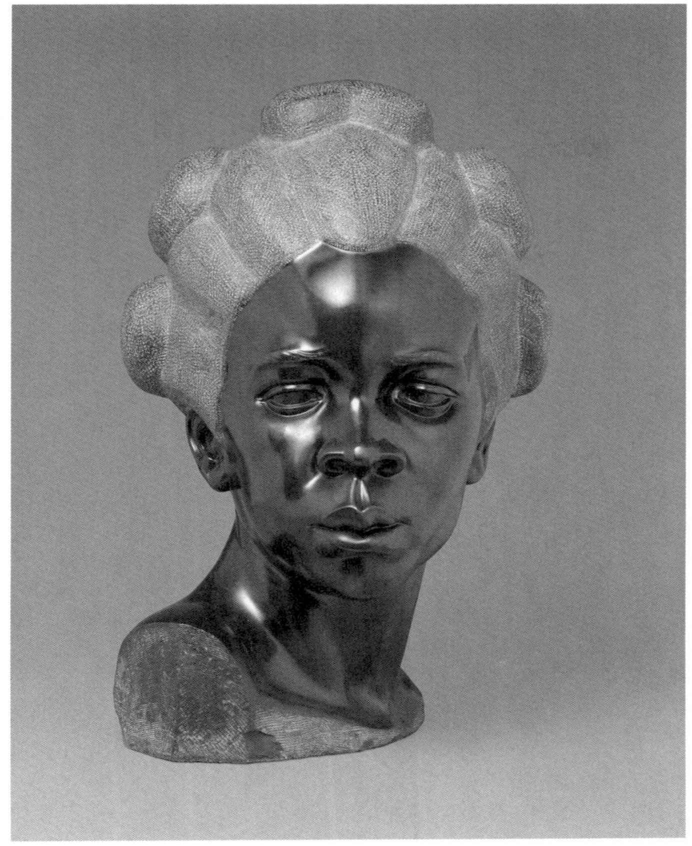

Martinique Woman, 1928

Although the name of this portrait suggests it is of a woman's head from the Caribbean island of Martinique, the sculpture carved out of black metamorphic stone is actually based on Hoffman's travels throughout the continent of Africa around 1928.

National Academy in 1924 and a gold medal of honor from the National Sculpture Society in 1964. She was also awarded five honorary doctorates. She has been called "America's Rodin" and is remembered for cataloging the works of her one-time mentor, Auguste Rodin, considered the founder of modern sculpture, for the Musee Rodin in Paris. Her awards for public service during World War I and World War II include the French Legion of Honor.

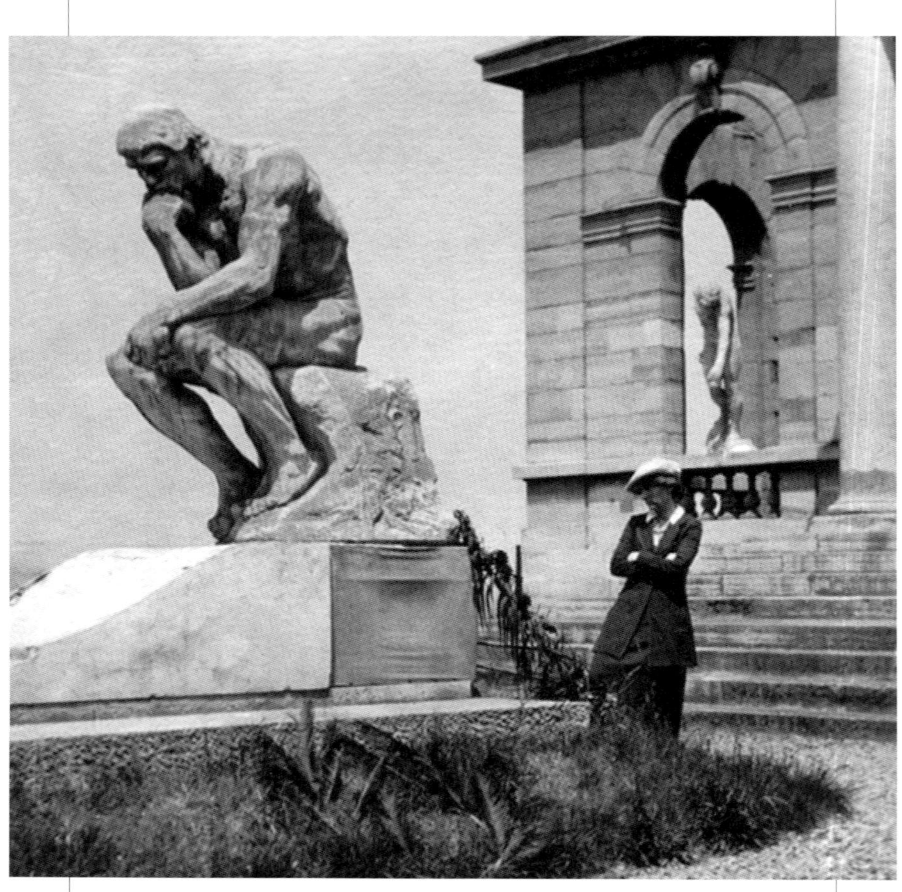

Malvina Hoffman

"Sculpture may be almost anything; a monument, a statue, an old coin, a bas-relief, a portrait bust, a lifelong struggle against heavy odds."[26]

Later in life, Hoffman made prosthetic limbs and medical models for prenatal study. She published *Sculpture Inside and Out* (1939), a book about the historical and technical aspects of bronze casting, and fifteen years later published her autobiography entitled *Yesterday is Tomorrow* (1965). She died of a heart attack at seventy-nine in New York City.

Augusta Savage
(1892–1962)

AUGUSTA SAVAGE was born in 1892 in northern Florida, the seventh of fourteen children of Cornelia and Edward Fells. Her father was a house painter and a Methodist minister. When she was six, Augusta angered her father by skipping school to model ducks out of red clay. He strongly opposed her interest in art based on his interpretation of the biblical concept of graven images or idolatry. To avoid her father's wrath, Savage learned to hide her work from him.

When Augusta was just fifteen years old, she married John Moore and, in 1908, gave birth to her only child, Irene. Moore died a few years later, and in 1915 Savage and her family moved to West Palm Beach, where a scarcity of clay prevented her from working until 1919 when a local potter provided her with clay. Also in 1915, Augusta married James Savage, whose name she kept after divorcing him in the early 1920s.

Encouraged to study in New York by the superintendent of the Palm Beach County Fair, where she had entered her sculpture and won a prize, Savage left her daughter with her parents and moved to New York City. She enrolled at the Cooper Union School of Art, where she studied with portrait sculptor George Brewster before she ran out of money. Savage was the first African American woman admitted to the school and was selected ahead of 142 men. Her talent so impressed the school's advisory board that they awarded her a scholarship to pay for her room and board, which allowed her to complete the four-year degree program in three years.

In 1923, Savage applied to a summer program sponsored by the French government to study art at the Fontainebleau School of Fine Arts in France but was rejected by the judging committee based on her race. She appealed to the media to shine a light on the discriminatory practice, but it was not enough to overturn the decision. After her father became paralyzed from a stroke and her family's Florida home was destroyed by a hurricane, Savage brought them all to live in her three-room apartment in Harlem. To support herself and her family, she worked in the steam laundries of Manhattan. The Harlem Renaissance had taken root, however, and Savage began to earn a reputation as a portrait sculptor. She spent a great deal of time studying artists and art history in the Harlem branch of the New York Public Library, where one of the librarians commissioned Savage to create a bust of W.E.B. Du Bois. Presented to the library in 1923, Savage earned critical acclaim for the work, and other commissions quickly followed.

Savage married for the third and final time in 1923, but her husband, Robert Lincoln Poston, died the following year. Savage continued to make and exhibit small figures of everyday African American people, such as her young nephew, Ellis Ford. Her bronze portrait of him, *Gamin* (1929), aroused so much admiration that she was able to obtain a Rosenwald Fund Fellowship when she was thirty-seven years old, which allowed her to finally fulfill her dream of studying in Europe. She enrolled and attended the Academie de la Grande

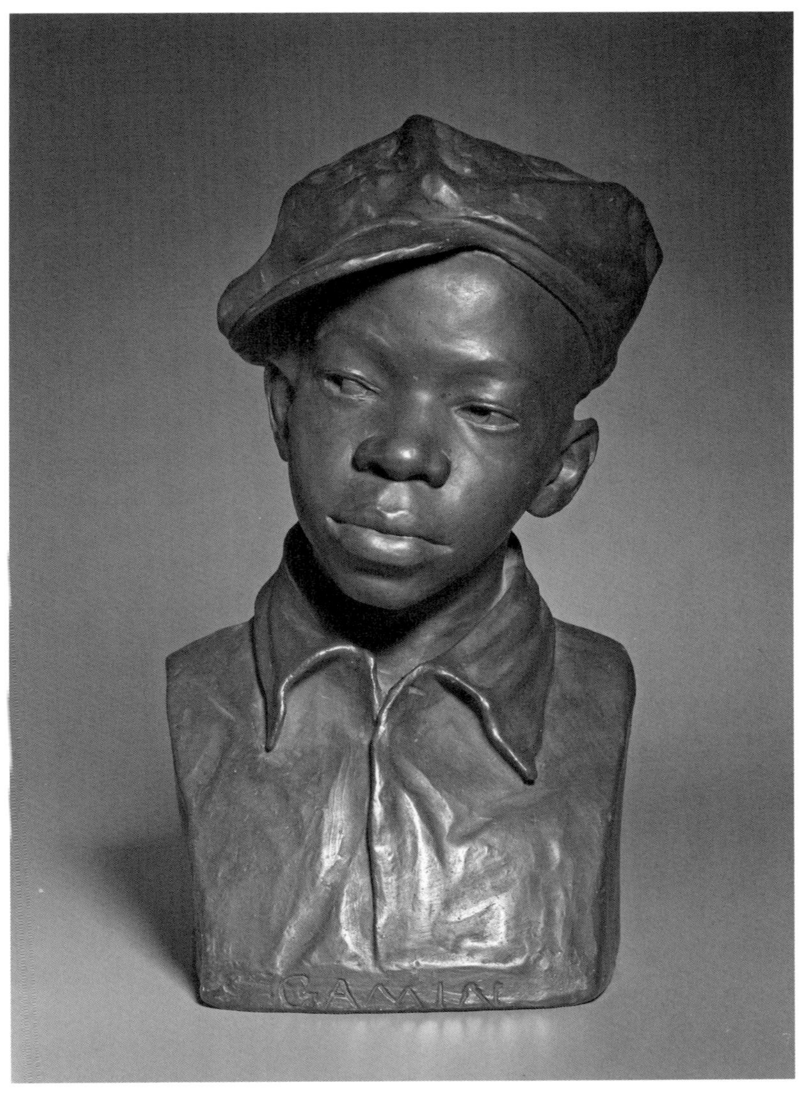

***Gamin*, 1929**

Gamin is the French word for a boy who lives on city streets. He peers from beneath a cap cocked to the side, which frames his cheeks and eyes. Savage was able to position his face and eyes so that they open upward to meet the viewer by arching his neck slightly and tilting his head for an approachable, informal air. Created early in her career, *Gamin* appeared on the cover of *Crisis* magazine in 1929. The sculpture increased her recognition as a leading African American artist.

Chaumiere, a leading Paris art school. Two years later, Savage won a second Rosenwald Fellowship and remained in Paris for another year. She was awarded a Carnegie Foundation grant to travel to France, Belgium, and Germany to research sculpture in cathedrals and museums.

Savage returned home to Harlem in 1932 during the Great Depression. While this took a toll on sales of her work, she was nevertheless able to establish the Savage Studio of Arts and Crafts, located in a basement on West 143rd Street in Harlem. In 1934, she became the first African American member of the National Association of Women Painters and Sculptors. Three years later, she was appointed the first director of the Harlem Community Art Center. She modeled busts of African American figures such as poet James Weldon Johnson and surgeon Walter Gray Crump.

Savage received a large commission to create *The Harp* for the 1939 New York World's Fair. Inspired by spirituals and James Weldon Johnson's poem, "Lift Every Voice and Sing," Savage's sixteen-foot sculpture depicts twelve stylized singers as the strings of an enormous harp, all held in a large hand. Small metal souvenir copies of *The Harp*, the most popular work at the fair, were sold, and many postcards of the piece were purchased. But like other temporary installations, *The Harp* was destroyed after the fair closed.

A well-established artist who had been active in the African American cultural explosion known as the Harlem Renaissance, Savage exhibited with other well-known artists such as Max Weber and Reginald Marsh. But the Depression resulted in few sales, and in 1945, she retired to a farm in rural Saugerties, New York, where she sold chickens and eggs and was employed as a lab assistant in a cancer research facility. She continued to teach art and sculpted friends and neighbors.

She visited the city occasionally to teach children in local summer camps and produced a few sculptures of tourists. She also wrote children's stories and murder mysteries. She is remembered today for breaking barriers facing African American women in the

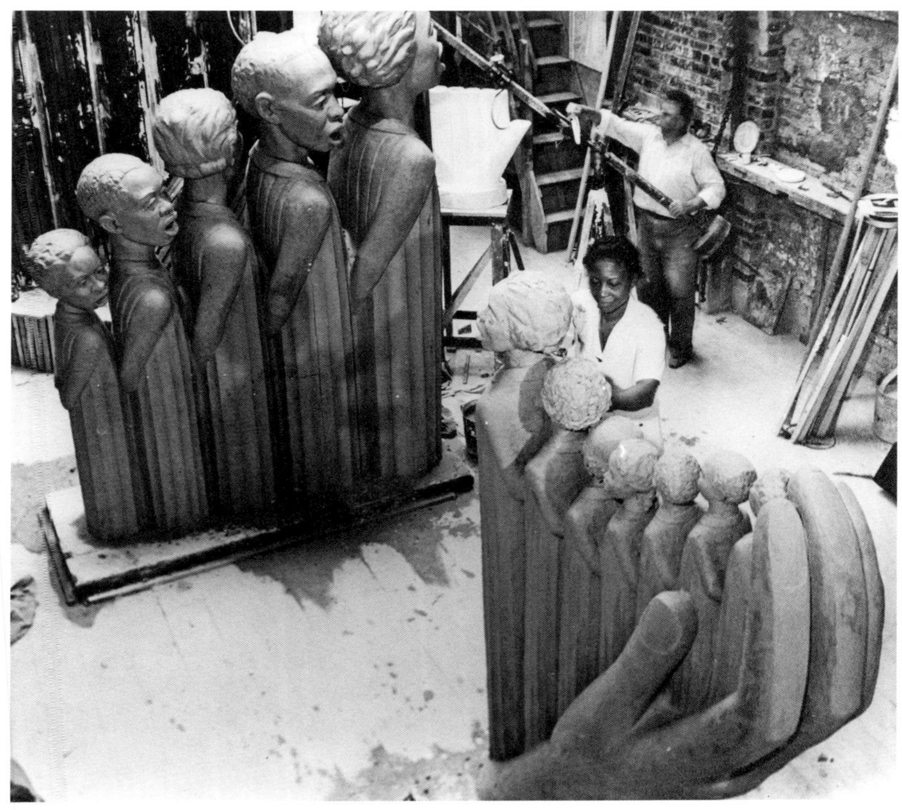

***The Harp*, 1939**

The commission of a lifetime, *The Harp* was exhibited in the court of the Contemporary Arts Building. It was one of the most popular and photographed pieces of art at the New York World's Fair. No funds were available to cast *The Harp*. Nor were there any facilities to store it. After the war it was demolished along with all the other art.

arts and remains an important figure of the Harlem Renaissance. In addition to being a great sculptor whose work reflects the humanity of African Americans, Augusta Savage was also a wonderful teacher whose studio was important to the careers of a generation of artists. She never regretted that much of her energy had been diverted to help talented young artists, such as Jacob Lawrence and Gwendolyn Knight. As she explained, "If I can inspire one of these youngsters to develop the talent I know they possess, then my monument will be their work ... No one could ask more than that."[27]

Savage died in 1962 at the age of seventy following a long bout with cancer. Her home and studio have been restored to evoke the time she lived there and are listed on the New York State and National Register of Historic Places. Her papers are available for study at the Schomburg Center for Research in Black Culture at the New York Public Library.

Elizabeth Catlett

(1915–2012)

Are we here to communicate? Are we here for cultural interchange? Then let us not be narrow. Let us not be small and selfish. Let us aspire to be as great in our communication as were our forefathers of our people, whose struggles made our being here possible.[28]

—ELIZABETH CATLETT

ELIZABETH CATLETT was born and raised in Washington, D.C. Her parents were children of freed slaves, and her grandmothers often shared stories with her about the struggles of slavery. Her father, a mathematics professor at the Tuskegee Institute, died shortly before her birth, so her mother, who was trained as a teacher, held down three jobs, including truant officer, to support Elizabeth and her two siblings.

Catlett knew at a young age that she wanted to be an artist, but at the time, it was rare for African American women to be allowed to forge successful artistic careers. After graduating with honors from Washington's Dunbar High School in 1931, she attended Howard University, where in 1935, she earned a Bachelor of Science in Art, cum laude. At Howard, she studied with artists Lois Mailou Jones, James Porter, James Herring, and James Wells. After graduation, Catlett moved to Durham, North Carolina, where she spent two years as an art teacher in the public schools.

Interested in the work of landscape artist Grant Wood, Catlett enrolled in the graduate program at the University of Iowa where she studied drawing and painting with Wood. Wood encouraged her to make art about what she knew best, and his mentorship was significant to her career. She also studied sculpture with Harry Edward Stinson. In 1940, Catlett earned the first-ever Master of Fine Arts degree from the University of Iowa. That same year her sculpture, *Negro Mother and Child*, won the First Award in Sculpture at the American Negro Exposition in Chicago.

For the next two years, Catlett taught art at Dillard University in New Orleans where she was chairman of the art department. During the summer of 1941, she studied ceramics at the Art Institute of Chicago and lithography at the South Side Community Art Center, which had opened earlier that year. It was in Chicago where she first experienced a community of socially engaged and politically active artists who were committed to creating art that encouraged social change. It was also in Chicago where she met her first husband, artist Charles White, whom she married in 1941.

In 1942 the couple moved to Harlem, where other African American intellectuals, such as Langston Hughes, Jacob Lawrence, Ralph Ellison, W.E.B. Du Bois, Paul Robeson, and Romare Bearden congregated and exchanged ideas. Catlett studied lithography at the Art Students League of New York and received private instruction from recently arrived Russian émigré sculptor Ossip Zadkine. In 1944, she joined the faculty of the George Washington Carver People's School in Harlem, an alternative night school where working people studied history, economics, and the arts. Here Catlett developed a greater understanding of how her students' lives were shaped by their economic circumstances and was deeply moved by what she called the "cultural hunger" of the students with whom she worked.

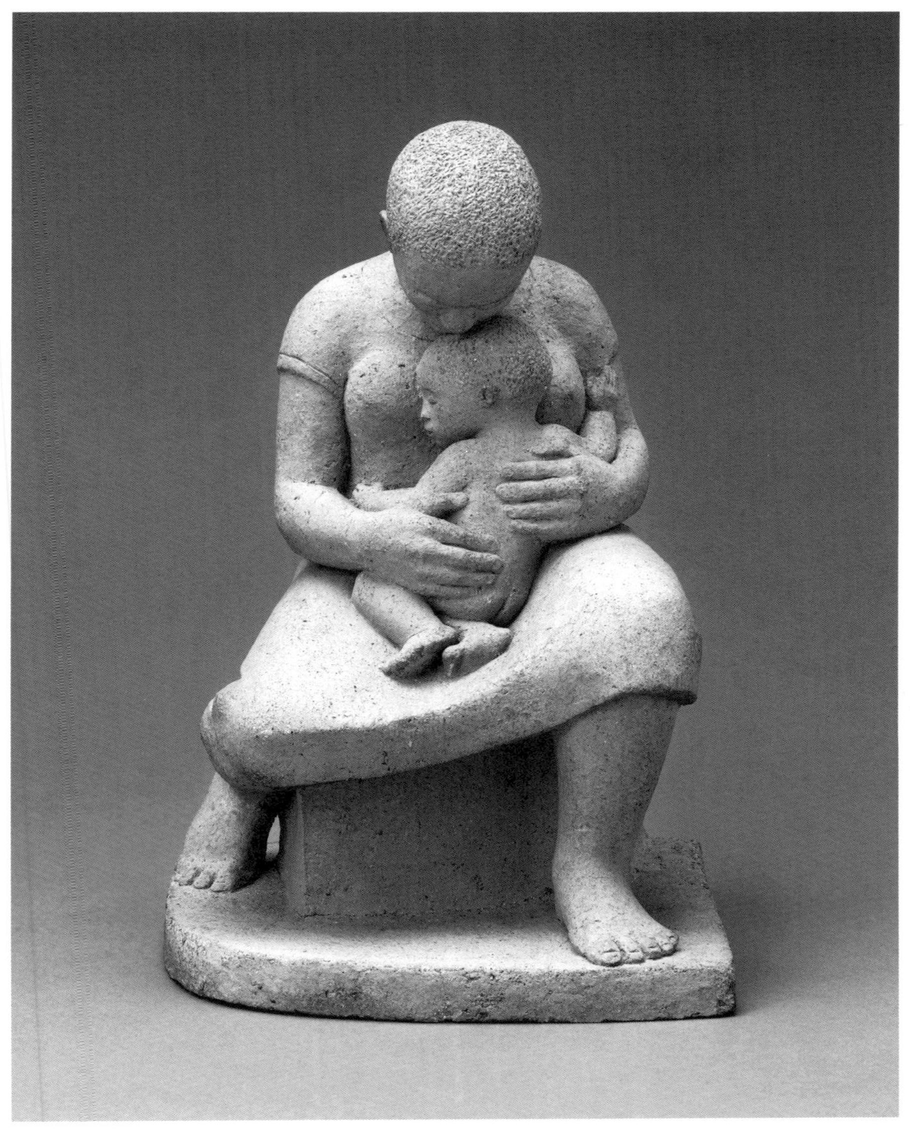

Mother and Child, 1956

Catlett was a successful printmaker while her children were young, but this was her first sculpture since becoming a mother herself. The mother looks down and nestles the head of the child in a protective embrace that shows the strength and vulnerability of the mother. Throughout her long and successful career, Catlett often addressed the subject of a mother and child.

In 1945, Catlett was awarded a two-year Rosenwald Fund Fellowship, which enabled her to travel to Mexico in 1946 with her husband to study painting, sculpture, and lithography. She and White divorced later that same year, but Catlett remained in Mexico City, where she worked with the Taller de Grafica Popular, a workshop dedicated to creating prints that promoted social causes and education. In 1947, Catlett met and married muralist and printmaker Francisco Mora, a fellow member of the workshop. The couple remained artistic and life partners until Mora's death in 2002, and their three sons all pursued careers in the arts.

When her children were young, Catlett focused on printmaking but eventually returned to sculpture and studied woodcarving with Jose Ruiz. In 1959, she became the first woman sculpture professor at the School of Fine Arts, National University of Mexico, serving as chair of the sculpture department until her retirement in 1976. She continued to live and work in Cuernavaca where she established permanent residency and concentrated on creating her wood and stone sculptures.

Catlett made *Mother and Child* (1956) when she returned to sculpture. The simplified round forms evoke pre-Columbian and African sculpture, as well as the work of socially-engaged German artist Kathe Kollwitz whose work Catlett studied. The monument to commemorate motherhood was completed in 1956 when Catlett returned to sculpture after the birth of her third son in 1951.

Catlett is known for her career as a teacher as well as an artist. During her lifetime, she received a host of awards, and her work can be found in major collections throughout the United States and Mexico, including the Museum of Modern Art, the Metropolitan Museum of Art, and the Palacio de Bellas Artes in Mexico City. She received honorary doctorates from Pace University and Carnegie Mellon, as well as the International Sculpture Center's Lifetime Achievement Award in contemporary sculpture. She had over fifty individual exhibitions during her lifetime, although her work did not begin to be shown regularly until the 1960s and 1970s.

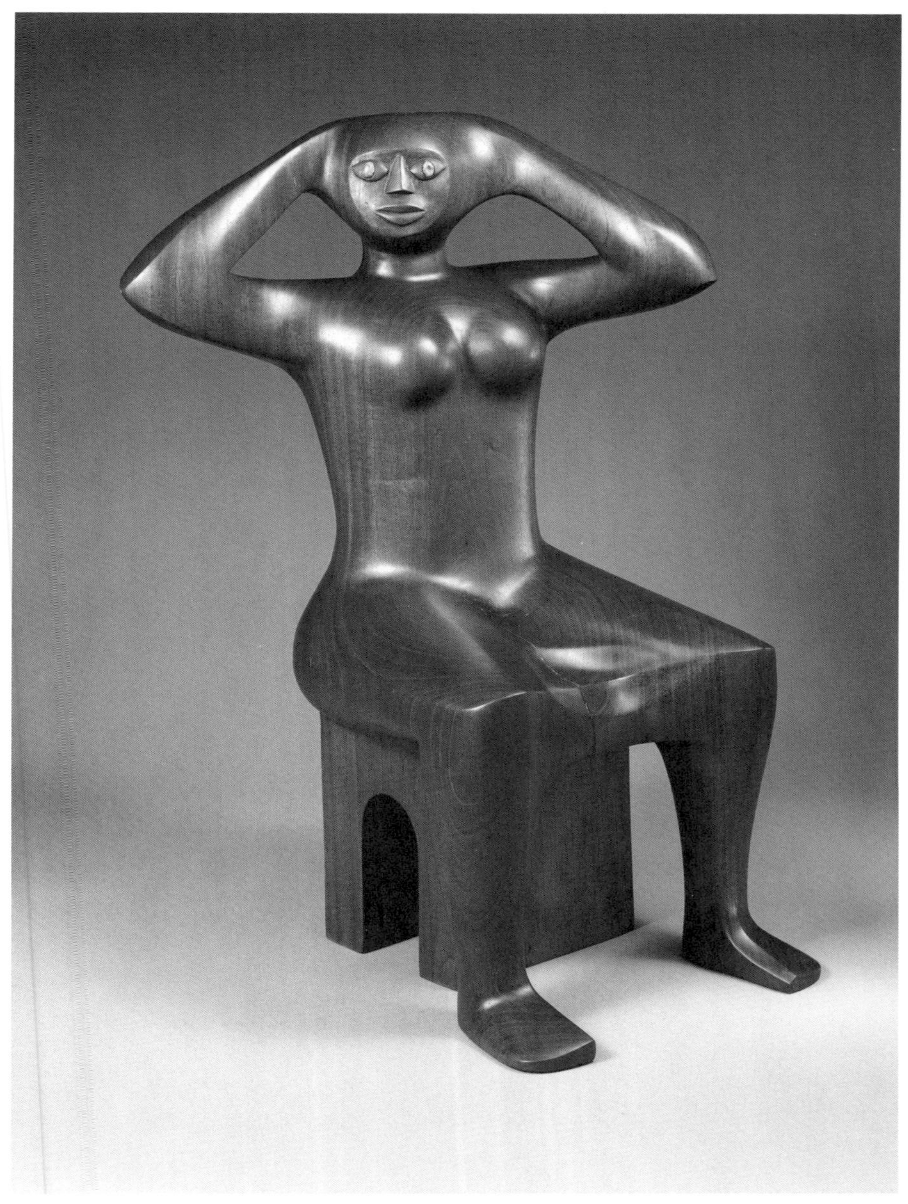

Woman Fixing Her Hair, 1993

This sculpture portrays a strong woman seated with her feet firmly planted on the ground. She lifts her arms and hands to fix her hair. The form is simplified with extraneous details eliminated so that the small figure feels larger than its actual size of 27 × 18 × 13 inches.

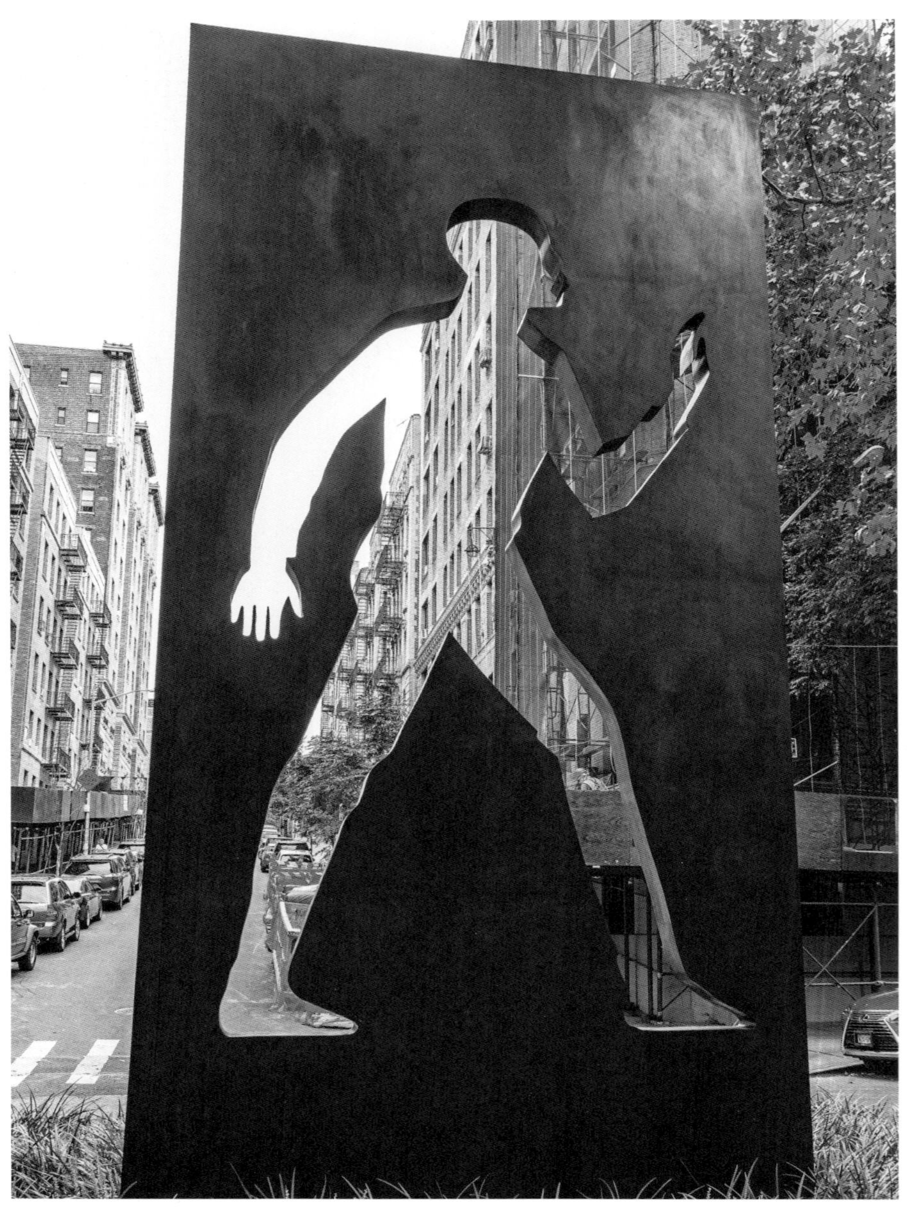

Ralph Ellison Memorial, 2003

The memorial refers to Ellison's epic novel *Invisible Man* (1952), which earned him international fame. One of the three inscriptions, a quote from his book, reads: "I am an invisible man. I am invisible, understand, simply because people refuse to see me."[29]

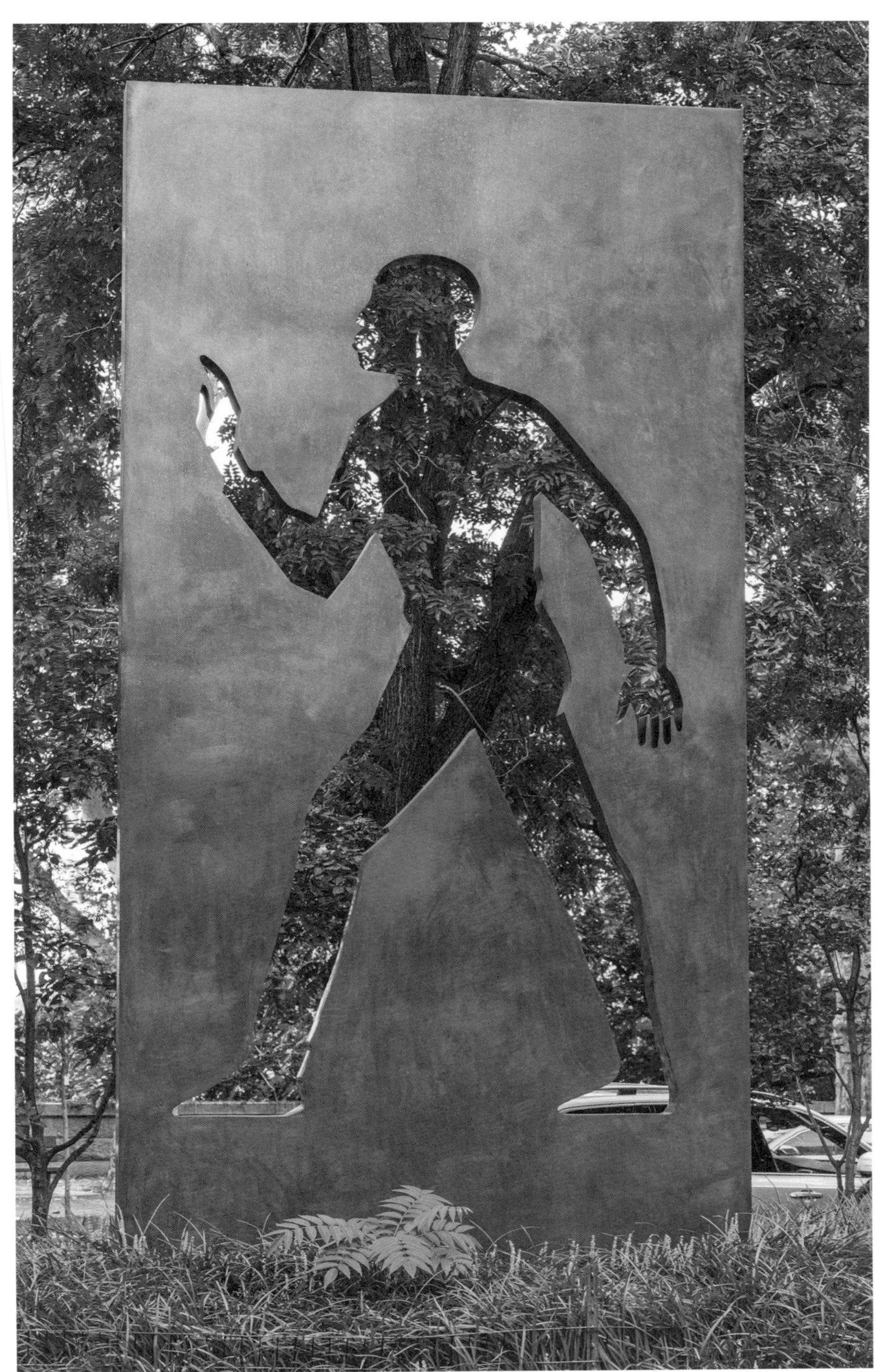

Catlett's work is primarily meant to convey social messages about race, gender, and class. As she explained:

> My purpose is twofold; one to present black people in their beauty and dignity for our race and others to understand ... two, to exhibit publicly where black people can visit and find art to which they can relate ...
>
> I have always wanted my art to service my people—to reflect us, to relate to us, to stimulate us, to make us aware of our potential. We have to create an art for liberation and for life.[30]

Woman Fixing Her Hair (1993), made of smooth polished mahogany and opals, is a blend of abstraction and realism depicting a woman involved in a daily act of toiletry. Catlett often used the African American female form for personal identity and artistic creativity to transcend racial discrimination, gender subordination, and national boundaries.

The *Ralph Ellison Memorial* (2003), a tribute to famed American novelist Ralph Waldo Ellison (1914–1994), is Catlett's only public commission in New York. The six-inch thick slab of bronze featuring a cut-out silhouette of a man stands fifteen feet high and seven and a half feet wide. The centerpiece of a restored area of Riverside Park is located at 150th Street, not far from Ralph Ellison's last and longest-standing home.

Catlett had become a Mexican citizen in 1962, and because of her social and political beliefs, was denied entry to the U.S. except on a visa. In 2002, her American citizenship was restored, and from then on, she divided her time between New York City and her home in Cuernavaca, Mexico, where she died peacefully in 2012 at the age of ninety-six, leaving a rich and powerful legacy.

Penelope Jencks
(b. 1936)

PENELOPE JENCKS was born in Baltimore, Maryland into a family of intellectuals and artists. She attended Swarthmore College to study art history but decided she would "rather make art than study it." She studied with painter Hans Hoffman and then attended the Skowhegan School of Painting and Sculpture, where she studied with sculptor Harold Tovish. This put her on the path to becoming a sculptor, and after earning a BFA in painting from Boston University in 1958, she continued to study sculpture at the Boston Museum School in 1959 and Stuttgart Kunst Akademie in Stuttgart, Germany, in 1960.

Much of Jencks's sculpture, particularly her images of large nude figures, relates to her experiences growing up on Cape Cod in the

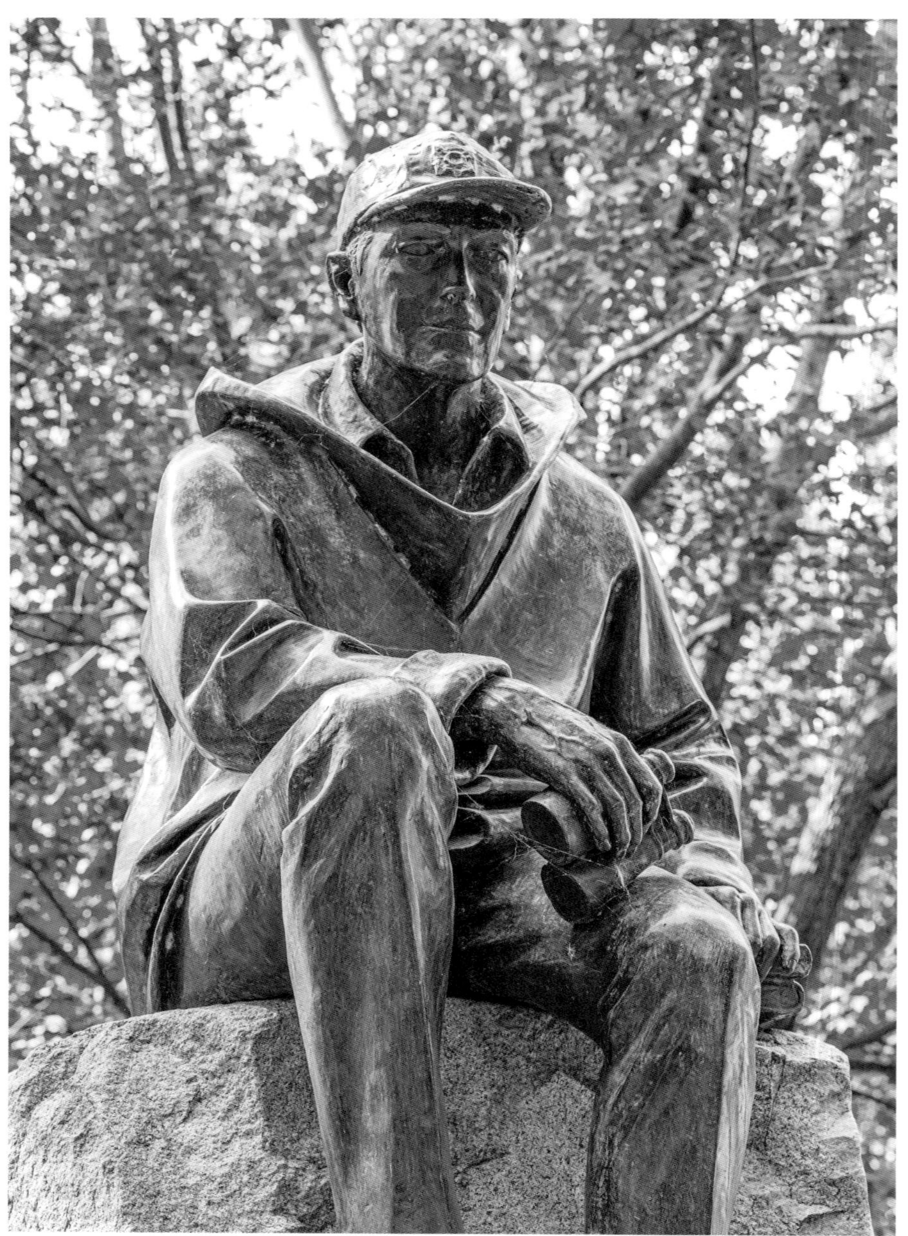

Samuel Eliot Morison, 1982

The statue of the military historian is installed along Boston's Commonwealth Avenue Mall. The bronze sculpture, installed on a granite base, shows Morison holding binoculars.

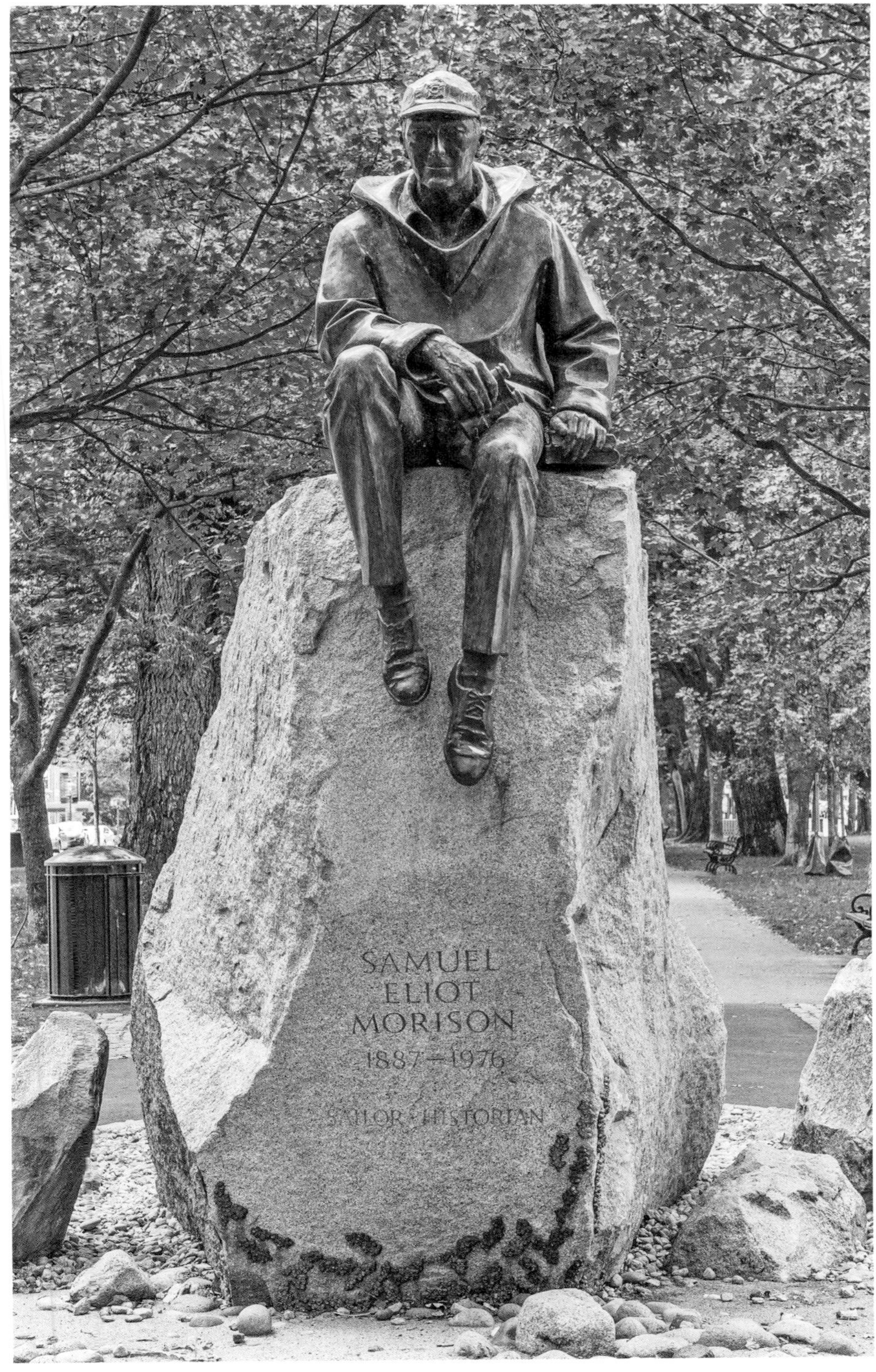
SAMUEL
ELIOT
MORISON
1887–1976
SAILOR • HISTORIAN

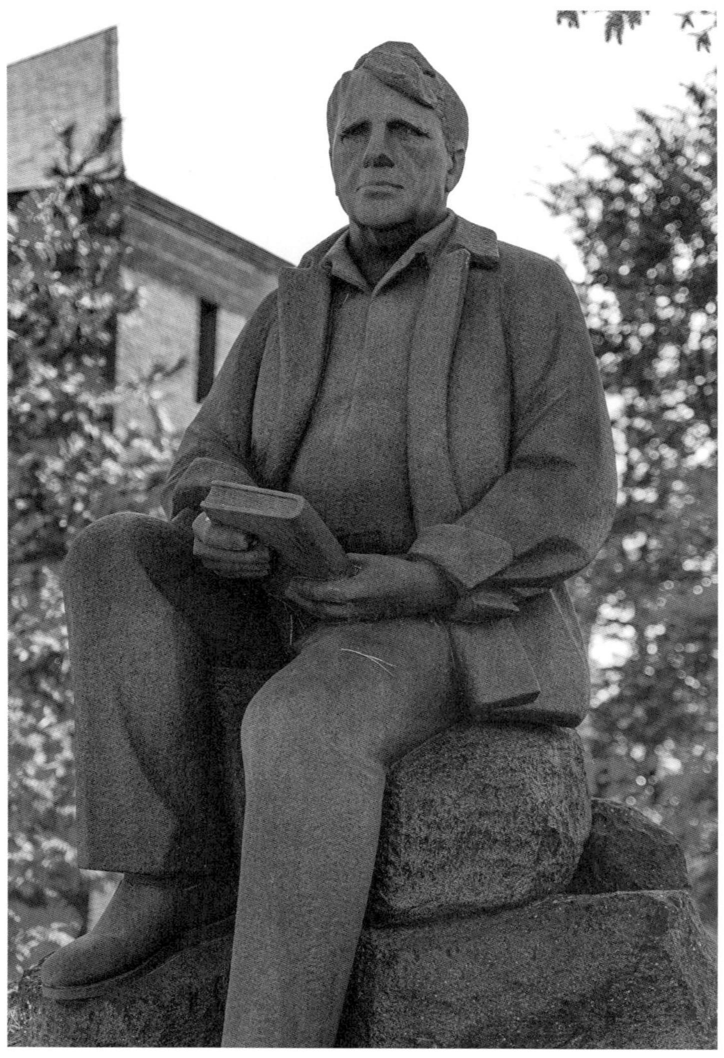

***Robert Frost*, 2007**

The eight-ton likeness of Robert Frost shows him sitting on a pile of rocks, looking ahead while holding a book.

years after World War II amongst a community of artists and intellectuals. A group of families would frequently gather on the beach, and the adults would shed their clothing, considering it a more natural state for swimming or lying on the beach, while the children were left to their own devices. Privacy, creativity, and individualism were highly valued aspects of life.

> As a child, the beach was a magical place to me. We spent the summers in Wellfleet. The slope of the land, with its curves and dips, was like the forms of a large human body. As children, it was as though we lived on a big shapely body that we could walk on, dig in, and pick flowers from. The sea, the sky, and the dunes were our constant.[31]

Her publicly commissioned granite and bronze monuments tend to show important people informally. For example, the statue of historian *Samuel Eliot Morison*, commissioned by the city of Boston, depicts a pensive Morison perched on a granite rock and wearing a cap and windbreaker (1982). Etched into the rock beside the sculpture is his advice to young writers, "Dream dreams, then write them aye, but live them first." Morison, the winner of two Pulitzer Prizes and the writer of over fifty books, is known mostly for his history of Christopher Columbus, as well as his fifteen-volume history of World War II.

Jencks's *Robert Frost* (2007) is located at Amherst College in Massachusetts. Presented to the college as part of a 50th reunion gift from the Class of 1957, the sculpture of the poet honors his role as a faculty member and symbolizes the importance of professors in shaping the lives of Amherst students. The sculpture, which took Jencks five years to complete, was conceived in Wellfleet, Massachusetts, created in Newton, Massachusetts, and carved in Pietrasanta, Italy.

Jencks's best-known sculpture, the eight-foot-tall *Eleanor Roosevelt Monument* (1996), located at the threshold of Riverside Park at 72nd Street and Riverside Drive in New York City, is the first monument dedicated to an American president's wife. It took Jencks ten years to complete and was unveiled by former First Lady Hillary

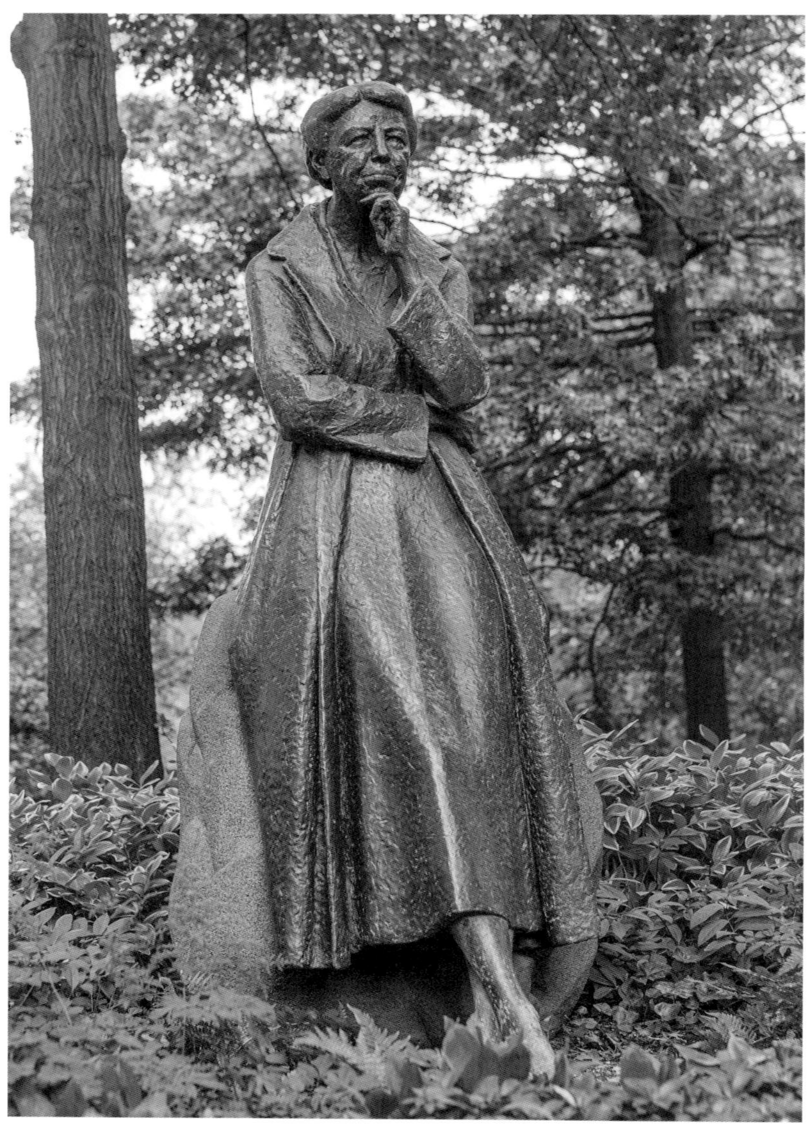

Eleanor Roosevelt, 1996

Jencks depicts Eleanor Roosevelt leaning on a granite rock while gazing thoughtfully with one hand resting on her chin. On the sidewalk in front of the statue is one of Roosevelt's quotes: "Where, after all, do universal human rights begin? In small places, close to home. Such are the places where every man, woman, and child seek equal justice, equal opportunity, equal dignity."[32] —ELEANOR ROOSEVELT, 1958

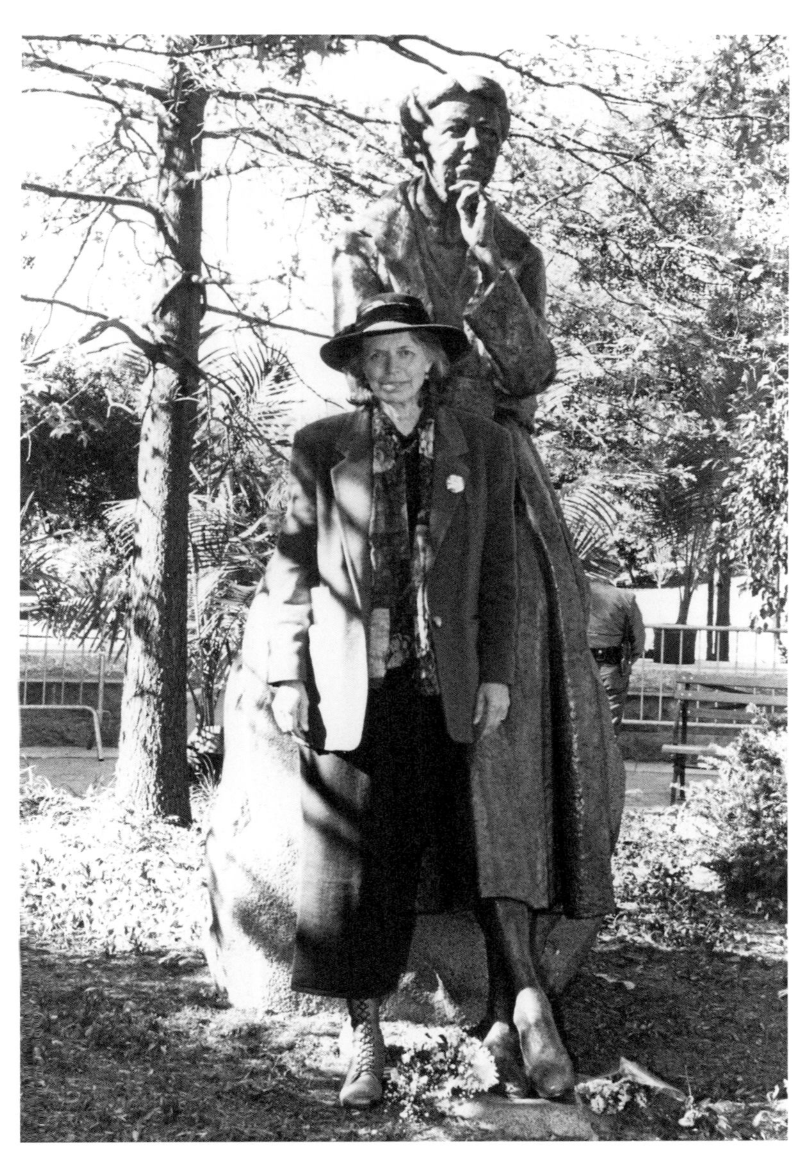

Penelope Jencks

"The intent of each piece, large or small, is I want them to be viewed from the perspective of a child's vision of an adult figure. Monumental like a force of nature."[33] —PENELOPE JENCKS

Rodham Clinton in 1996. The sculpture remains an important component of New York City's public artscape and is a popular focal point for residents and visitors alike.

Eleanor Roosevelt (1884–1962) maintained active involvement in social and political organizations, such as the League of Women Voters, the American Red Cross, and the Women's Trade Union League, while raising five children. First Lady from 1933–1945, Roosevelt was also a successful diplomat and dedicated humanitarian activist. After her husband Franklin Delano Roosevelt was stricken with polio, Eleanor became his representative at many public functions and was the leader of the women's platform committee for the 1924 Democratic National Convention. She held weekly press conferences, championed the cause of racial equality, and supported programs to fight poverty and unemployment.

Jencks studied hundreds of photographs of Roosevelt before choosing a contemplative pose to suggest her complicated inner life, dignity, and humanity. Jencks identified strongly with Roosevelt because she had grown up in a household where Roosevelt was revered and quoted often. The statue, the boulder on which it leans, and the footstone on which it rests form the center of a heavily planted circular memorial designed by landscape architects Bruce Kelly and David Varnell, who are also responsible for their work on "Strawberry Fields," the monument to John Lennon in Central Park. Inscriptions surrounding the granite pavement include Roosevelt's 1958 United Nations speech advocating universal human rights. A bronze tablet in the planting bed summarizes her achievements.

Jencks's career spans more than forty years. Sculptures of Aaron Copland and Leonard Bernstein are both at Tanglewood in Lenox, Massachusetts. Other commissions are at the Federal Courthouse in Danbury, Connecticut, in Chelsea Square, Chelsea, Massachusetts, and Bunker Hill Pavilion, Charlestown, Massachusetts, as well as around the world. She is a member of the National Academy of Design and the Royal British Society of Sculptors and a Fellow of the National Sculpture Society.

Meredith Bergmann
(b. 1955)

Meredith Bergmann grew up in Montclair, New Jersey, the middle of three children born to secular Jewish parents who encouraged social awareness and artistic ability. She studied at Wesleyan University and graduated with a Bachelor of Fine Arts from Cooper Union in 1977, where she discovered sculpture. She then traveled around Europe, settling in Pietrasanta, Italy, where she further developed her sculpting skills. Today Bergmann lives in Connecticut with her husband Michael, a writer and director, and their son, and is well-known as a sculptor, poet, and essayist. Her articles, essays, and poems have appeared in many journals, including *The American Arts Quarterly* and *The New York Review of Art*.

Bergmann's work often explores issues of history, race, human rights, disabilities, and the power of poetry and music. She derives great satisfaction from the knowledge that her sculptures make a difference in people's lives. It is her hope that all people will be inspired by scenes of women of different races, religious backgrounds, and economic status working together to change the world. Her empathetic representations of diverse, inspiring people have appeared in over twenty-four exhibitions and ten institutional collections.

Her largest public commission was the *Boston Women's Memorial,* unveiled in 2003 on Commonwealth Avenue Mall. It includes statues of Phyllis Wheatley, the first African American poet; First Lady Abigail Adams, wife of President John Adams; and Lucy Stone, an abolitionist and suffragist. The three historic figures are commemorated for their writing and their impact not only on the history of Boston but on society overall.

Phyllis Wheatley (1753–1784), born in West Africa and sold as an enslaved person, became a literary prodigy. Her 1773 volume entitled "Poems of Various Subjects, Religious and Moral" was the first book published by an African writer in America. Lucy Stone (1818–1893), a suffragist, abolitionist, and respected orator, was one of the first women in Massachusetts to earn a college degree. Abigail Adams (1744–1818), wife of the second president of the United States, was committed to the advancement of women. In a letter to her husband written in 1776, she wrote:

> Remember the Ladies, and be more generous and favorable to them than your ancestors. Do not put such unlimited power into the hands of the husbands. Remember all Men would be tyrants if they could[34] ...

In 2006, Bergmann presented her statue of the famous opera singer and civil rights icon Marian Anderson on the campus of Converse College in Spartanburg, South Carolina. In 2012, she completed a commission commemorating the events of September 11, 2001, for New York City's Cathedral of St. John the Divine. Entitled *Memorial to September 11th,* the monument was made with bronze, steel, and glass fragments from the rubble of the World Trade Center.

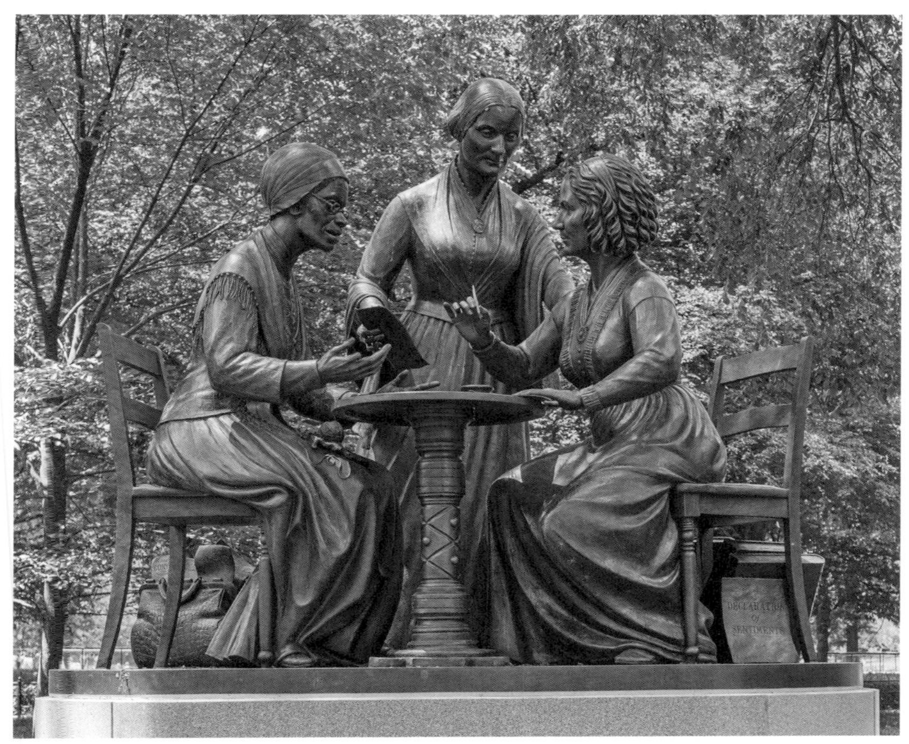

Women's Rights Pioneers Monument, 2020

The *Women's Rights Pioneers Monument* sculpture in Central Park in Manhattan, New York City, commemorates (L–R) Sojourner Truth (c. 1797–1883), Susan B. Anthony (1820–1906), and Elizabeth Cady Stanton (1815–1902), pioneers in the suffrage movement for women's right to vote.

In 2020, on the 100th anniversary of the ratification of the Nineteenth Amendment to the United States Constitution which granted women the right to vote, Bergmann's fourteen-foot high sculpture of Sojourner Truth, Susan B. Anthony, and Elizabeth Cady Stanton became Central Park's first statue depicting real women. Truth is speaking, Anthony is organizing, and Stanton is writing to showcase three essential elements of activism. The *Women's Rights Pioneers Monument* represents the interior of a home where much of women's political work originated in the nineteenth century.

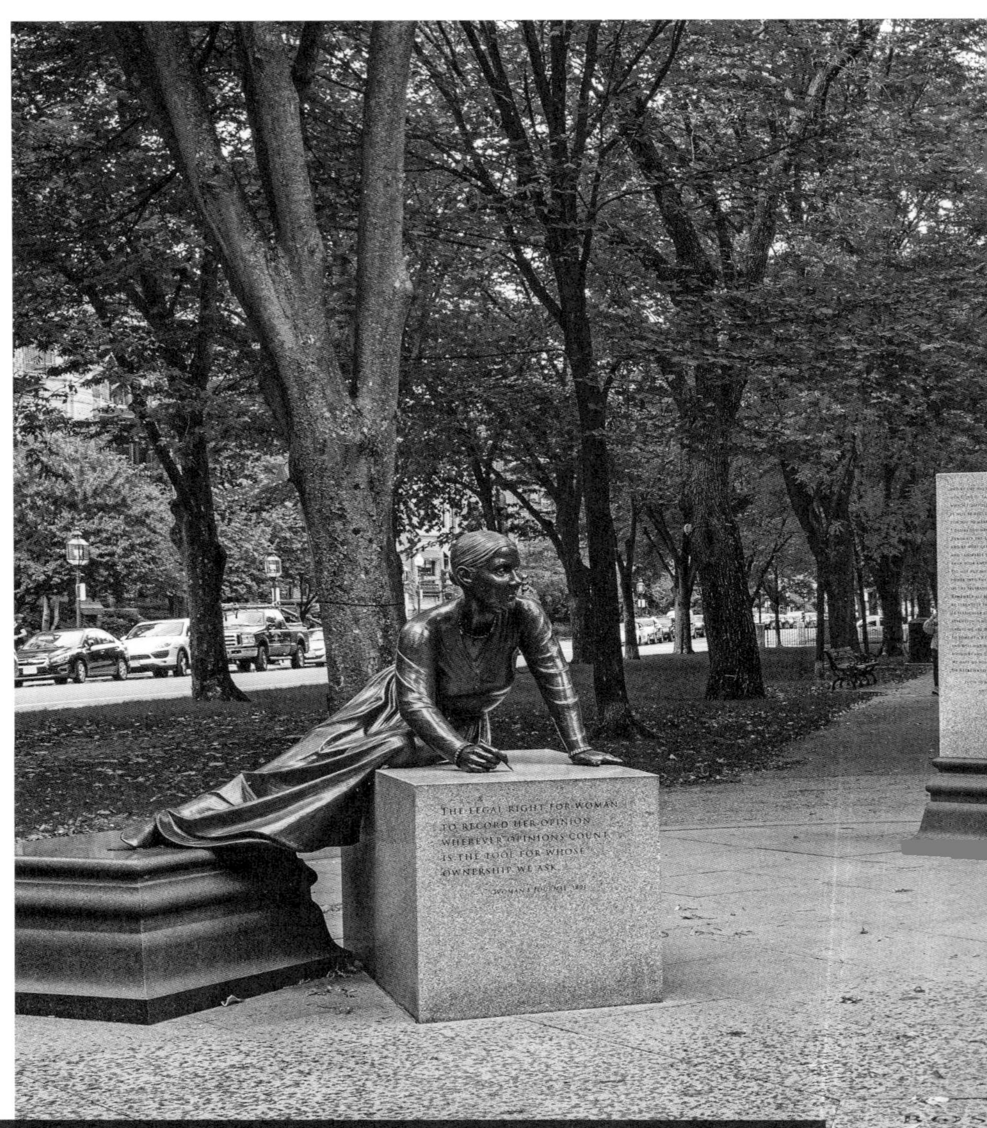

Boston Women's Memorial, 2003

The *Boston Women's Memorial* on the Commonwealth Avenue Mall in Boston, Massachusetts, is a trio of sculptures commemorating three women who helped shape the city's history. (L–R) Lucy Stone, Abigail Adams, and Phillis Wheatley.

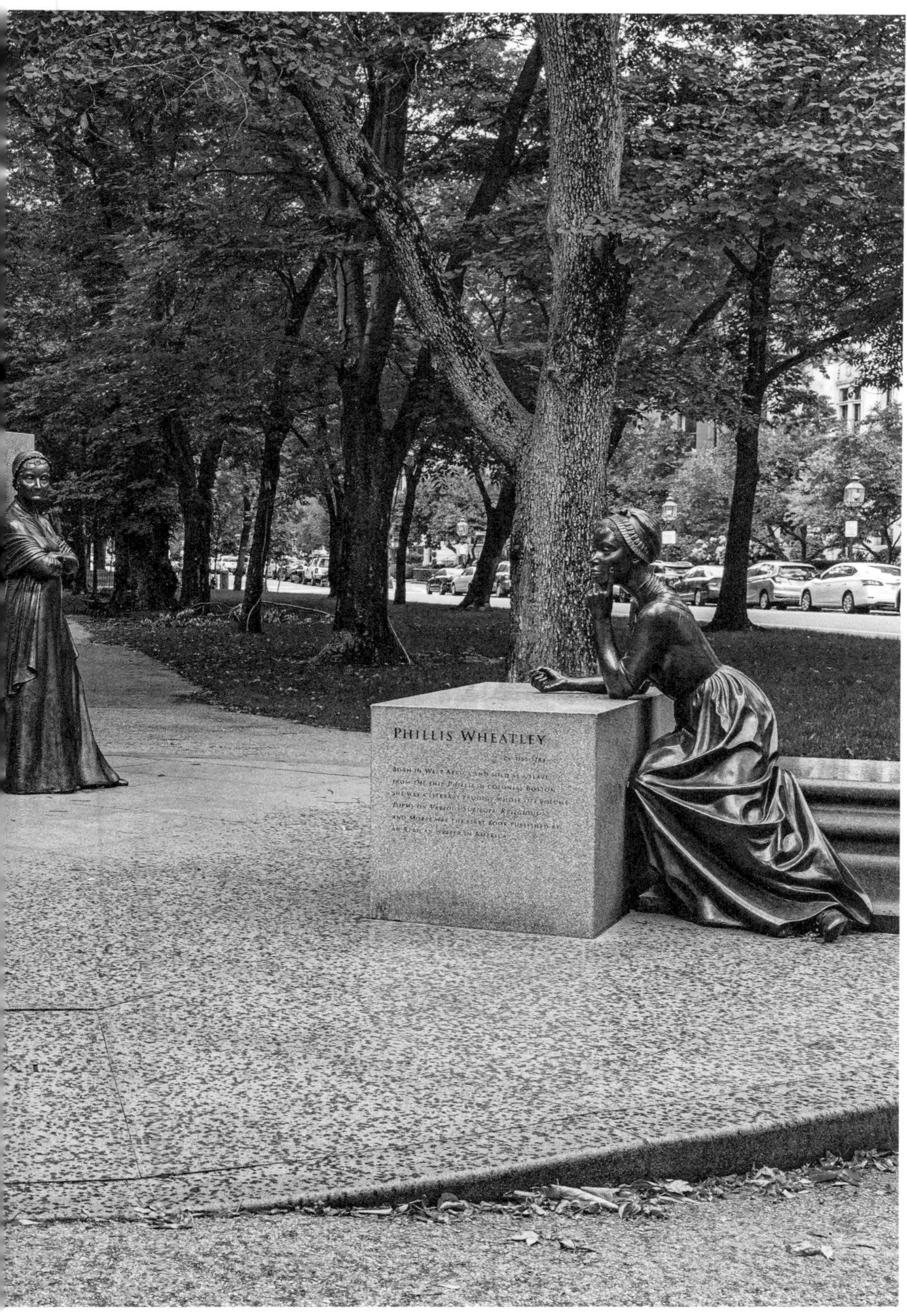
PHILLIS WHEATLEY

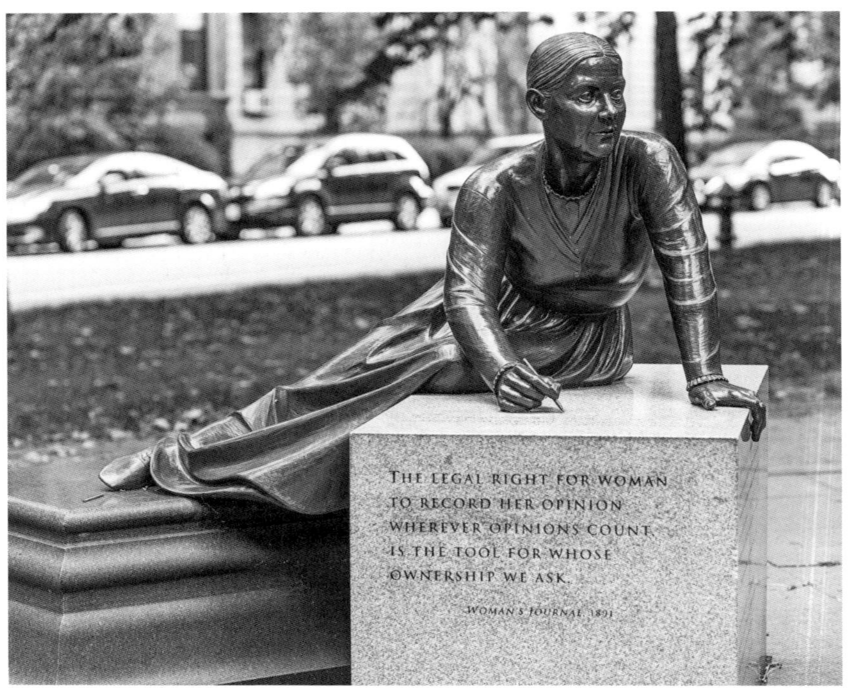
THE LEGAL RIGHT FOR WOMAN
TO RECORD HER OPINION
WHEREVER OPINIONS COUNT
IS THE TOOL FOR WHOSE
OWNERSHIP WE ASK.
WOMAN'S JOURNAL 1891

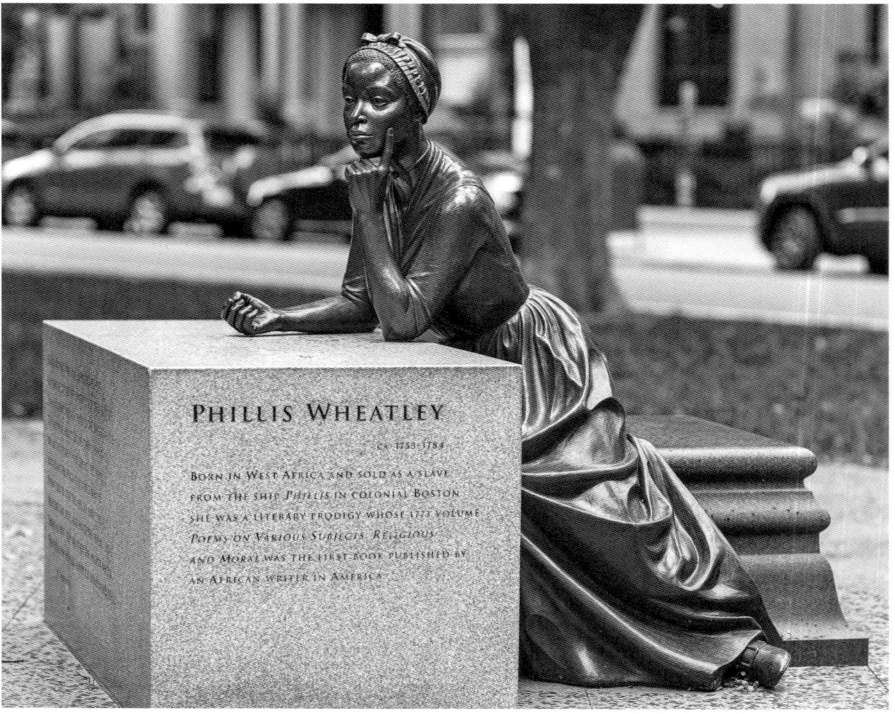
PHILLIS WHEATLEY
CA 1753-1784
BORN IN WEST AFRICA AND SOLD AS A SLAVE
FROM THE SHIP PHILLIS IN COLONIAL BOSTON
SHE WAS A LITERARY PRODIGY WHOSE 1773 VOLUME
POEMS ON VARIOUS SUBJECTS, RELIGIOUS
AND MORAL WAS THE FIRST BOOK PUBLISHED BY
AN AFRICAN WRITER IN AMERICA.

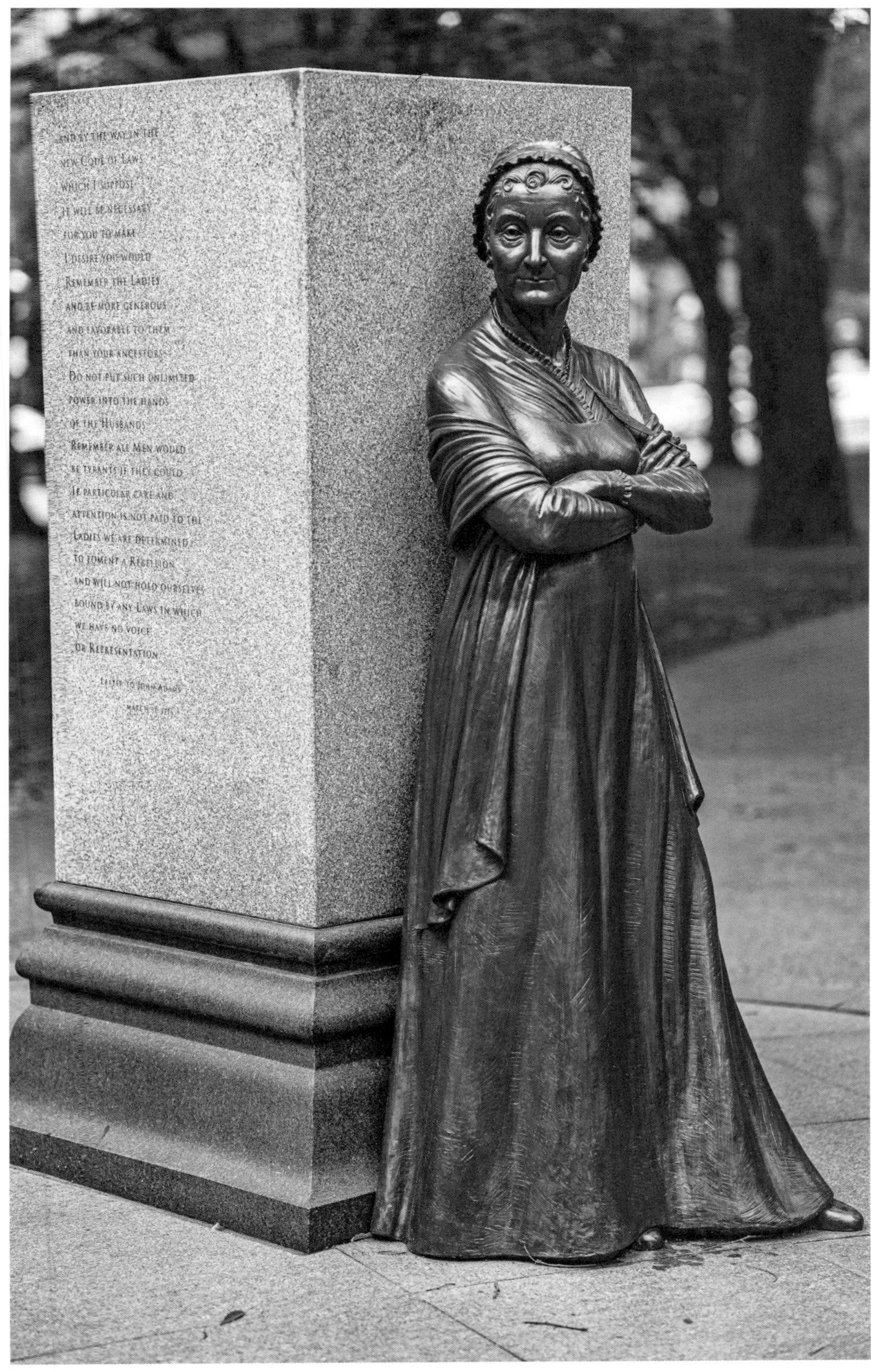
and by the way in the
new Code of Laws
which I suppose
it will be necessary
for you to make
I desire you would
Remember the Ladies
and be more generous
and favorable to them
than your ancestors
Do not put such unlimited
power into the hands
of the Husbands
Remember all Men would
be tyrants if they could
If particular care and
attention is not paid to the
Ladies we are determined
to foment a Rebellion
and will not hold ourselves
bound by any Laws in which
we have no voice
or Representation
Letter to John Adams

The *Women's Rights Pioneers Monument* was unveiled by Monumental Women, an all-volunteer, not-for-profit organization. Members were responsible for "breaking the bronze ceiling" and creating the first statue of real women in Central Park, which is visited by over forty-two million people each year. With the goal of increasing awareness of women's history and the history of people of color, Monumental Women is dedicated to a nationwide education campaign of creating public spaces that reflect and respect all people.

Bergmann relied on her knowledge of history and art history to forge links between the past and present. She conducted a wealth of research before creating the monument, and she read a great deal and spoke with Elizabeth Cady Stanton's great-great-granddaughter for more insight. Bergmann then spent months creating the clay models, getting them approved, and casting different molds for the molten metal. She used some of the vocabularies of existing Central Park statuary by having her figures sit and stand on a granite pedestal that holds inscriptions. But she departed from the other monuments by having all three figures sharing a pedestal and relating to one another.

Bergmann feels a responsibility to create art that is not only beautiful, but that reflects the reality of the lives of all those who see it. Her statues have layers of meaning that unfold over time. Rather than copying photographs of the three women, she studied all available photographs in order to render faces that express more than a single moment in their lives. The resulting figures depict hints of their youthful faces, their old faces, their angry faces, and their happy faces. The portraits show the women's respect for one another but also the tensions among them, aptly capturing their sisterhood along with their differences. Truth sits with Stanton at a small table while Anthony stands beside the table. Bergmann's intention is that viewers should decide for themselves what Sojourner Truth is saying, what Elizabeth Cady Stanton is thinking, and what Susan B. Anthony wants them to consider.

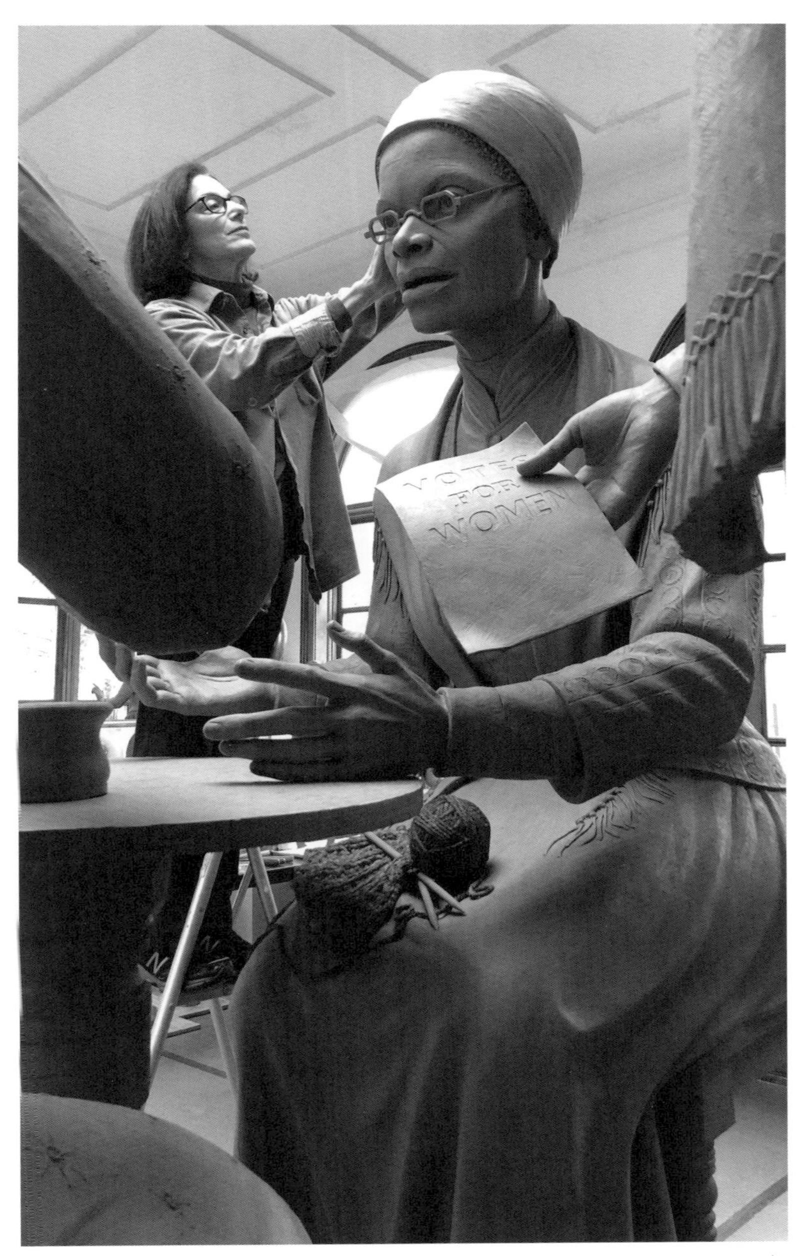

Meredith Bergmann

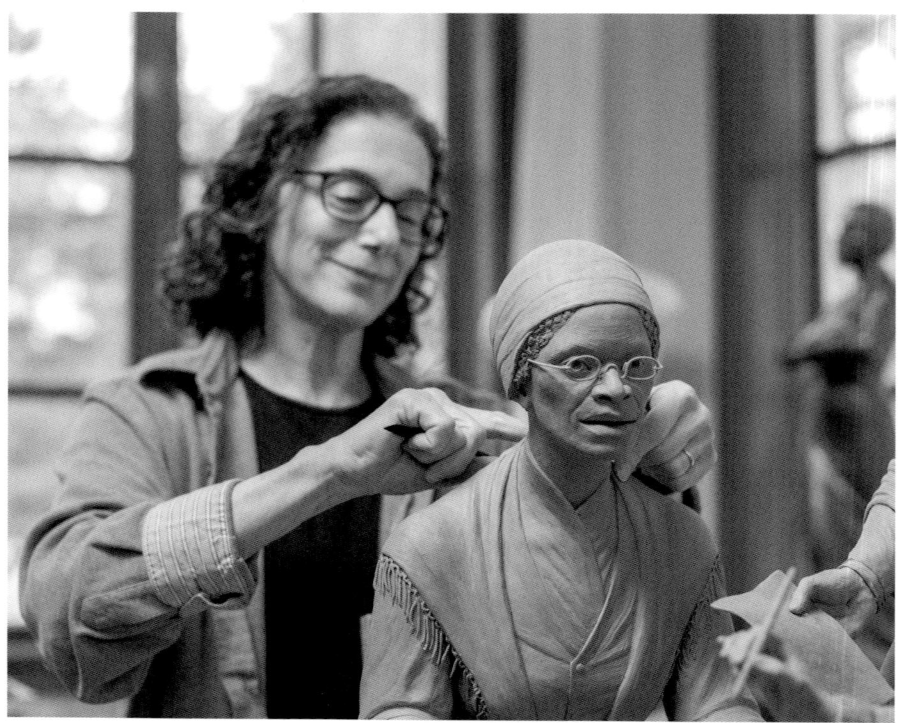

Regarding the *Women's Rights Pioneers Monument*, Bergmann states:

> None of the women depicted on the monument lived to see the ratification of the Nineteenth Amendment, let alone the Voting Rights Act of 1965, whose work is still incomplete. But as we struggle towards greater justice, we need and deserve a monument commemorating some of the important work that has come before us.[35]

Alison Saar
(b. 1956)

ALISON SAAR was born in 1956 in Los Angeles, California, to well-known African-American sculptor Betye Saar and art conservationist and ceramicist Richard Saar. Her mother was involved in the 1970s Black Arts Movement, and when Alison and her two sisters were children, Betye often took them to museums and art openings. Saar credits her mother with cultivating her fascination with spiritual traditions and mysticism, as well as fostering her admiration of artists who create beauty out of found objects. As the daughter of two artists, she developed a love of nature and an interest in folk art. She worked for many years, beginning in high school, with her father in his restoration shop, where she learned about different techniques, styles, and materials while restoring works of art ranging from ancient Chinese frescoes to African sculpture.

Saar studied art history and studio art at Scripps College in Claremont, California, earning a BA in 1978 and an MFA three years later from the Otis Art Institute (now Otis College of Art and Design)

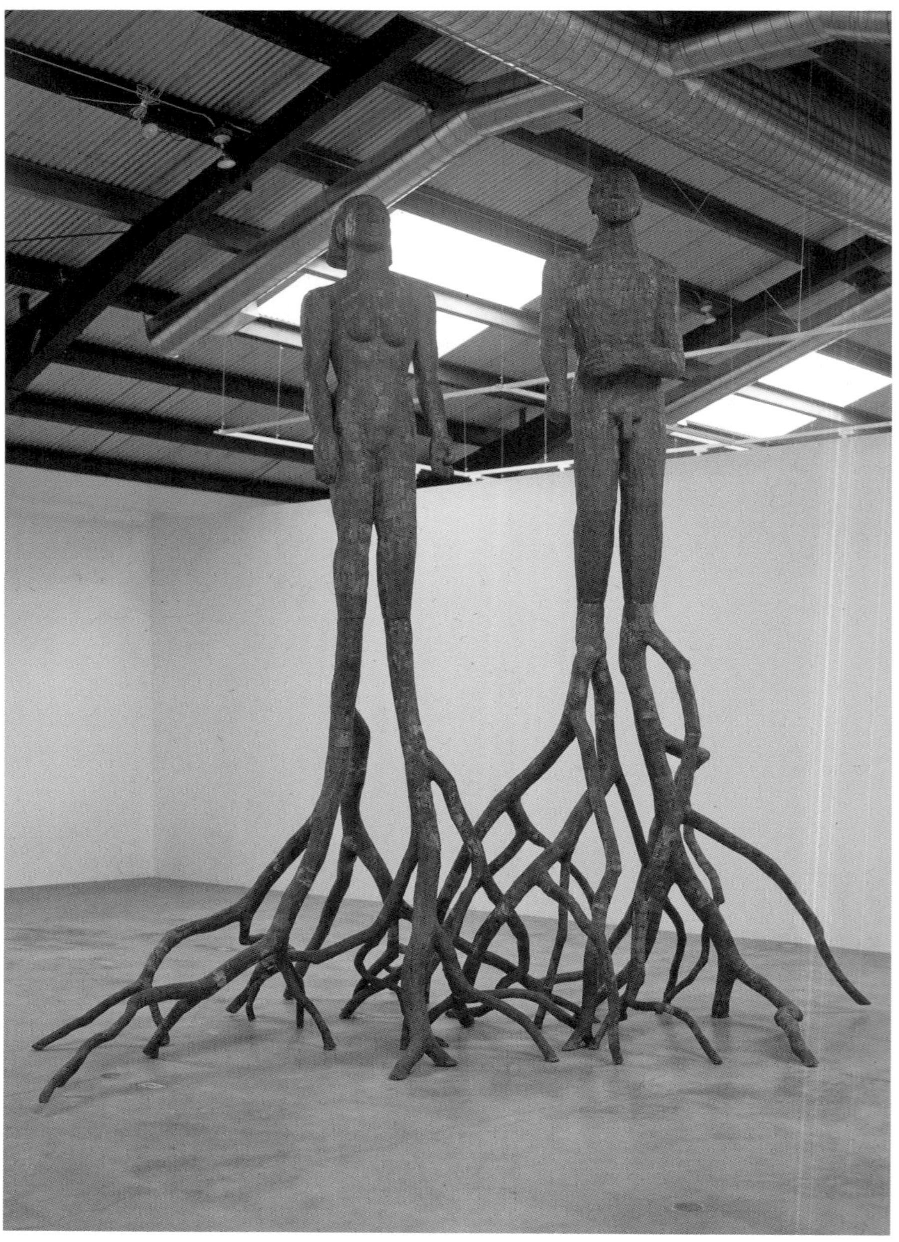

Tree Souls, 1994

The narrative of the installation follows nineteenth-century accounts of runaway slaves who traveled through Florida swamps and hid in the roots of mangrove trees.

in Los Angeles. Saar and her husband, Tom Leeser, a digital media artist, educator, and curator, then moved to New York, where in 1983 Saar became an artist-in-residence at the Studio Museum in Harlem. Two years later, she completed another residency in Roswell, New Mexico, where she augmented her urban style with Native American and Mexican influences.

Like her mother, Saar devotes her attention to the marginalization of both women and minorities. Often working with female nudes, she acknowledges historical injustices and uses mythological narratives to present defiant figures that seem to transcend their pasts. Incorporating found objects like old tin ceiling panels, pottery shards, glass, and urban detritus, her sculptures are powerful totems that explore issues of gender, race, and heritage. Her work has been exhibited in museums, private collections, and galleries throughout the United States, and she has received many awards.

In *The Woods Within* (1995) at the Brooklyn Museum of Art, Saar's *Tree Souls* sculptures depict figures rising from a long tangle of root-like forms. Included as part of the installation are boulder-shaped sculptures with human forms emerging called "Stone Souls," which allude to fertility rites in certain cultures.

Since childhood, Saar has believed that plants, trees, and other forms of nature possess spirits. Inspired by African American folklore and African-Caribbean tales, Saar uses materials that reflect these cultural and artistic traditions.

In *Sweeping Beauty* (1997), a naked woman hangs upside down by her feet, and her long hair appears to have morphed into a broom. The manner of the work recalls lynchings that occurred in the South.

The role of women in society is a recurring theme in Saar's work. Being a mother has been formative to her art.

> Children have a certain experience and wisdom from the day they are born. They open their eyes and look at you like, 'Who are you?' That makes me interested in the soul and the spirit.[36]

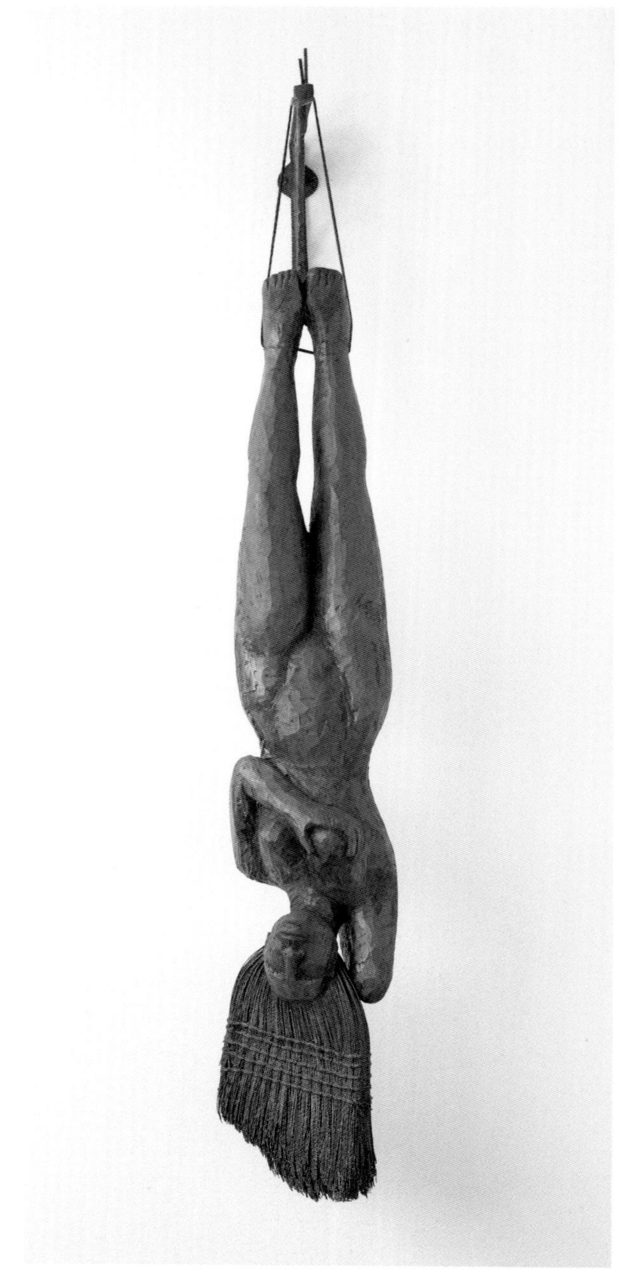

***Sweeping Beauty*, 1997**

Saar notes that women "are the psychic strength within the family who sweep up the messes in life and clear out the bad spirits."

In 2008, Saar was commissioned to create *Swing Low* (2008), a monument to famous abolitionist Harriet Tubman (1822–1913), runaway slave and conductor of the Underground Railroad. Tubman was called Moses by the hundreds of people she helped free during her thirteen trips between the South and the North. Her nightly expeditions with the North Star as her guide began in the slave-holding state of Maryland and ended in Canada. Tubman also fought for the Union Army during the Civil War, and later in life supported women's right to vote.

Located at the intersection of St. Nicholas Avenue and Frederick Douglass Boulevard at West 122nd Street in Harlem, the two-ton, thirteen-foot bronze and granite sculpture depicts Tubman striding forward despite the tangled roots that pull on the back of her skirt, roots that represent slavery. Embedded in her skirt are stylized images that represent the slaves who Tubman helped to escape, as well as objects carried North by fugitive slaves. The base of the statue features illustrations from Tubman's life.

The statue faces south, which initially caused some debate, but Saar explained,

> She [Tubman] is best known for her sojourns north, but what is most impressive to me are her trips south, where she risked her own freedom. As impressive as her courage and commitment were, what is amazing to me is her compassion. Harriet Tubman is calling on all of us to look at the compassion within each of us.[37]

Located at the Hall of Justice in downtown Los Angeles is a twelve-foot bronze depiction of Justice known as *Embodied* (2014). She needs no sword, blindfold, or scale, but instead, she weighs and balances the book of law, which she equates to freedom and peace, as affirmed by the dove taking flight from her upheld hand. Etched onto the fabric of her nine-foot-tall dress are over two hundred uplifting words that signify the spirit of Justice. These words

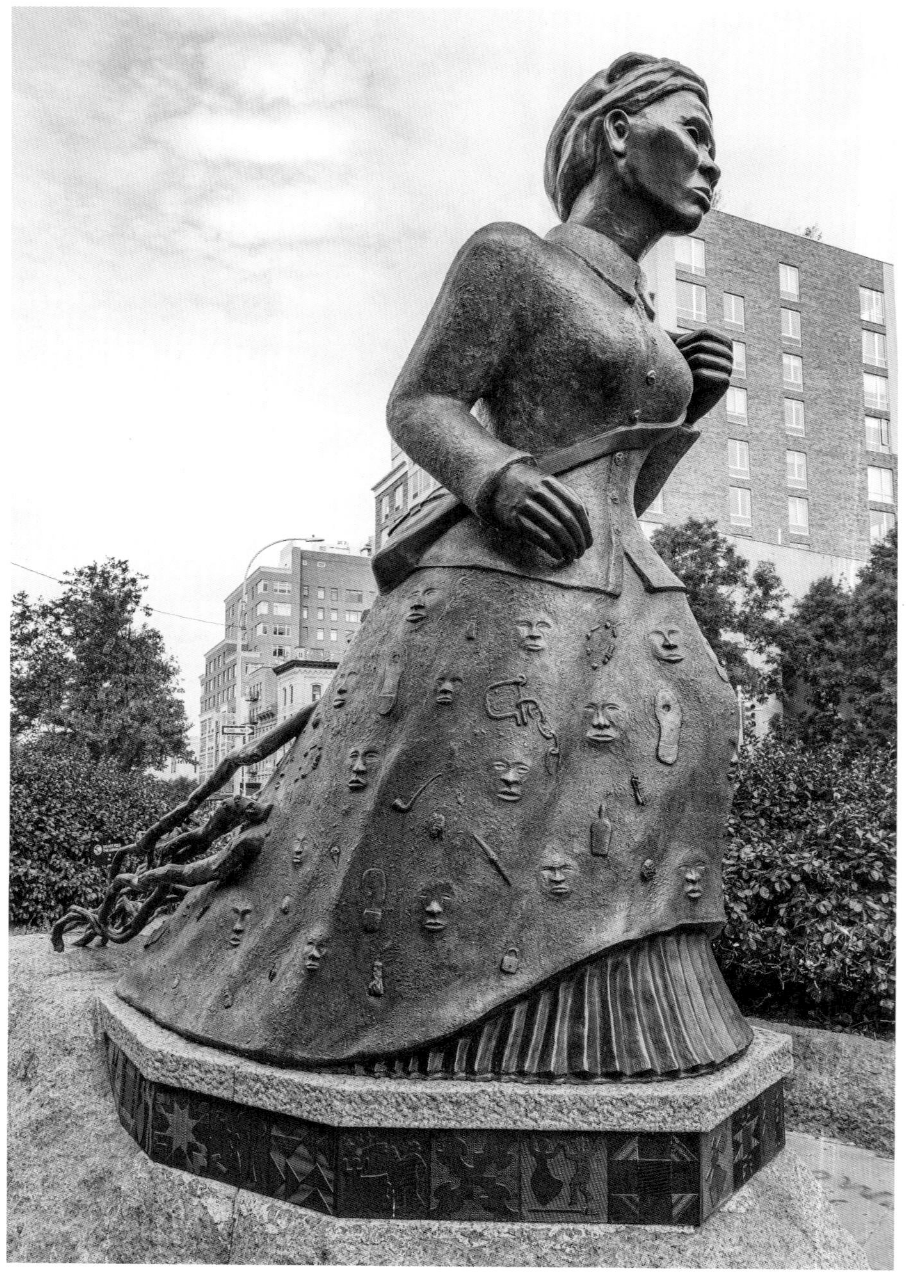

***Swing Low*, 2008**

The Harlem statue is the city's first public monument to an African American woman.

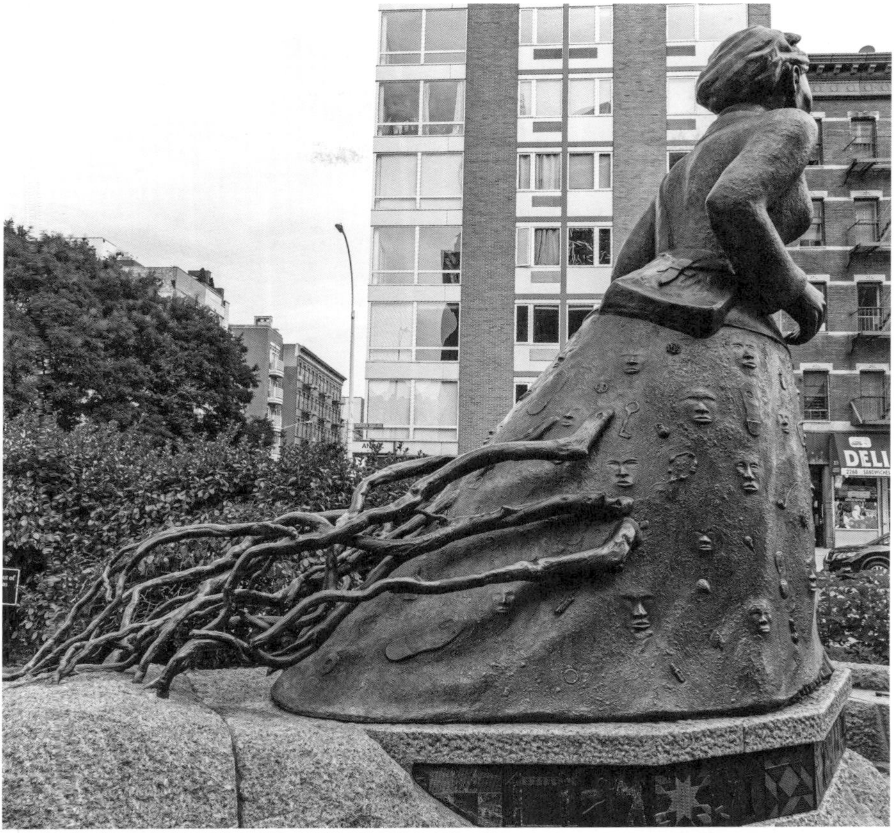

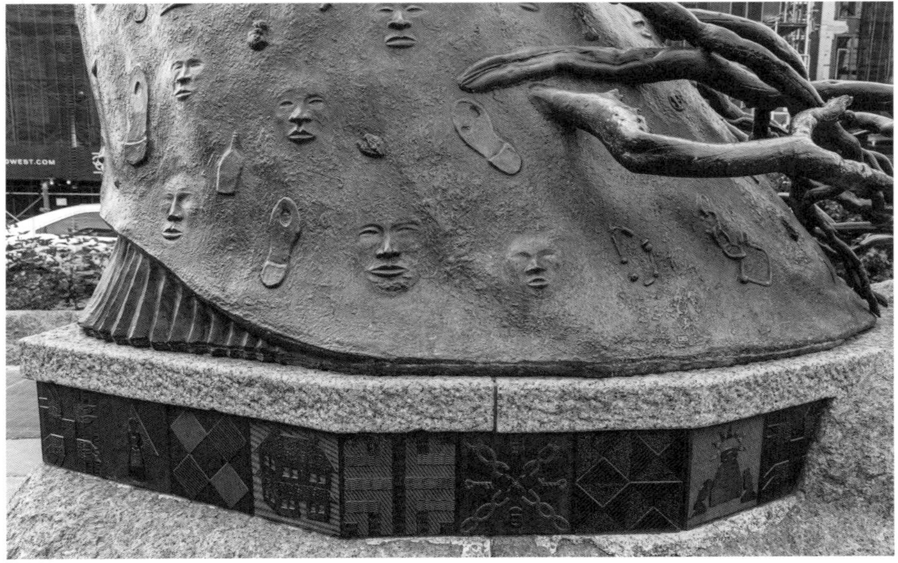

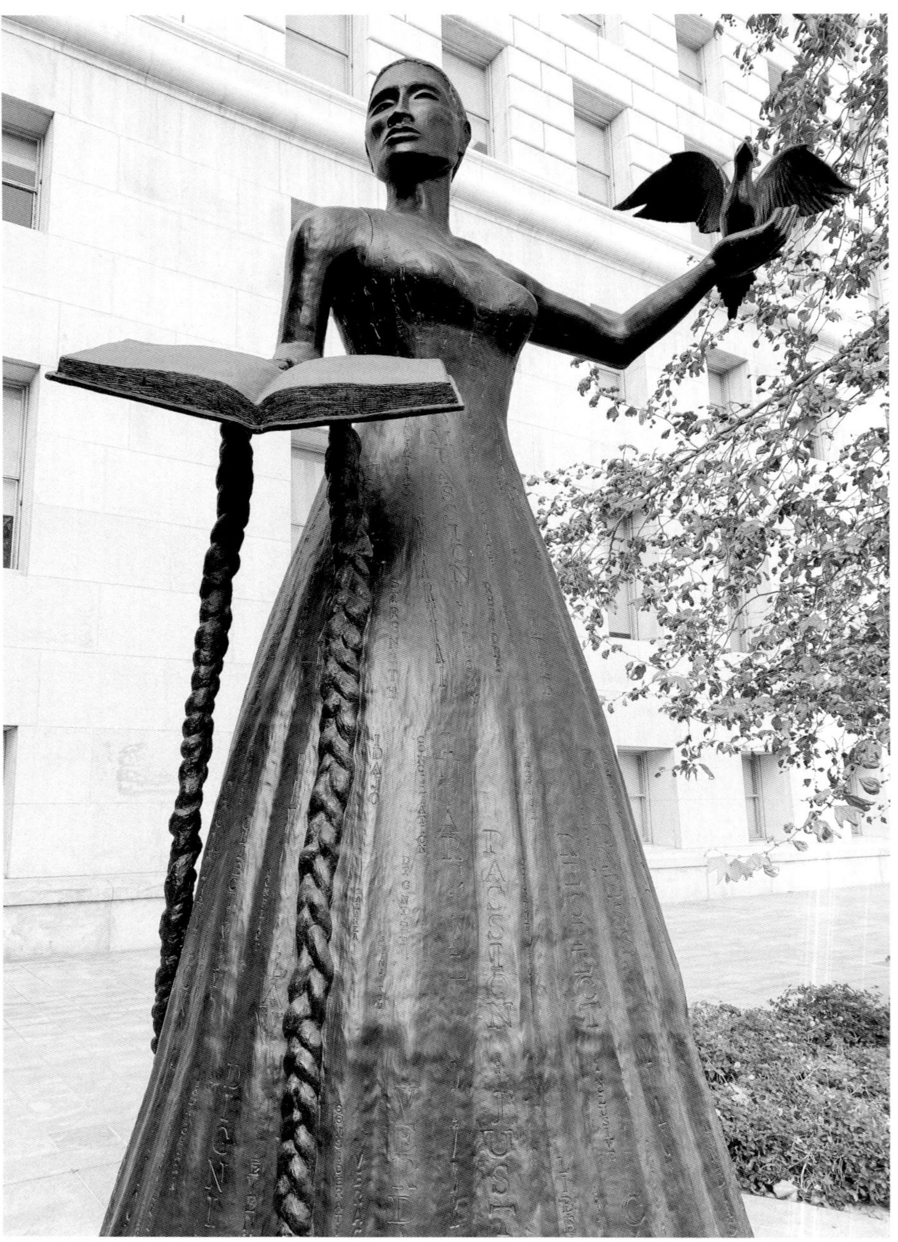

Embodied, 2014

Wearing a dress etched with over 200 words about justice in more than a dozen languages, the female figure *Embodied* has a commanding presence at the center of the Hall of Justice Plaza in Los Angeles.

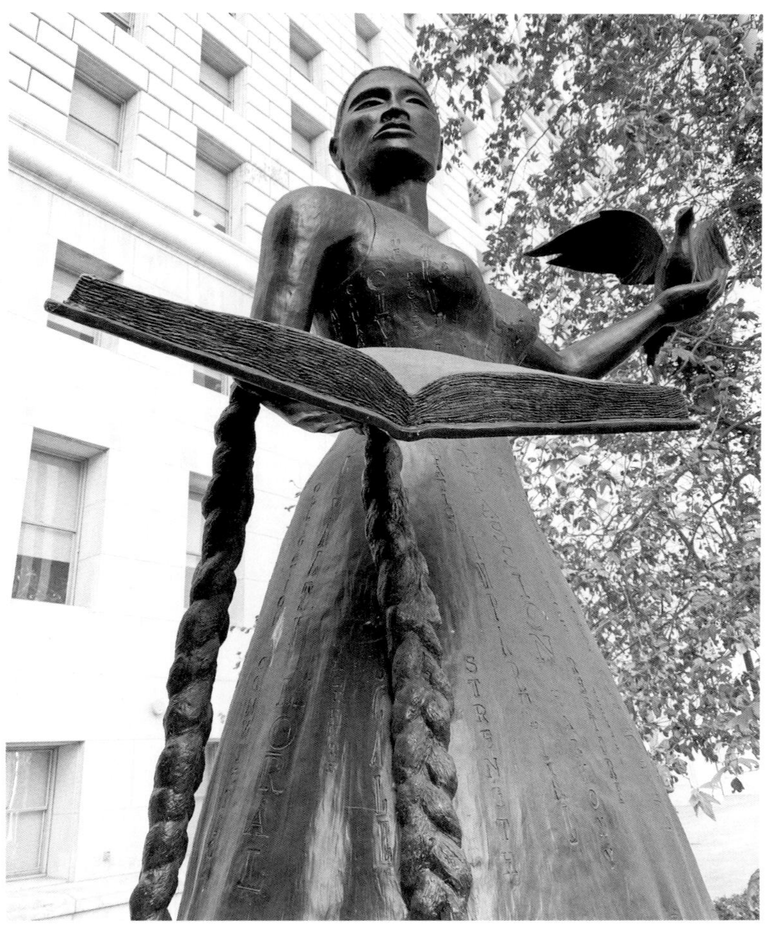

were collected from employees of the Los Angeles County Sheriff's Department and District Attorney's Office, as well as from students and the general public.

Imbue (2019–2020) is a twelve-foot cast bronze sculpture of a woman carrying water vessels. The figure balancing a tower of tubs, basins, pans, and pitchers is the embodiment of Yemaja, a Yoruba deity found throughout Africa and the Americas. As the goddess of all waters and mother of all living things, Yemaja, also known for cleansing and healing powers, is the protector of women and children. The work was commissioned by Benton Museum of Art at Pomona College in Claremont, California, to accompany Saar's

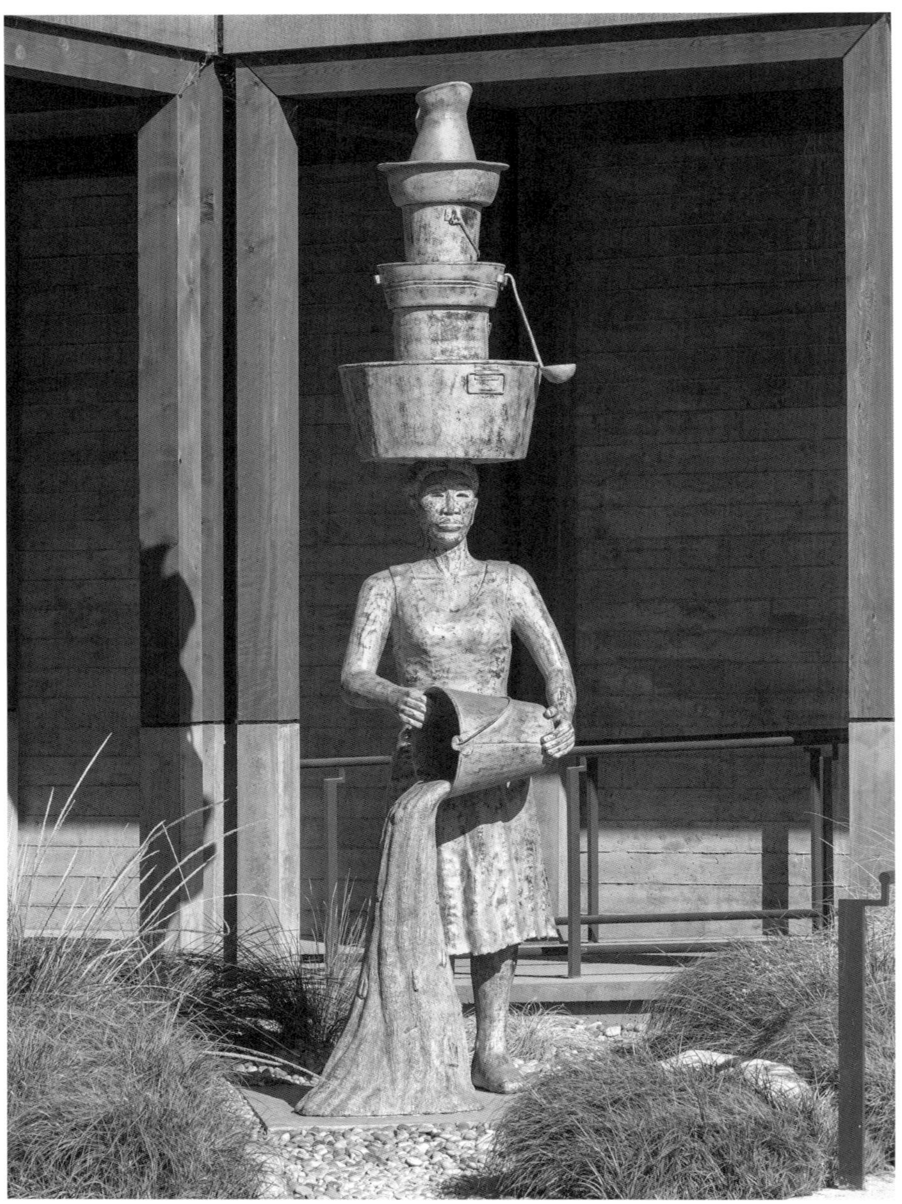

***Imbue*, 2019–2022**

The sculpture *Imbue* standing in the exterior courtyard on the Pomona College campus evokes the life-giving spirit of the Yoruba water goddess associated with childbirth and rivers. A balancing act between anger and serenity, she carries a stack of heavy pails on her head.

upcoming exhibition at the Museum. The title reflects Saar's own experiences of college in Claremont as "being nourished and filled with knowledge." Her choice of goddess relates to the location of the Museum itself, which is near an area that once regularly flooded from runoff from heavy snowmelt in the nearby mountains. "Now this goddess seems particularly appropriate," she muses. "Right now ... we are all in need of cleansing and healing."

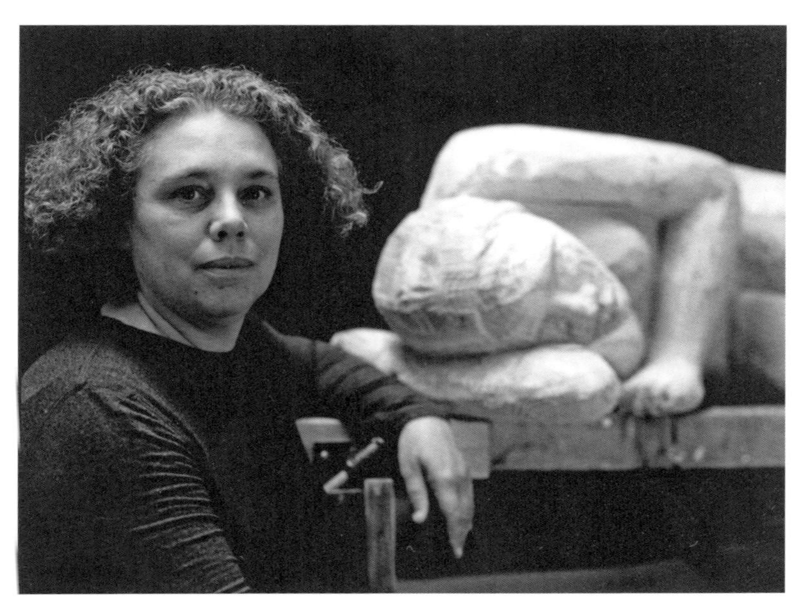

Alison Saar

"I wanted to make art that told a story, that would engage people. I wanted them to be moved by my work, whether it was specifically what my intentions were or not did not matter. I wanted them to be drawn in and affected by my sculpture."[38]

Postscript

EARLY ON in the history of our nation, women artists made sculptures, often against tremendous odds. Repeatedly ignored, patronized, and disapproved of privately and publicly, these hardworking sculptors responded by turning their backs on conventions and creating art with bravery and resilience. Often, they had to make sacrifices because they could not juggle marriage, motherhood, and a career.

The statues these artists created—and continue to create—show a desire for humanistic ideals: the affirmation of human worth and dignity, compassion, equality between the sexes, social justice, higher education for all, individual freedoms, democracy, a free press, and global harmony and peace. Whether the sculptures represent real people or mythological beings, or creatures from fairy tales, they reveal psychological strength, a desire to make the world a better place, a love of humanity, and faith in humankind. What follows are notable examples of recent sculptures by women artists prompting us as viewers to reflect on the achievements of women in art, literature, and other facets of life:

- *Fearless Girl* by Kristen Visbal was commissioned by a financial firm to push for more gender diversity in the corporate world.
- The sculpture of pioneer photographer *Diane Arbus*, located presently in Central Park, New York City, highlights the importance of representing all kinds of people.
- *The Girl Puzzle* monument on Roosevelt Island in New York City honors investigative reporter Nellie Bly and four other women based on Bly's depictions of patients inside the island's asylum. She went there to write an expose on the treatment of mental illness. More than ever, with the knowledge that women's role in history is often overlooked, the sculptures being made by women artists today represent real women who overcame great barriers to accomplish major achievements.
- At Battery Park in New York City, one of the most recently made monuments honors *Mother Cabrini*, the patron saint of immigrants who supported her fellow Italian immigrants to the United States. During her lifetime, she founded sixty-seven orphanages, schools, and hospitals in New York and throughout the world.
- In Provincetown, Massachusetts, Penelope Jencks is creating a sculpture commemorating journalist, labor activist, social critic, and novelist *Mary Heaton Vorse* that will be located on the grounds of her historic home at 466 Commercial Street.
- With the creation of a bronze gateway, Meredith Bergmann brilliantly honors the contributions made by Lexington, Massachusetts, residents who struggled since before the American Revolution to pursue social justice. Portrayed as silhouettes which were a popular way to remember loved ones during the eighteenth and nineteenth centuries, the bold outlines of these women are easy to see yet exude a sense of mystery, reminding us we still have much to learn about Margaret Tulip, Venus

Moore, Caroline Wellington, and other abolitionists and suffragists whose local actions advanced the liberty of our nation. Surrounded at the gateway by these women's profiles among flowers and birds, we are invited to stand for a while, examine a more spacious view, not only of our shared past but of what lies before us, and resolve to take steps forward that will make a difference.

—MARIA AUSHERMAN

Questions

1. *How does sculpture reflect a time period?*
2. *What story is being told?*
3. *What purpose does sculpture serve society?*
4. *What does sculpture reveal about the people who make it?*
5. *What influenced sculptors to select their subject matter?*
6. *Why are sculptures made?*
7. *Where does sculpture belong?*
8. *Should sculpture be representational or abstract?*
9. *What is your favorite sculpture?*
10. *Why do you like it so much?*
11. *How have women sculptors shaped the way we understand the past?*
12. *How have women sculptors used their art to change society?*
13. *Why should we remember the achievements of women sculptors?*

Notes

1. Jennifer Harlan, "Overlooked No More: Emma Stebbins, Who Sculpted an Angel of New York," *New York Times*, May 29, 2019.
2. "History of American Women: Anne Whitney" womenhistoryblog.com
3. Nathanial Hawthorne, *French and Italian Notebooks*, ed. Thomas Woodson, Vol. 14. *The Centenary Edition of the Works of Nathaniel Hawthorne* (Columbus: Ohio State University, 1980), 77–78.
4. "Portrait Bust is Discovered of a Remarkable Victorian Activist by American Sculptor Margaret Foley" – ArtFIXDaily, June 22, 2021.
5. Dolly Sherwood, *Harriet Hosmer: American Sculptor*, 1830–1908. (Columbia: University of Missouri Press, 1991), 213.
6. Collection: Papers of Harriet Goodhue Hosmer, 1834–1959. Harvard Library, 57–63. See also Sarah Knowles Bolton, *Lives of Girls Who Became Famous* (first published in 1886), 141.

7. Henry James, *William Wetmore Story and His Friends: From Letters, Diaries, and Recollections* (New York: Houghton, Mifflin, 1903), 1:257.

8. Cornelia Carr, *Harriet Hosmer: Letters and Memories* (New York: Moffat, Yard and Co., 1912), 35.

9. Cornelia Carr, 35.

10. Percy Bysshe Shelley, *The Cenci*, V.iii, 1–3.

11. Hosmer to Crow, August 1854 (Rome), *Harriet Goodhue Hosmer Papers*, Schlesinger Library, Radcliffe Institute, Harvard University, Cambridge, Mass. See also Cornelia Carr, 35.

12. Lydia Marie Child, "Edmonia Lewis," *Broken Fetter,* 3 March 1865, 25.

13. Henry James, *William Wetmore Story and His Friends: From Letters, Diaries, and Recollections* (New York: Houghton, Mifflin, 1903), 1:257.

14. Edmonia Lewis, *National Anti-Slavery Standard*, February 27, 1864.

15. Gordon Langley Hall, *Vinnie Ream: The Story of the Girls Who Sculpted Lincoln* (New York: Holt, Rinehart & Winston, 1963), 33.

16. Vinnie Ream. Interview. *Sunday Star,* 9 February 1913.

17. Vinnie Ream, from an *Address Given to the International Council of Women*, 1909. See Vinnie Ream Hoxie, "The Field of Sculpture for Women," Box 5, Vinnie Ream and R.L. Hoxie Papers, Manuscript Division, Library of Congress, Washington D.C.

18. Janet Scudder, *Modeling My Life* (New York, 1925), 155.

19. Bessie Potter Vonnoh, "Tears and Laughter Caught in Bronze: A Great Woman Sculptor Recalls Her Trials and Triumphs," *Delineator,* October 1925, 8.

20. Henry McBride 1942 Memorial Essay. See Clarice Stasz, *The Vanderbilt Women: Dynasty of Wealth, Glamour and Tragedy* (Lincoln, Nebraska: Excel Press), 1991.

21. J. Walker McSpadden, *Famous Sculptors of America* (New York: Dodd, Mead & Co., 1925), 347.

22. Doris E. Cook, *Woman Sculptor: Anna Hyatt Huntington* (1876–1973) (Hartford, Conn., 1976), 13.

23. Malvina Hoffman, *Yesterday is Tomorrow: A Personal History* (New York: Crown Publishers, 1965), 33.

24. Ibid, 108.

25. Malvina Hoffman, *Heads and Tales* (New York: Charles Scribner's & Sons, 1936).

26. Malvina Hoffman, *Sculpture Inside and Out*, (New York: W.W. Norton & Co., 1939).

27. T.R. Poston, "Augusta Savage," *Metropolitan Museum*, January 1935, n.p.

28. Elizabeth Catlett, "Keynote Address to the Third Annual Meeting of the National Conference of Negro Artists in Washington D.C., 1961." See Melanie Anne Herzog, *American Art*. Vol. 26, #3, 2012.

29. Ralph Ellison, *Invisible Man* (New York: Random House, 1952), 1.

30. Riverside Park Monuments, *Ralph Ellison Memorial*, NYC Parks, July 17, 2021.

31. Penelope Jencks website, penelopejencks.com

32. Eleanor Roosevelt, Speech on the Tenth Anniversary of the Universal Declaration of Human Rights, 1958.

33. Penelope Jencks website, penelopejencks.com

34. Abigail Adams, Letter to her husband, John Adams Family Papers: An Electronic Archive, Massachusetts Historical Society.

35. Meredith Bergmann, Sculptor's Page – Monumental Women. monumentalwomen.org

36. Alison Saar, LA Louver Gallery website. lalouver.com

37. "Why is Harriet Tubman Facing South?" *New York Times*, November 13, 2008. www.cityroom.blogs.nytimes.com

38. Alison Saar, LA Louver Gallery website. lalouver.com

Bibliography

Aronson, Julie. *Bessie Potter Vonnoh: Sculptor of Women.* Cincinnati Art Museum, 2008.

Borzello, Frances. *A World of Our Own: Women as Artists Since the Renaissance.* New York: Watson-Guptill Publications, 2000.

Chadwick, Whitney. *Women, Art, and Society.* London: Thames and Hudson, Ltd., 1996.

Chiarmonte, Paula. *Women Artists in the United States.* Boston: G.K. Hall & Co., 1990.

Craven, Wayne. *American Art: History and Culture.* Madison, Wisconsin: Brown & Benchmark, 1994.

Cronin, Patricia. *Harriet Hosmer: Lost and Found, A Catalogue Raisonne.* Milan: Edizioni Charta, 2009.

Dabakis, Melissa. *A Sisterhood of Sculptors: American Artists in Nineteenth-Century Rome.* University Park, Pennsylvania: The Pennsylvania State University Press, 2014.

Driskell, David C. *Hidden Heritage: Afro-American Art, 1800–1950.* San Francisco: The Art Museum Association of America, 1985.

Greenthal, Kathryn; Kozol, Paula M. and Ramirez, Jan Seidler. *American Figurative Sculpture in the Museum of Fine Arts Boston.* Boston: Museum of Fine Arts, 1986.

Heller, Nancy. W*omen Artists: An Illustrated History.* New York: Abbeville Press, 1997.

Hill, May Brawley. *The Woman Sculptor: Malvina Hoffman and Her Contemporaries.* New York: Berry-Hill Galleries, Inc., 1984.

Jencks, Penelope. *Eleanor Roosevelt on Riverside Drive.* Create Space Independent Publishing Platform, 2015.

Jencks, Penelope. *Frost in Granite.* Create Space Independent Publishing Platform, 2016.

Kasson, Joy S. *Marble Queens & Captives: Women in the Nineteenth-Century American Sculpture.* New Haven: Yale University Press, 1990.

Rubinstein, Charlotte Streifer. *American Women Sculptors: A History of Women Working in Three Dimensions.* Boston: G.K. Hall & Co., 1990.

Scudder, Janet. *Modeling My Life.* New York: Harcourt Brace & Co., 1925.

Seidler, Jan and Kathryn Greenthal. *The Sublime and the Beautiful: Images of Women in American Sculpture.* Boston: Museum of Fine Arts, 1979.

Sherwood, Dolly. *Harriet Hosmer: American Sculptor, 1830–1908.* Columbia: University of Missouri Press, 1991.

Slatkin, Wendy. *Women Artists in History: From Antiquity to the 20th Century.* Englewood Cliffs, New Jersey: Prentice Hall, 1990.

Photo Credits

	Bergmann, Meredith	*Memorial to September 11th*	Installed 2011	Steven Taylor
1	Visbal, Kristen	*Fearless Girl*	2017	Steven Taylor
2	Stebbins, Emma	*Horace Mann*	1865	Steven Taylor
3	Stebbins, Emma	*Angel of the Waters*	1873	Steven Taylor
4	Stebbins, Emma	*Portrait of Emma Stebbins*	1815–1882	Library of Congress
5	Whitney, Anne	*The Lotus Eater*	1868	Newark Museum of Art
6	Whitney, Anne	*Lady Godiva*	1862	Dallas Museum of Art
7	Whitney, Anne	*Roma*	1869	Davis Museum, Wellesley College
8	Whitney, Anne	*Samuel Adams*	1876	Steven Taylor
9	Whitney, Anne	*Charles Sumner*	1875	Steven Taylor

10	Whitney, Anne	*Portrait of Anne Whitney*	1821–1915	Library of Congress
11	Lander, Louisa	*Nathanial Hawthorne*	1858	Concord Free Library, Concord, Mass.
12	Lander, Louisa	*Virginia Dare*	1860	Noah Ausherman
13	Foley, Margaret	*Head of Prophet Zephaniah*	1868	Brooklyn Museum of Art
14	Foley, Margaret	*Pascuccia*	1865	Brooklyn Museum of Art
15	Foley, Margaret	*Jenny Lind*	1865	Ben Elwes Fine Art, London; photography by Matthew Hollow
16	Foley, Margaret	*Jessie White Mario*	1867–1868	Ben Elwes Fine Art, London; photography by Matthew Hollow
17	Foley, Margaret	*Cleopatra*	1876	Smithsonian American Art Museum
18	Hosmer, Harriet	*Clasped Hands of Robert and Elizabeth Barret Browning*	1853	National Portrait Gallery, London/Art Resource, NY
19	Hosmer, Harriet	*Daphne*	1854	The Metropolitan Museum of Art/Art Resource, NY
20	Hosmer, Harriet	*Puck on a Toadstool*	1856	Smithsonian American Art Museum
21	Hosmer, Harriet	*Beatrice Cenci*	1857	Art Gallery of New South Wales, Australia
22	Hosmer, Harriet	*Zenobia*	1859	Wadsworth Atheneum Museum of Art, Hartford, CT
23	Hosmer, Harriet	*The Sleeping Faun*	1870	Cleveland Museum of Art

24	Hosmer, Harriet	*Portrait of Harriet Hosmer*	1830–1908	Library of Congress
25	Lewis, Edmonia	*Indian Combat*	1868	Cleveland Museum of Art
26	Lewis, Edmonia	*Hagar*	1875	Smithsonian American Art Museum
27	Lewis, Edmonia	*The Death of Cleopatra*	1876	Smithsonian American Art Museum
28	Lewis, Edmonia	*Minnehaha*	1868	The Metropolitan Museum of Art/Art Resource, NY
29	Lewis, Edmonia	*Hiawatha*	1868	The Metropolitan Museum of Art/Art Resource, NY
30	Lewis, Edmonia	*Portrait of Edmonia Lewis*	1844–1907	National Portrait Gallery Washington, DC
31	Ream, Vinnie	*Sappho*	1865–1870	Library of Congress
32	Ream, Vinnie	*Lincoln*	1870	Library of Congress
33	Ream, Vinnie	*Farragut*	1875	Steven Taylor
34	Ream, Vinnie	*Portrait of Vinnie Ream*	1847–1914	Library of Congress
35	Scudder, Janet	*Pan Playing Pipe*	1916	Library of Congress
36	Scudder, Janet	*Frog Fountain*	1901	The Metropolitan Museum of Art/Art Resource, NY
37	Scudder, Janet	*Seated Faun*	1924	Brooklyn Museum of Art
38	Scudder, Janet	*Young Diana in Garden*	1918	Library of Congress
39	Scudder, Janet	*Portrait of Janet Scudder*	1869–1940	Library of Congress

40	Vonnoh, Bessie Potter	*A Young Mother*	1896	The Metropolitan Museum of Art/Art Resource, NY
41	Vonnoh, Bessie Potter	*The Dance*	1897	Newark Museum of Art/Art Resource, NY
42	Vonnoh, Bessie Potter	*His First Journey*	1901	The Metropolitan Museum of Art. Art Resource, NY
43	Vonnoh, Bessie Potter	*Burnett Memorial Fountain*	1936	Steven Taylor
44	Whitney, Gertrude Vanderbilt	*Fountain of El Dorado*	c.1915	Library of Congress
45	Whitney, Gertrude Vanderbilt	*Titanic*	c.1915–1920	Steven Taylor
46	Whitney, Gertrude Vanderbilt	*Washington Heights–Inwood War Memorial*	1922	Steven Taylor
47	Whitney, Gertrude Vanderbilt	*Portrait of Gertrude Vanderbilt Whitney*	1875–1942	Library of Congress
48	Huntington, Anna Hyatt	*Reaching Jaguar*	1906	Steven Taylor
49	Huntington, Anna Hyatt	*St. Joan of Arc*	1915	Steven Taylor
50	Huntington, Anna Hyatt	*El Cid*	1927	Steven Taylor
51	Huntington, Anna Hyatt	*Jose Marti*	1965	Steven Taylor
52	Huntington, Anna Hyatt	*Portrait of Anna Hyatt Huntington*	1876–1973	Library of Congress

53	Hoffman, Malvina	*Boy and Panther Cub*	1915	Steven Taylor
54	Hoffman, Malvina	*La Gavotte*	1915	Cleveland Museum of Art
55	Hoffman, Malvina	*Bacchanale Russe*	1912	Steven Taylor
56	Hoffman, Malvina	*Martinique Woman*	1928	Brooklyn Museum of Art
57	Hoffman, Malvina	*Portrait of Malvina Hoffman*	1885–1966	Private collection of Derek Ostergard
58	Savage, Augusta	*Gamin*	1929	Cleveland Museum of Art
59	Savage, Augusta	*The Harp*	1939	The New York Public Library/Art Resource, NY
60	Catlett, Elizabeth	*Mother and Child*	1956	The Museum of Modern Art/Licensed by SCALA/Art Resource, NY
61	Catlett, Elizabeth	*Woman Fixing Her Hair*	1993	The Metropolitan Museum of Art/Art Resource, NY
62	Catlett, Elizabeth	*Ralph Ellison Memorial*	2003	Steven Taylor
63	Catlett, Elizabeth	*Portrait of Elizabeth Catlett*	1915–2012	National Portrait Gallery
64	Jencks, Penelope	*Samuel Eliot Morison*	1982	Steven Taylor
65	Jencks, Penelope	*Robert Frost*	2007	Steven Taylor
66	Jencks, Penelope	*Eleanor Roosevelt*	1996	Steven Taylor

67	Jencks, Penelope	*Portrait of Penelope Jencks*	b.1936	Penelope Jencks/NY Parks Department
68	Bergmann, Meredith	*Boston Women's Memorial*	2003	Steven Taylor
69	Bergmann, Meredith	*Women's Rights Pioneers Monument*	2020	Steven Taylor
70	Bergmann, Meredith	*Portrait of Meredith Bergmann*	b.1955	Laney Lloyd
71	Saar, Alison	*Treesouls*	1994	L.A. Louver, Venice, CA
72	Saar, Alison	*Sweeping Beauty*	1997	The Metropolitan Museum of Art/Art Resource, NY
73	Saar, Alison	*Swing Low*	2008	Steven Taylor
74	Saar, Alison	*Embodied*	2014	Chloe Chapman
75	Saar, Alison	*Imbue*	2019–2020	Steve Comba, Pomona College, Claremont, CA
76	Saar, Alison	*Portrait of Alison Saar*	2005	Paul O'Connor, L.A. Louver, Venice, CA

About the Author & Contributors

Maria Ausherman is a teacher and the author of *The Photographic Legacy of Frances Benjamin Johnston* and *Behind the Camera: American Women Photographers Who Shaped How We See the World*, as well as co-author with Patricia Jennings of *Georgia O'Keeffe's Hawaii.* She completed her BA in Geography from the University of North Carolina at Chapel Hill, her MA in Cinema Studies from the City University of New York, and her MEd in Social Science Education from the University of Georgia in Athens, where she obtained a graduate certificate in historic preservation and completed coursework and a dissertation for a PhD in Art.

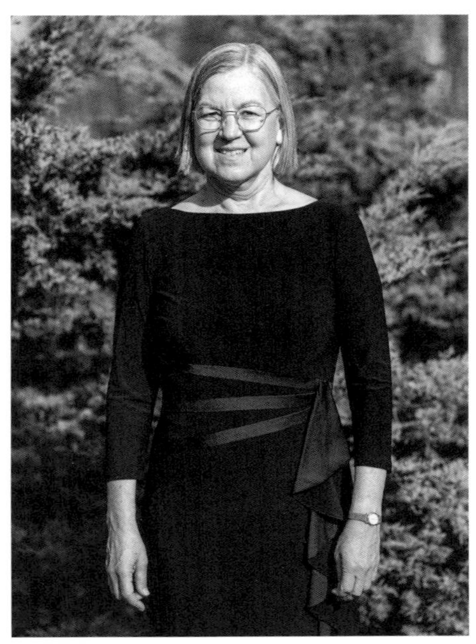

Kristen Visbal is a bronze sculptor who specializes in lost-wax casting and manages a clay modeling studio. She has created numerous public monuments, and her realistic work is often preoccupied with motion and the sea. Visbal's *Cradle of Coaches* is a collection of ten larger-than-life Hall of Fame coaches. Her rendition of historical figure *Alexander Hamilton* is the largest to date. Her multiple large-scale marine life works dot the southeast. Her most famous work, *Fearless Girl,* is an iconic symbol inspiring the empowerment of women worldwide and symbolizing the call for gender diversity in leadership. The figure can be seen in New York, Melbourne, and Oslo. Kristen Visbal remains a member of the National Sculpture Society, founded in 1893 as the first organization of professional sculptors.

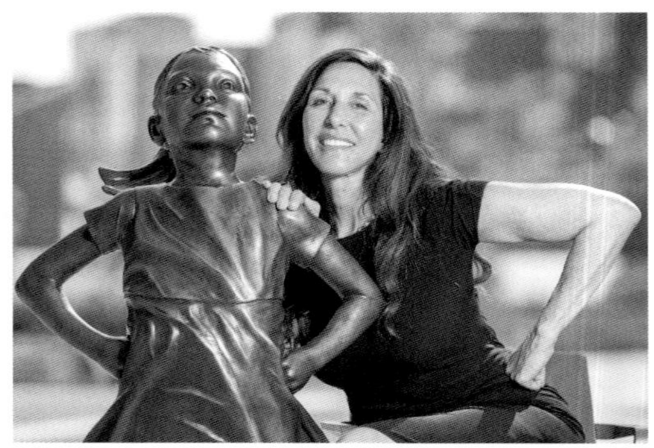

Carol S. Ward has twenty years of collaborative leadership in for-profit and non-profit management, financial oversight, fundraising, strategic planning, board relationships, and grant-winning cultural program development. She is currently Executive Director of the Lexington Historical Society, having previously been the Director of One River School of Art and the Executive Director of the Morris-Jumel Mansion.

Ms. Ward is an art historian with her BA from Mary Washington College and two Masters Degrees; her first in Museum Education from the College of New Rochelle and her second in Art History from Hunter College. She has presented the keynote address at CLHO (Connecticut League of Historic Organizations) on connecting a historic site to the community, the annual NYCMER (New York City Museum Educators Roundtable) conferences on bringing contemporary art into a historic house museum, at Mary Washington College about the future of careers in art history and the museum field and the New-York Historical Society on Alexander Hamilton (the man and the musical).

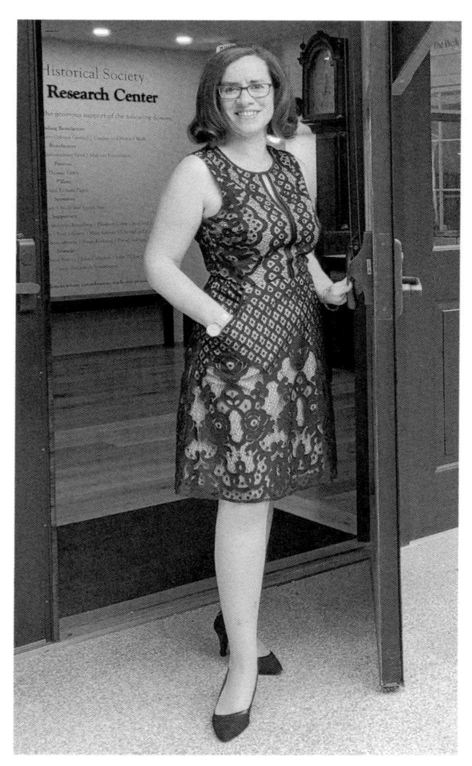

Articles she has written have been published in *The Magazine Antiques*, *Historic House Trust* journal, *American Alliance of Museums* magazine, *Antiques Weekly*, and catalogs for the Bruce Museum, Morris-Jumel Mansion, and Keno Auctions. Her book *Visions of America: The Morris-Jumel Mansion* was published in 2015, and she has recently appeared in the documentary on the making of the hit musical "Hamilton."

Steven J. Taylor is a retired New York City finance professional. He lives upstate in Stuyvesant, New York, with his wife, Maria Ausherman. He enjoys cycling and snowboarding. Steven has an interest in photography, especially event photography–music, dance, theatre. Taking photos of sculpture is similar to photographing individuals; choosing the right angle, separating and uncluttering the background, bringing up shadows, tightening or widening the composition to capture the sculpture in its intended environment. The hard part is selecting one photo to represent the artist's meaning.

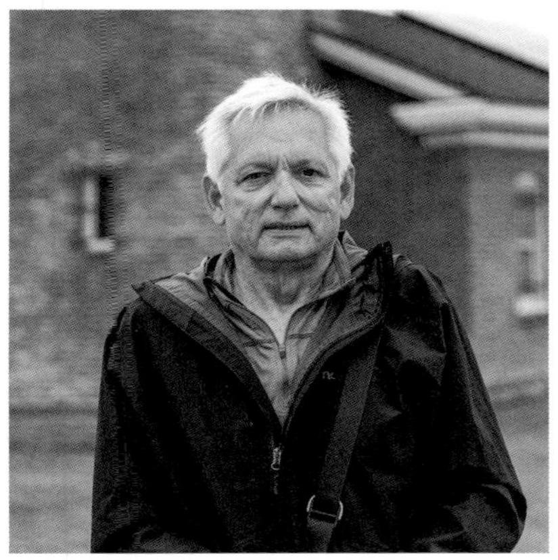